MAADI

MAADI

THE MAKING
AND UNMAKING
OF A CAIRO SUBURB
1878–1962

Annalise J.K. DeVries

The American University in Cairo Press

Cairo New York

First published in 2021 by
The American University in Cairo Press
113 Sharia Kasr el Aini, Cairo, Egypt
One Rockefeller Plaza, 10th Floor, New York, NY 10020
www.aucpress.com

Dar el Kutub No. 22297/19
ISBN 978 977 416 978 6

Dar el Kutub Cataloging-in-Publication Data

DeVries, Annalise J.K.
        Maadi: The Making and Unmaking of a Cairo Suburb, 1878–1962 / Annalise J.K.
    DeVries.—Cairo: The American University in Cairo Press, 2021.
        p. cm.
        ISBN 978 977 416 978 6
        1. Cities and towns – Egypt – Maadi
        2. Maadi (Egypt) – History – 20th century
        3. Maadi (Egypt) – Social life and customs – 20th century
        307.10962

1 2 3 4 5   25 24 23 22 21

Designed by Adam el-Sehemy
Printed in the United States of America

CONTENTS

ACKNOWLEDGMENTS

When I arrived in Cairo to begin research on this project in the autumn of 2009, I was not sure what kind of materials I would find, and I prepared myself for an arduous process of applying to archives while also combing through newspapers and tracking down oral histories. While several of those avenues proved promising, my real research breakthrough came the following year, after longtime Maadi resident Samir Raafat donated a large portion of his materials on the history of the area to the Rare Books and Special Collections Library at the American University in Cairo. Mr. Raafat's book, *Maadi, 1904–1962: Society and History in a Cairo Suburb*, was the first history of Maadi, and while we never had the opportunity to meet in person, his work offered the foundation for my own and I remain greatly indebted to him. I am additionally grateful to Stephen Urgola, the university archivist at AUC, and his staff, who assisted me throughout the research process, identifying resources from Mr. Raafat's collection and locating additional materials that further aided my efforts.

This project additionally owes a great deal to Maadi's environmental activists, whom I was introduced to by Sallie Kishk. I am grateful to Nadia Salem, Maggie Safwat, Ingy Safwat, Samia Zeitoun, Maggie Zaki, and 'Adl Nimatallah, who were all especially gracious as they shared their recollections of their home with me.

My research came during a revolutionary period in Egypt's history. The events of 25 January 2011 and their aftermath necessitated that I leave the country, and I heard the news of Hosni Mubarak's downfall from England, where I continued my research for several months as conditions in Egypt remained unstable. I found an especially welcoming environment at Oxford University, where the Middle East Centre Archive at St. Antony's College provided ample materials. The centre's archivist, Debbie Usher, offered invaluable assistance as I continued my work. In England I also had the opportunity to conduct oral history interviews with some of Maadi's former residents, and I thank Gabriel Josipovici and his cousin Anna Joannides for allowing me into their homes and for sharing their memories with me.

Also in Cairo, I remain grateful to Paul-Gordon Chandler, who provided valuable resources on the history of the Church of St. John. Amy Widener was not only my first friend in Maadi, but also paved the way for my first research breakthrough when she put me in touch with the gardening enthusiasts of the Maadi Women's Guild. This project would not have been possible without the ongoing kindness of Mike and Marty Reimer, whose Digla flat became home to me. I remain grateful to them for their ongoing support and to Mike for chances to continue collaborating.

Craig Encer and his Levantine Heritage Foundation introduced me to the many nuances and ongoing legacy of eastern Mediterranean life. Through his work, I was introduced to Alithea Lockie, whom I thank for offering additional details on the Williamson family and for allowing me to include some of her family photos here. I am additionally grateful to Nona Orbach and her recollections of her grandfather Isaac Kipnis, as well as the photos she shared with me.

This project received support from the US Fulbright Scholarship to Egypt, as well as predissertation small grants through the Mellon Foundation and the Graduate School-New Brunswick at Rutgers University. I am especially grateful for the mind-sharpening instruction I gleaned from the history faculty at Rutgers University. Seth Koven offered sustained assistance throughout my processes of research and writing, as well as great personal kindness when I evacuated Cairo. Bonnie Smith, Toby Jones, and David Cannadine opened up my eyes to the various facets of global history, Mediterranean trade networks, and the complexity of class relations in the Middle East. They each helped me refine my thinking and focus my analysis as I put my ideas into writing. Al Howard offered the kind of friendly, consistent, and patient support that I hope to emulate in my own career. Special thanks to Nova Robinson and her ongoing friendship and collaborative spirit. Any success I enjoyed at Rutgers and since would also not have been possible without the ongoing comradery of Elizabeth and

Zach Churchich, Kat Mahaney, and Alex Gomez-del-Moral. Thanks, also, to Carol Helstosky, whose early mentorship paved the way for many of my professional achievements.

While writing my dissertation from Birmingham, Alabama, I also benefitted from the rich academic communities at Birmingham-Southern College, the University of Alabama, and my current academic home at Samford University. I am especially grateful to Jonathan Bass for his mentorship and to Jason Wallace for sharpening my thinking. I am additionally thankful for the friendship of Michelle Little, whose passion for oral histories has helped confirm my own conviction that local histories allow little places to tell big and important stories.

Special thanks go to Nadia Naqib at the American University in Cairo Press for believing in and supporting this project from our earliest conversations. I am grateful for reviewer comments, especially those for the full manuscript, which were instrumental in refining my thinking and keeping my analysis on track. Thank you also to AElfwine Mischler for her thoughtful notes and careful editing as it drew to a close. Part of my research on Maadi's environmentalists was previously included in an article in the *Journal of Social History* and I am grateful for permission to include that material here.

My own personal story ultimately became a small part of Maadi's ongoing history. I would not have known the town existed had my Aunt Tina, Uncle Sam, and cousins Micah and Mark not moved there in the early 1990s. My extended family bears the imprint of Maadi's international legacy with three marriages and four grandchildren (and counting) who all come from matches made south of Cairo. My parents and siblings Matt, Jessica, and Joel have been the stable base of my support network. I am ever grateful for my dad's charge since childhood to pursue my dreams, and my mom's constant faith that such achievements are possible. I am also grateful to my grandmothers, whose legacies of education, hard work, a love of history, and insatiable curiosity planted the seeds for my career from my earliest years.

My life today is another instance of the global ties that formed in Maadi. Like so many residents before me, I met and eventually married another global traveler after our paths briefly crossed in this small suburban space. Because our story began in Maadi, it seems only fitting that I dedicate the following to my companion on life's adventures, Stephen DeVries.

NOTE ON TRANSLITERATION

I have followed the *International Journal of Middle East Studies* system for transliterating words from Arabic, but in simplified form by omitting diacritical marks except for the *hamza* glottal stop (') and the letter *'ayn* ('). The exception to this is for the transliteration of Maadi, where there is no diacritical mark for the *'ayn*, reflecting the more common and accepted English spelling of the area's name. The transliteration guidelines also do not apply to personal names and place names that have well-established English spellings.

ABBREVIATIONS

AARR	Asia and Africa Reading Room, British Library, London, United Kingdom.
AWM	Australian War Memorial
BNA	British National Archives, Kew, Surrey, United Kingdom.
BT	Board of Trade, BNA, Series BT 31.
EUL	University of Exeter Library
FO	Foreign Office, BNA, Series FO 141, FO 307, FO 370, FO 371, FO 383, FO 407, FO 841, FO 847.
IWM	Imperial War Museum, London, United Kingdom. Private papers.
IR	Board of Inland Revenue, BNA, Series IR 40.
MECA	Middle East Centre Archives, St. Antony's College, Oxford, United Kingdom. Private papers.
NAA	National Archives of Australia, Canberra, Australia.
SCP	Samuel Comfort Papers, No. C0407, Rare Books and Special Collections, Firestone Library, Princeton University, United States.
SRCARMPC	Samir Raafat Cairo Architecture Research Materials and Photograph Collection (formerly Maadi Collection), Rare Books and Special Collections Library, American University in Cairo, Egypt.

INTRODUCTION

When the Arab conquest reached the Nile in 642 CE, the river's eastern bank was already peppered with Jewish and Christian settlements. The Arabs would establish Fustat just north of Qasr al-Sham, which remained home to Orthodox Greeks, Jews, and Coptic Christians. Further south, Jews and Christians established Qasr al-Babiliyun, now known as Old Cairo.[1] Beyond that were the villages of Maadi, Tura, and Helwan. While these villages would later be defined by their relationship to the emerging Egyptian capital, they remained distinct from Cairo for more than a millennium. In these places, villagers established agricultural enclaves, fished, and traded. In Maadi, the Nile's annual flood brought silt-rich deposits that sustained the land's fertility.

For the Coptic community, Maadi had long held special significance. Coptic tradition across generations told of how the Holy Family took refuge in the village during their flight from Palestine to Egypt. According to the story, Jesus, Mary, and Joseph stayed in Maadi for ten days before setting sail for Upper Egypt in a papyrus boat. Maadi's Church of the Holy Virgin (al-'Adhra' bi-l-Maadi) was believed to be on the exact location of their departure. The location was also believed to be the place where Pharaoh's daughter pulled Moses from a basket in the reeds of the Nile waters.[2] As the stories indicate, from its earliest history, Maadi was long associated with the Coptic and Jewish communities that would become minorities in Egypt. Maadi's modern history was no different.

Maadi remained a village outside of Cairo throughout the reign of Saladin, Mamluk rule, the Ottoman invasion, and the rise of the Ottoman governor Mehmed Ali. Elements of modern urban development

1

only began near the end of Mehmed Ali's reign, when in 1843, Cairo's then-governor 'Abbas Pasha created a Council of Tanzim (Arabic for plan), which oversaw a scheme for widening Cairo's streets and developing new utilities.[3] It was not until the khedive's son Isma'il came to power in 1863 that a larger plan for Cairo's development became a significant factor in ambitions to modernize Egypt. Construction of the Suez Canal had already begun, after the 1854 concession was granted to Ferdinand de Lesseps. Isma'il would look to incorporate the capital fully into modernization efforts that had previously prioritized industrialization and utility development.[4]

With a plan to unveil a new city to a mass of international visitors when the Suez Canal opened in 1869, Isma'il appointed 'Ali Mubarak, a French-educated Egyptian engineer, to direct a newly formed Tanzim. Isma'il drew inspiration from a meeting with Georges-Eugène Haussmann, who was then undertaking his massive renovation of Paris, and the khedive hoped similarly to update Cairo with wide boulevards that radiated off of large public squares. While Mubarak initially planned to incorporate the older medieval city into the redesign, time constraints forced him to focus on largely uninhabited areas to the west and north of Cairo's existing quarters. This uneven development established districts like Ismailiya, which had wide avenues and European-styled building façades that appealed to Cairo's growing class of European expatriates. The new districts abutted the older areas of Old Cairo and Bulaq, which retained their medieval shapes and fell into further disrepair. Ultimately, Isma'il's scheme proved financially unsustainable and directly contributed to the bankruptcy that would justify the British invasion in 1882. By then, the Ottoman sultan had conceded to British pressure and deposed Isma'il and replaced him with his son Tawfiq. Instead of creating a fully integrated modern city, Isma'il's nineteenth-century plans made Cairo into "two cities"—the increasingly dilapidated medieval city, with its winding, unpaved roads, and the new, European-styled city with its wide avenues and Western-inspired design.[5]

In this context, the village of Maadi would be developed into one of the suburbs of Cairo's European city.[6] The history of how it was made pushes past the machinations of local and colonial officials to reveal how foreign capital made a home not just in Egypt's businesses and banks, but also in its streets, houses, and gardens. What Maadi became exposes how international investment capital and the people representing it shaped local society and culture, creating a vision for modern Egypt that incorporated a range of global influences.

The expansion of Cairo required infrastructure that could reliably move goods and people into and out of the capital, so suburban development followed the growth of Cairo's rail networks. Egypt's first railroad connected the capital to the more cosmopolitan port city of Alexandria in 1858. Afterward, Cairo quickly grew into a major railway junction that helped integrate communications and transportation across the country.[7]

Railway development, like the construction and management of the Suez Canal, was undertaken by foreign companies that received concessions from the Egyptian government. These companies had a special advantage because of the benefits guaranteed by the Capitulations. The Capitulations offered foreigners in Egypt and their businesses extraterritorial status, exempting them from local taxes and the jurisdiction of local courts. The system dated back to the sixteenth century, when the Ottoman sultan established the Capitulations to regulate trade with Europe.[8] Throughout Ottoman territories, including Egypt, the policies exempted foreign subjects and foreign-registered businesses from local laws and taxes, which, in turn, encouraged foreign domicile in Egyptian cities and other commercial hubs under Ottoman authority across the eastern Mediterranean. In Egypt, these policies were further institutionalized by the Mixed Courts, which established a separate legal system for foreign nationals that remained in place from 1876 until 1949, thus preserving the Capitulations benefits well after the fall of the Ottoman empire.[9] While the Mixed Courts were created to keep a preponderance of foreign consuls from overrunning Egypt's legal system, they also allowed each of the world's "Great Powers" and "middle powers" to have a representative judge in the country. This meant that most European countries, including England, France, Italy, Germany, Austria, and Russia, as well as the United States, had a hand in Egyptian governance for the first half of the twentieth century.[10]

The legal protections guaranteed by the Capitulations and Mixed Courts provided much of the justification for the British invasion and subsequent occupation. The royal fleet landed at Alexandria under the aegis of protecting British investments in the Suez Canal and elsewhere in Egypt. Yet, British authorities made a habit out of deploring the systems, rightly identifying how detrimental they were to the formation of independent Egyptian economic and political strength. Sir Evelyn Baring, Lord Cromer, who served as the British consul-general of Egypt from 1883 to 1907, considered the Capitulations part of Egypt's "heterogeneous mass of international cobwebs"—elements that he believed the Englishman, whose "mission was to save Egyptian society," had arrived to combat, not benefit from. Cromer acknowledged, however, that the delicate balance of power worked out among the governments invested in the Mixed Courts made their abolition diplomatically unfeasible.[11] As long as the Mixed Courts remained in place, the Capitulations continued protecting foreigners' privileged status.

Rather than combatting the Capitulations, the British occupation actually intensified their impact. Britain's administration of the country, especially its finances, made Egypt appear like a more stable investment.[12] While many expatriates had long made homes in Alexandria, more and more moved to the Egyptian capital, which offered the promise of new profits. Historians have referred to this growing class of expatriates by a range of names to indicate their dual identity as both locals and foreigners: foreign-resident bourgeoisie, local foreign minorities, or, in the case of this book, resident foreigners.[13] With this growing population looking to reside in Cairo long term came demand for new residential spaces, and companies previously focused on transportation began new endeavors in land development that looked to profit from resident foreigners' domicile in Cairo.

During a general meeting in London on 22 December 1903, the Egyptian Delta Light Railways Company Ltd. (Delta Railways) announced its intention to form a new company that would undertake projects in land development. Land values, the company explained, had "significantly increased," and Delta Railways hoped to capitalize on those growing values through the new venture.[14] The company established the Egyptian Delta Land & Investment Co., Ltd. (Delta Land) in April of the following year.[15] Because both Delta companies were registered in England, they enjoyed protections under the Capitulations. As English entities, they might appear straightforward products of imperialism. The London announcement was made by Delta Railways' chairman Sir Auckland Colvin, who previously represented British interests in Egypt when he managed the country's debt under Khedive Tawfiq, a subject examined in Chapter Two.[16] Yet the inner workings of the companies reveal deep local ties to some of Egypt's most prominent families.

The Capitulations and Mixed Courts not only attracted foreign businesses and their employees to Egypt, but also made acquiring foreign nationality profitable for locals. France and Italy, which were heavily invested in preventing Britain from gaining full control over Egypt's affairs, regularly granted their respective nationalities to Egyptians with the means to pay for it. For European powers, this gave them more influence within the Mixed Courts. What is more, Egypt had no nationality law of its own until 1929.[17] This meant that many people born and raised in Egypt were technically foreign subjects, even if their families had resided in the country for generations. Such was the case with the local families that helped establish Maadi, who were longstanding Egyptian Jewish families that retained foreign nationality in order to ensure that their various banking and commercial endeavors enjoyed the benefits of the Capitulations.[18] So while Maadi was founded by Italian, Austro-Hungarian, and English passport holders, that foreign status was not divorced from deep and longstanding local attachments, and in fact represented a kind of Egyptian identity that remained prominent in the country's affairs until the mid-twentieth century.[19] More than representing foreign interests, these Jewish families profoundly shaped the Egyptian economy. Their influence often incorporated local and foreign interests and eventually served as a platform for Egyptian independence from the British.

The Delta companies' Egyptian Jewish connections were integral to establishing Maadi. While the names of both companies indicated an earlier focus on transporting goods in Lower Egypt, Delta Land made its most substantial impact south of Cairo. In December 1904, Delta Railways purchased the Cairo–Helwan light rail line and announced plans to extend the narrow track from the Muqattam hills in the east to the Nile in the west, allowing them to move stone to the river for bridge construction. This track traversed Maadi al-Khabiri, and it is no coincidence that Delta Land simultaneously announced its purchase of seven hundred feddans of land (294 hectares or 726 acres).[20] Less than three years later, Delta Land definitively made Maadi its biggest investment when it purchased all of the land that the Messrs Suarès Frères et Compagnie owned at Maadi al-Khabiri.[21] The Suarèses were among Egypt's most prominent Jewish families, and they, along with the Mosseris, Menasces, Cattaouis, and Rolos, led much of the country's banking and transportation ventures. All of these families became involved in Maadi from the beginning, and in doing so, incorporated Delta Land's new development into local commercial networks that were integral to the Egyptian economy.

According to popular legend, the Suarès patriarch Felix—whose former property at Maadi al-Khabiri became the basis for Delta Land's development—first envisioned the development of the area into a distinctive "garden city."[22] The garden city concept was created by Sir Ebenezer Howard at the turn of the twentieth century and combined urban and rural elements into a town-and-country satellite.[23] For Delta Land, the garden city offered a method for a creating a well-controlled and aesthetically pleasing space conveniently situated a short train ride from the capital.

When Howard first developed the garden city plan, he believed that the greatest crisis facing the world was the growth of metropolitan slums and the related impoverishment of rural areas. To address the crisis, he proclaimed, "Town and country *must be married*, and out of this joyous union will spring a new hope, a new life, a new civilization."[24] Howard believed that modern technology could liberate humanity from grueling, unskilled toil, and that the railroad was integral to allowing for the dispersion of humanity into more harmonious, semirural establishments.[25] In his plan, Howard created a series of diagrams to explain how the garden city was to be carefully zoned. The town centered on a single commercial center, which was surrounded by residential space that comprised the majority of the development. Outside of the residential area was an industrial sector, and finally a rural greenbelt that served as an agricultural buffer. A rail line attached the garden city to the larger metropolitan center and to neighboring towns. It also provided an ideal outlet, in Howard's consideration, for farmers, manufacturers, and artisans to more widely market their goods.[26]

Significantly for Delta Land and other land development companies, Howard's plan relied on the activities of a private business that could independently manage the town. He devoted nearly two-thirds of his 1902 *Garden Cities of To-morrow* to the financial workings of the project.[27] He envisioned a private company functioning as the town's local municipality, providing guidance and keeping it in line with the long-term garden city plan. He explained that the administration of the town would be "modeled upon that of a large and well-appointed business, which is divided into various departments."[28] The company would serve as the local governor and in that role would be responsible for building roads, parks, and schools, and creating sanitation, water, and electric utilities. In order to ensure that the company remained in control of land use, residents would rent land rather than buy it outright. Howard stipulated that the company would use those rents to pay for the land and provide for the town's municipal needs.[29]

Howard intended the whole garden city system to be cooperative in nature—with the company depending on residents' rents and the residents relying on the company to appropriately reinvest their funds.[30] Residents would not own their homes and Howard dictated that the land's increased value be held in common, rather than being part of the company's profit.[31] These cooperative elements proved serious barriers to the complete implementation of Howard's plan, making it challenging to find investors and residents. What is more, Howard did not anticipate that the garden city would appeal to bourgeois residents who wanted to distance themselves from industry rather than incorporate small-scale manufacturing into their country life. When garden cities quickly gained appeal on a global scale, most of them failed to undertake the entirety of Howard's original ideal.[32]

In the first decade of the twentieth century, companies established suburban "garden cities" throughout continental Europe, the United States, and Japan.[33] Egypt and especially Cairo proved to be an especially hospitable climate for these kinds of developments. Municipal authority in early twentieth-century Cairo only extended to street planning and development, allowing Delta Land and its competitors to design and build new communities and administer them according to their own standards and interests.[34] While Delta Land's plans for Maadi established the capital's first garden city, they were quickly followed by two competitors. In 1905, the global transportation magnate Belgian Baron Edouard Empain, who designed the Paris and Cairo tramways, founded the Heliopolis Oasis Company and established Heliopolis along the desert tramline, just under ten kilometers (six miles) northeast of Cairo.[35] That same year, the Nile Land & Agricultural Company founded the aptly named Garden City southwest of Cairo's European quarter, along the eastern bank of the Nile.[36] All three companies focused on building garden cities of villas where upper middle-class foreigners and Egyptians might make a home.

In Heliopolis, Empain made his tramway the basis for a new garden city that he believed would help alleviate Cairo's overcrowding. Architecturally, the town blended Continental European building façades with Arab-Muslim motifs, reflecting his early aims to create a multiethnic, socially integrated space.[37] Empain created a "two-oases project" that was supposed to offer Cairenes of all social ranks a new space to live. The larger, first oasis centered on the luxurious Heliopolis Palace Hotel, a cathedral, and a racetrack—all designed to attract Cairo's wealthy resident foreigners and elite Egyptians. Surrounding this center were residential plots available for purchase or rent. Factories were to be situated along the town perimeter. The second oasis was to stand as a separate development from the first. It offered housing to the Egyptian workers who helped construct the town, worked on the tramway, and were employed in the factories surrounding the first oasis. These two communities were to share quick and easy access to Cairo by tram. After the 1907 financial crisis, however, Empain opted to cut expenditures and limit the scope of his scheme. He abandoned the worker oasis and focused instead on the more elite development.[38] The change in plans likely reflected the growing conflict between Empain and tramway workers, who went on strike in 1908.[39] As the development of Heliopolis continued, it would be Maadi's biggest competitor.

In contrast to Maadi and Heliopolis, the Nile Land & Agricultural Company established Garden City adjacent to Cairo's existing downtown. Rather than standing as a true satellite, it immediately extended the urban environment and required no railway connection to the city center. French engineer José Lamba designed the town in an art nouveau style, with twisting and turning streets that made it difficult to navigate for those who did not live there.[40] Overall, the area remained a garden city in name more than function.

Ultimately, Maadi proved to be Cairo's most enduring marker of Howard's influence. As the population of Cairo continued to rise, the other two areas were more quickly absorbed into the city's sprawl. Heliopolis saw an especially rapid rise in population, growing from ninety-two hundred in 1921 to two hundred and twenty-four thousand in 1928.[41] While Garden City and Heliopolis were more quickly drawn into the larger metropolis, Maadi remained most firmly established as a separate, semirural retreat throughout the first half of the twentieth century.

The following chapters explore Maadi's ongoing development as Delta Land's garden city south of Cairo. Where the village of Maadi al-Khabiri was previously set apart from the capital, Maadi garden city, as the company regularly referred to it, would be drawn into Cairo's expanding orb.

The new Maadi would simultaneously belong to Cairo, yet also be defined by its verdant distinctions. Events in Maadi were regularly described as *fi Maadi, bi-l-Qahira*, or "in Maadi, in Cairo." This moniker captures the town's altered status, as it lost its position as a village that predated the city center, to a modern space that now belonged to and depended on Cairo. Placing Maadi in Cairo, however, was a process. Examining how this small place became incorporated into the national whole, which was itself in the making, exposes a sustained vision for a particular kind of modern Egypt that lasted for the first half of the twentieth century. Maadi would be defined by the domicile of resident foreigners and the Capitulations that protected them. Those influences made the town possible. Yet, Egyptians, too, would see Maadi as an ideal of the nation's natural beauty and its potential for international collaboration. The history of Maadi, then, captures a story of modern Egypt that was never exactly at the center of national politics, but, in drawing ever closer to it, remained deeply influential. To overlook it would be to miss the very meaning of Egypt to a large number of people who considered themselves locals, whether or not they bore Egyptian nationality.

Maadi would be known for its villas and gardens. It became home to a number of memorable personalities, many of whom are recalled here. Yet what follows is not an attempt to catalogue each facet of Maadi's past. Such an undertaking would not only be impossible but also fail to interpret the significance of Maadi's history. For those familiar with Maadi, this book will hopefully present context and nuance regarding the area's history and offer a way to situate one's memories within Egypt's larger story. For those more broadly interested in modern Egypt, Maadi's history offers a detailed picture of how foreign economic influences shaped an ideal of the Egyptian nation that was swept away amid global and regional conflicts, as well as by Cairo's demographic transformation.

PART ONE: FOUNDATION

The verdant garden suburb of Cairo that developed at Maadi was rooted in the international financial influences that shaped the Egyptian economy and increasingly its society and culture from the mid-nineteenth century forward. Before the town's streets were laid, its villas built, or its gardens cultivated, this area south of Cairo was Maadi al-Khabiri, a rural village situated between the Nile and the rocky Muqattam hills. The modern suburb that drew its name from the ancient village would rely on a range of innovations for its construction. The building of the Suez Canal, the renovation of Cairo along the lines of Haussmann's Paris, and a new vision for town-and-country planning known as the garden city all informed Maadi's early development. What is more, Maadi could not exist without a place in the Egyptian economy. Networks of foreign investment—especially by Greeks and Levantine Europeans—went hand-in-hand with the town's early establishment.

1

FINANCIAL CORNERSTONE

In the early years of construction, Delta Land created a map of Maadi that depicted a space carefully planned to meet the specifications of Ebenezer Howard's garden city model. Delta Land neatly organized Maadi into blocks, which were divided into a clean grid of residential roads. Each of these streets was numbered, with Road 9—the garden city's sole commercial district—at the center and home to the rail station that anchored the town. Maadi's small streets were then crisscrossed by a network of wider avenues that intersected at large *mayadin* (plural for *midan*), or roundabouts. The names on these roads and roundabouts related to the town's earliest founders. The avenues bore mostly English names—Colvin, Palmer, and Williamson—while the *mayadin* indicated Maadi's Jewish founders—Suarès, Mosseri, and Menasce. The map captured a network of connections. Avenues Palmer and Williamson met at Midan Suarès, while Avenue Mosseri crossed Avenue Colvin as it passed southeast toward the irrigation canal that bisected Maadi.

The network of names on Delta Land's map reflected the relationships that formed between the colonial civil servants, local bankers, and foreign capitalists who brought Maadi into existence.[1] The history behind these street names exposes how the landscape of greater Cairo developed into a modern town-and-country place in the early years of the twentieth century. Here, politics and commerce collided as competing empires vied for influence in Egypt and a range of public and private interests looked to turn a profit.

Before names like Palmer, Suarès, and Menasce were etched into Maadi's built environment, the people they represented were influential figures in the intricate financial dealings that set the terms for banking, land ownership, and access to wealth in Egypt for more than a half-century. The personal and professional connections that formed between these men and their families were also at the heart of a scandal that threw into question the reputation of the British empire's financial administration of Egypt.

Two roads in Maadi—Avenues Colvin and Palmer—most clearly linked the town to the British empire in Egypt, indicating founders who had been involved in Egyptian finance since before the British occupation began.[2] Sir Auckland Colvin, Delta Land's founding chairman, was integral to shaping the terms of the British occupation, particularly in regard to establishing financial reform at the heart of the administration. Later, Sir Elwin Palmer, a founding board member, would take up Colvin's mantle as financial advisor to the khedive. Over the course of their respective careers, both men would transition from work in the colonial administration to private commercial ventures, eventually amassing significant personal wealth through business arrangements that grew out of their work as British officials.

Sir Auckland Colvin first arrived in Egypt from India in January 1878 as the head of a cadastral survey, researching the country's real estate and property ownership boundaries. His goal was to find a more effective means of extracting taxes from the countryside in the wake of Egypt's bankruptcy two years earlier. The disarray of Egyptian finances opened up the country to the intervention of a variety of foreign powers. As described in this chapter, Khedive Isma'il incurred the majority of Egypt's debts through his personal expenditures and the renovation of Cairo.[3] To help cover the arrears, Isma'il sold his shares in the Suez Canal Company to the British government, which resulted in more direct British involvement in the country's financial administration—an intrusion Colvin arrived to represent.

Colvin was one among some thirteen hundred Europeans who moved to Egypt in the late-1870s and 1880s to join the government's employ, their salaries comprising some 5 percent of the budget.[4] In his new role, the former Anglo-Indian found himself working amid a range of international interests, with Egyptian nationalist, British, French, and Ottoman claims all struggling for supremacy. For the next five years, Colvin watched Egypt's political situation deteriorate as it faced ongoing financial duress, a growing nationalist movement, a tangle of intervening foreign powers, popular revolt, and, eventually, British military invasion and occupation.

Colvin carried with him a kind of imperial pedigree. His grandfather first moved the family to India in 1778 when he joined the employ of the East India Company. His father John Russell Colvin served as the lieutenant-governor of the North-Western Provinces until the collapse of company rule in 1857.[5] Auckland was born in the Punjab province in 1838 and later continued the family line of imperial representation in India, starting his career as an official in the North-West and then becoming undersecretary of the Indian government's home department before moving to Cairo.[6]

Colvin's work in Indian regional financial management paved the way for his movement to Egypt. The transfer was also indicative of a larger British imperial belief that Egypt might be reformed along the same lines as India.[7] A large number of British officials in Egypt came by way of India for that purpose, including Sir Elwin Palmer and Sir Evelyn Baring.

Soon after Colvin relocated, the Egyptian government underwent an overhaul from the top down. After the sultan deposed Isma'il in 1879 and established the khedive's more passive son Tawfiq in his place, the Egyptian budget and other financial concerns were placed under the Anglo-French Dual Control. While the changes met the demands of foreign governments (the primary holders of Egyptian debt), the combination of a weakened khedivate and budgetary changes that increased taxes and cut military spending fueled nationalist fervor and further destabilized state authority. Colvin became the British representative in the Dual Control in the summer of 1880, making him one of Britain's chief representatives in Egypt at a time when the country looked increasingly on the brink of revolution.[8]

Initially, Colvin advocated for a modernization effort infused with orientalist paternalism. He believed that through close interaction with Europe, Egypt would eventually be "emancipated" from the supposed inferiority of intellect and ideology instilled by Ottoman rule.[9] Here, Colvin's prejudices mirrored his existing beliefs about South Asians. In his biography of his father, Colvin wrote that Indians have a "corrupt character" that could only be corrected by the adoption of Western values.[10] Once in Egypt, Colvin's ethnocentric presumptions proved untenable. When it became increasingly clear that Egyptian nationalists were going to revolt against the khedivate and wholly reject the Anglo-French Dual Control, Colvin quickly turned from his emphasis on paternalist cooperation to advocating military invasion.

The revolutionary impulse in Egypt largely came from village notables and military leaders. Both groups had cause for seeking to overthrow the existing state of affairs. The new budget imposed heavy taxes on rural areas, and, in devoting half of state funds to debt payment, severely cut funding for the military. The budget changes most severely impacted Egyptians, whose primary avenues for social and economic advancement were agriculture and military service. The formidable nationalist fervor centered on the leadership of Ahmad 'Urabi Pasha, a former army general, who led the call for checks on khedival power and the creation of a parliamentary government.[11] 'Urabi's demands had already met with some success in early 1881, when he led a series of military disturbances that September. His call for the creation of an Egyptian chamber of delegates was granted. In turn, the chamber spearheaded opposition to Anglo-French control of the budget.[12]

While Colvin initially advocated limited cooperation with 'Urabi, he reversed his position by January 1882. Writing to the Foreign Office, he argued that yielding to any of the chamber's demands would only increase the call for the full-scale removal of the Anglo-French Control, risking default on Egypt's debts. Making his beliefs about Egyptians explicit, he stated, "The Egyptians . . . are not capable of governing the country." He believed only military intervention would solve the crisis, and as to when, "it is merely a question of time and manner."[13]

By May 1882, the British and French had stationed gunboats off the coast of Alexandria. When Egyptians revolted, targeting European expatriate homes and businesses, the French fleet returned to Europe while the British invaded. 'Urabi, now leading the Egyptian army in mutiny against Khedive Tawfiq, withdrew from Alexandria as the British continued their pursuit. By September, the British defeated 'Urabi's army at Tal al-Kabir. The invasion crushed the Egyptian military and what little popular support remained for the khedive. In turn, the British found themselves propping up a weakened Ottoman regime in what was supposed to be a brief intervention.

Colvin, for his part, did not remain in Egypt for the occupation. That same year he returned to India, where he served out the remainder of his career in the colonial civil service, retiring in 1892. After retirement, however, Colvin's interests returned to Egypt—this time with an eye for commerce rather than governance. He began collaborating on new business ventures closely tied to imperial development goals, working with fellow Anglo-Indian Elwin Palmer, one of his successors as financial advisor.

The move to private business was indicative of a larger paradigm shift. Colvin's Anglo-Indian plans for Egypt failed. While the British became the dominant foreign power in the country, they never secured unilateral control. Colvin likely saw his move to private business as a negotiated continuation of his imperial claims. He wrote in his 1906 opus to British colonialism, *The Making of Modern Egypt*, that "Cairo of the Muski, and of mediaevalism, is disappearing; and villadom, begirt with bougainvillaes, and bright with the lustre of Oriental bloom, is stretching out along the Nile an ever-advancing arm."[14] The "villadom" he identifies was due in part to his own business ventures—something he never explicitly identified. The new means of modernization meant substantial personal profit for Colvin, earnings that would have been impossible without connections to others involved in Egyptian finance, both inside and outside of government service.

In 1885, Palmer came to Cairo from India as the director-general of accounts, where he undertook the intricate project of reviewing Egyptian government finances and separating public spending from the khedive's private expenditures. This was not his first time in Egypt. Palmer undertook the same financial work for a brief spell in 1877 before returning to India to resume his position in the Financial Department, where he began his career in 1870 at just eighteen years old.[15] Once back in Egypt, Palmer served as director-general of accounts for four years before he became financial advisor to the khedive. Palmer remained in the khedive's government until 1898, when he left to serve as the founding governor of the National Bank of Egypt.[16]

Although Egyptian in name, the National Bank was modeled after the Bank of England. In England, the bank controlled the money supply and interest rates, functioning as a private institution with significant public responsibilities. The National Bank of Egypt was established similarly to centralize the country's banking system. While not officially the central bank of Egypt, it issued currency and set interest rates on cotton, Egypt's most valuable export.[17]

With his move to the newly formed National Bank, Palmer appeared to have rounded out a fairly straightforward resumé in imperial finance. He exhibited many of the consummate qualities of the "gentlemanly capitalists," who historians P.J. Cain and A.G. Hopkins argue were integral to building the British empire through networks of financial interest and banking expertise.[18] To label him a clear servant of empire, however, would mean ignoring the intricacies of Egypt's political and financial situation, as well as the actions that Palmer appeared to take in his own self-interest. In particular, Palmer's move to the National Bank of Egypt in 1898 was fraught with conflict, giving the impression that he used his detailed knowledge of the khedive's accounts—especially those involving land values—to secure a profitable new position for himself and enormous wealth for his new colleagues.

The issue of land value and the khedive's ongoing debt crisis was at the heart of Palmer's seemingly surreptitious deal. In an attempt to cover his debts, the khedive sold half a million feddans—some 10 percent of Egypt's cultivatable land—to the Egyptian government in 1880. These lands, known as the *da'ira saniya*, were sold as part of the Law of Liquidation, a scheme for Egyptian debt repayment authored by an international commission that included representatives from Italy, France, Germany, Austria, Russia, and Turkey. It was administered by three comptrollers, one British, one French, and one Egyptian.

Eighteen years after the *da'ira saniya* was initially created, Palmer advised the government to sell the three hundred thousand feddans of remaining land to the newly formed Daira Sanieh Company for £6,250,000. Four days later, the same group that owned the Daira Sanieh Company established the National Bank of Egypt and appointed Palmer as its founding governor.[19] The sale became all the more conspicuous when it was made public that Harry Crookshank Pasha, who worked with Palmer in the finance department as the British comptroller of the *da'ira saniya*, had issued a report that assessed the value of the estates at £10 million.[20] It was no coincidence that Palmer also became the chairman of the board for the Daira Sanieh Company.[21]

The sale and Palmer's subsequent resignation from the khedive's employment did not escape the attention of the news media or the general public, though an outright conflict of interest was never proven. American journalist A.B. de Guerville wrote in his 1906 book *New Egypt*, "There was some ill-natured comment on [Palmer's] appointment, but I have been unable to find any confirmation of the suggestion that it was connected in some way with the Daira's transactions."[22] At the least, a reputation for corruption appears to have stuck with Palmer. In January of the same year,

Palmer died unexpectedly of "enteric fever," or typhoid. Reporting on his death, the *Egyptian Gazette*, which often took pains to describe British affairs in a positive light, described Palmer as "a very lucky man," identifying his career successes with his fortunate position as successor to more laudable civil servants. The *Gazette* continued that Palmer "could not be termed a popular man and some of his business methods have been subject to much criticism. Whether he administered the National Bank with that scrupulous regard for financial 'tone,' such as should characterise the conduct of a great State Bank, it is not for us to decide."[23] Nor did Palmer appear to have the respect of his peers. Sir Eldon Gorst put a finer point on his colleague's character, stating that Palmer was "a man of inferior capacity who, like, all inferior people, preferred to do everything badly himself, rather than let it be done well, under his superintendence, by others."[24] Perhaps reputation was of little concern to Palmer because of the wealth he was able to amass after joining the bank. Upon his death, Palmer's estate was valued at £144,037, the equivalent of roughly $18.8 million today.[25]

For his own part, Palmer considered his work at the National Bank one of his life's greatest achievements. His headstone on the Isle of Wight highlights his career in Egypt, listing his most important accomplishments as "Financial Adviser to H.H. the Khedive of Egypt, 1889–1898" and "Governor of the National Bank of Egypt, 1898–1906."[26] The two titles point to Palmer's movement between varying forms of British influence in Egypt, and their interconnection, as he transitioned from public servant to private citizen, between British imperialist to the more locally embedded resident foreigner, without seeing any contradiction between the two roles. Yet, there is a tension in Palmer's involvement in these different facets of foreign influence. In particular, his work in private commerce made him a clear beneficiary of the foreign privileges established by the Capitulations and Mixed Courts, which gave resident foreigners tax exemptions and extensive legal protections that British imperialists were purported to work against.

Instead, both Palmer and Colvin might have looked to fulfill colonial aims through these local systems. Yet, these negotiations with the colonial context led to compromises and even a kind of assimilation, particularly in areas that afforded them greater private wealth. Perhaps the greatest irony came from Colvin, who went so far as to condemn Egypt's European resident foreigners because of their dependence on the Capitulations:

Almost domiciled in a strange land, he yet prizes above all things his nationality, which throws over the aegis of its protection. Living on privileged terms among the people of the country, he does not feel the pressure of their needs, nor the yoke of maladministration. The presence of a numerous and powerful but independent foreign body of this nature in Egypt, enjoying privileges, but claiming exemption from public burdens and duties, adds enormously to the difficulties of administration.[27]

The wealth that Colvin accrued as he penned his criticism depended on the very financial privileges he condemned. Likewise, the "villadom" that he lauded as evidence of British imperial successes came through collaboration with the very class of foreigners he publicly denounced.

For Palmer and Colvin, their involvement in private business ventures at the turn of the twentieth century worked against the financial reform efforts they had previously been employed to establish on the government's behalf. This was not a case of building empire through banking and finance, as though they were motivated by some guiding imperialist ideology. These were men who capitalized on the financial opportunities wrought by empire and, in turn, amassed significant private wealth. The results of their efforts would help substantiate networks of local finance that predated the British occupation. And their profitable modernization projects—the railway and suburban developments—would come to depend on the financial protections granted to foreigners that the imperial administration was supposed to amend.

If Palmer did not publicly address the accusations leveled against him, popular perception remained central to the profitability of his new ventures, and his business partners, a cohort of Egypt's most prominent Jewish families, appeared most concerned with establishing a good name for the National Bank of Egypt and the Daira Sanieh Company. When de Guerville identified Palmer's questionable financial dealings, he also published a defense from Raphael Suarès, one of Egypt's most powerful bankers and transportation magnates. Suarès related a sequence of events that detailed how he became involved with both the land and the banking ventures and selected Palmer as the bank's founding governor. His account also details how the global financial powerhouse Sir Ernest Cassel became involved in the deal.[28]

Suarès explained that he was the one who obtained the government concession for not only the creation of the National Bank but also the option of purchasing what remained of the *da'ira* for £6 million. Seeking additional capital, he said he was then introduced to Cassel on a trip to England. Suarès continued:

> I told him I looked for a profit of something over £1,000,000, when he said he would trust to me; and the affair was concluded. The concession for the Bank seemed to please him more, and he asked who we should place at the head. It was then that I proposed Palmer, whose name, so well known as Financial Adviser, was bound to carry weight.[29]

Cassel's introduction to Egyptian finance had widespread effects. He not only provided significant capital for the creation of the bank and Daira Sanieh Company, but also issued the loan behind the construction of the Aswan Dam.[30] Cassel's relationship with Suarès made these ventures possible. But that was not his only connection to Egypt. Cassel was a close business associate of Cromer's brother, Lord Revelstoke, who as the head of Baring Brothers arranged the loan for the dam and profited substantially.[31] Here again private capital served imperial aims. Fulfilling those goals, however, required close local partnerships, and it was Suarès and the larger network of local banking expertise that he represented that substantiated Cassel's ongoing investment in Egypt, rather than Palmer's influence.

The history of the Suarès family cannot be parsed from that of Egypt's other leading Jewish families—the Rolos, Cattaouis, Menasces (also spelled Menashe), and Mosseris. Shared business ventures and intermarriage intertwined their interests in such a way that by the late nineteenth century each family's respective history became inseparably connected to that of the others. Together these families formed the upper echelon of Jewish society in Egypt, with various branches remaining heads of the Jewish communities in both Cairo and Alexandria for generations. By the time that the National Bank of Egypt was formed in 1898, their influence was felt not only through significant business dealings with the British, but also through the khedive's court, where prominent women like Valentine Rolo and Alice Cattaoui—both members of the Suarès family—served successively as first ladies-in-waiting to the khediva.[32] Their local expertise allowed them to continue effectively working within existing Ottoman systems while also profiting from growing European investment in Egypt. In this way, they not only established financial practices that put locals in close connection with foreign partners, but also created a pattern within local society for the incorporation of multinational cultural influences.[33]

As Sephardic Jews, these families' leadership of Cairo's and Alexandria's Jewish communities was representative of Egypt's Sephardic majority, with smaller Ashkenazi and Kairate populations forming their own separate, smaller communities. Sephardic leadership, however, only provided a limited basis for creating a cohesive group identity. The majority of Egypt's local, indigenous Jewish population remained in the Jewish quarter, or *hara*, near Cairo's downtown, where men wore Arab-style dress—a long shirt known as a *gallabiya*—spoke Egyptian Arabic, and earned their living through small trade and traditional crafts. The Sephardic elite, in contrast, adopted the European tastes and customs of their respective nationalities, and generally spoke either Italian or French.[34] The Jewish community remained complex and often segmented by class, language, religious tradition, and culture, so that it was not a singular entity.[35] Yet, even as the Sephardic elite embraced a class identity that often tied them not only to European resident foreigners but also to the royal family, they also remained connected to the broader Jewish communities in their respective cities and took their leadership roles seriously.

When Raphael Suarès partnered with Palmer, he brought with him his brothers Felix and Joseph, Moise de Cattaoui Pasha, and Simon Rolo. For these men, the formation of the National Bank of Egypt served as a continuation of their families' long histories of banking, which began generations earlier with money changing and lending in Cairo's *hara*. Finance and banking were particularly important opportunities for Jewish families because the Muslim majority did not traditionally pursue service professions in banking.[36] For example, by the mid-nineteenth century, Moise de Cattaoui's father Yacoub used the capital he had amassed through moneylending to be the first to leave the Jewish quarter and move to Shubra, then a rural suburb north of Cairo. By that time, he served as Egypt's leading moneylender under Khedive Isma'il.[37] Yacoub Cattaoui established a trend in linking Jewish capital with suburban development. The Mosseris and then the Suarèses, Menasces, and Rolos all similarly moved into wealthier suburbs, and took up residence in new palatial villas on the outskirts of Cairo and Alexandria.

While these families lived in Egypt across generations and ingratiated themselves to the khedive's circle, they also maintained foreign citizenship. The Cattaouis possibly claimed the longest connection to Egypt. Multiple histories of the family exist, with some saying they came to Egypt from Holland in the early nineteenth century and others contending that their lineage dates back to the Fatimid period of the tenth and eleventh centuries.[38] If these millennial connections to Egypt are true, then their name likely derives from the village of Qat'a, located near present-day Zamalek, west of downtown Cairo.[39] The opaque roots of the Cattaoui family speak of these families' complicated histories. In some ways, they existed as *mutamassirun*, or "Egyptianized," while also relying on the privileges granted to them by their status as foreign subjects. Their sustained presence in Egypt across the nineteenth century became integral to the deep local influence that so-called foreign actors had on Egyptian modernization efforts, which began in the finance sector and moved to technological and land development initiatives.

These Jewish families' divergent forms of citizenship grew out of Egypt's location among a range of imperial rivalries, with each of the Great Powers looking to increase its influence in the country by granting citizenship to wealthy Egyptians.[40] The Mosseri, Suarès, Menasce, and Rolo families' foreign status all indicated Egypt's checkered landscape of competing imperial regimes. Urban areas became especially profitable spaces in this context because of the layered impact of British and Ottoman influences on the country, with the Ottoman Capitulations offering financial and legal advantages while the British presence created a perceived economic stability that attracted more European investment.[41]

Although born in Egypt, these families possessed foreign nationalities that served as more than external or legal identities. Each family mingled local, regional, and foreign modes of identification, so that while they intermarried and remained closely tied to one another, they also maintained a connection to their respective nation of citizenship. Italian and Austro-Hungarian citizenship were particularly common among this Sephardic elite. The Suarèses were Spanish Jews with Italian citizenship. Isaac Suarès, the father of Joseph, Felix, and Raphael, arrived in Cairo in the early nineteenth century from Livorno, Italy, where the family landed after fleeing Spain in the fifteenth century.[42] The Mosseris were also Italian subjects, and maintained a particularly strong allegiance to the country's culture and politics, which often separated them from the Suarès, Cattaoui, Menasce, and Rolo cohort.[43] It was not until the late nineteenth century that the Mosseri family became more firmly connected to the rest of the Sephardic elite. Their integration was initiated more through marriage than business, when Nissim J. Mosseri Bey married Hélène Cattaoui, followed by Elie Nissim Mosseri's marriage to Felix Suarès's daughter Laura.[44]

The Menasces and Cattaouis were Austro-Hungarian citizens and both acquired the status of baron, indicated by the "de" that preceded their surnames. They maintained connections to the wider Austro-Hungarian community in Egypt until the end of the First World War, after which they became either stateless or acquired nationality from another foreign power.[45] These families also maintained close relationships with the khedive. Before the family relocated to the Mediterranean coast, Jacoub Levi Menasce became Khedive Isma'il's leading banker. With the khedive's support, the Menasce family later founded the Banque Turco-Egyptienne, which strengthened their regional ties to Istanbul.[46]

The Rolos were similarly well connected to the khedival court. As mentioned above, Valentine Rolo was a first lady-in-waiting. When the family first came to Egypt remains unknown, but they acquired British nationality. They maintained a strong sense of Anglophilia, educating their sons in England and fostering close relations with the British colonial government.[47] That the Rolos simultaneously participated in Ottoman courtly culture points to the kinds of complex negotiations these families undertook, as they connected to the Ottoman and British elite. Rather than a kind of juggling act, however, these multinational connections were an existing part of Egypt's urban landscape—linkages that the relationships between these powerful families helped fortify and perpetuate.

Rather than standing in a kind of paradoxical or contradictory position, the Sephardic elite were located amid complex geographical networks that defied Egypt's national boundaries. Their significant local impact on Egypt's banking sector, which culminated in the establishment of the National Bank, derived from the Capitulations.[48] Those privileges were part of their local identity and additionally helped associate economic prowess and elite status with a local culture of cosmopolitan exclusivity.

The construction of Maadi further intertwined the locally embedded, multinational financial relationships behind the National Bank and the Daira

Sanieh Company with new modern development projects in Egypt. In 1897—one year before he resigned his post in the khedive's government—Palmer was appointed as the government representative on the board of the newly formed Delta Railways, where Colvin served as chairman.[49] Delta Railways appeared distinct in its English-ness, and especially its Anglo-Indian pedigree. Other board members included Sir Charles Fremantle, the director of the Suez Canal, Francis Langford O'Callaghan, the former secretary of public works for the Indian government and director of the Burma Railways Co. Ltd., as well as E.L. Marryat and Robert Miller, who were both employed in other Indian railway ventures.[50] The founding board stands out in its apparent lack of representation by the local commercial elite. After Palmer joined the National Bank and the Daira Sanieh Company, however, this earlier light rail venture became incorporated into local networks of capital and expertise that served as the basis for developing Maadi.

Much of Egypt's transportation industry was already dominated by the Suarès family and its cohort.[51] The family created Egypt's first public transport company, a network of horse-drawn carriages known as the Suarès Omnibus Company, which served Cairo's Muski Street until 1940.[52] The vehicles were so ubiquitous that author Naguib Mahfouz depicted them as part of the everyday sights and sounds of Islamic Cairo in the 1910s. In his first installment of the Cairo Trilogy, *Palace Walk*, he describes a draft of air bringing "with it the grinding wheels of the mule-drawn Suarès omnibus, the voices of workmen, the cry of the hot-cereal vender."[53] The omnibus company was just the beginning. In another partnership with Moise de Cattaoui, the Suarès family later pursued the development of light railways throughout Egypt.[54]

A year before the creation of Delta Railways, the Egyptian government had already granted the Suarèses, Cattaouis, Menasces, and Belzadis a concession to build a light railway system in the eastern provinces of Sharqiya, Daqaliya, and Qalyubiya. They subsequently developed the railway system as part of the Sharq Economic Railways Company. In 1900, the company resigned its concession and granted it to Delta Railways. At this same time, La Société Egyptienne des Chemins de Fer Agricole, also known as the Egyptian Company, resigned its concession to build light railways in the provinces of Beheira and Gharbiya to Delta Railways.[55] Once the concessions were transferred, Delta Railways controlled the light rail from Cairo throughout the Lower Egyptian Delta.

If the Suarès cohort established control over much of the transportation industry by 1900, the question of land development remained. The activity of the Daira Sanieh Company became just one facet of how Suarès, Palmer, Menasce, and others became involved in land use. As part of the government sale, the company was responsible for selling the remaining *da'ira* land to pay the balance of the government's loan of £6,431,500 by October 15, 1905, with a minimum 20 percent profit.[56] A year before the deadline, the company had already sold the land and paid the loan.[57] Colvin lauded its success in *The Making of Modern Egypt*, reporting that the company's sales gained an additional £7 million in profit, which was split between the government and the company—a far larger profit than the £1 million Suarès initially promised Cassel. Colvin also noted that the company had the good fortune of purchasing the land just as Egyptian real estate surged in value.[58] Suarès began running a number of sugar refineries on former *da'ira* lands, which were eventually consolidated into the Société du Wadi Kom Ombo, a joint venture between the Cattaoui, Suarès, Menasce, and Rolo families that controlled some seventy thousand feddans (a bit under thirty thousand hectares) by 1904.[59]

With the profitable sale of the *da'ira* lands helping to shore up real estate prices, investment in other land development projects progressed beyond the khedive's former estate, as discussed in the Introduction. When Delta Railways expanded to form Delta Land in 1904, it created the new company with the express purpose of developing lands along the rail line, and Maadi would become its most significant endeavor.

As Delta Land constructed Maadi's streets, the names of the roads reflected the foreign capital and local business expertise that established the garden city. The roads showed the financial relationships that made Maadi possible, but they did not reflect the residents who lived there—the people whose lives made Maadi an increasingly significant part of the landscape of greater Cairo. That is, except for Avenue Williamson, which intersected with Avenue Palmer at Midan Suarès.

Financial arrangements between Colvin, Palmer, and Suarès made Maadi possible, but they did not sustain the town into the future. Palmer died in 1906, and Colvin resigned from Delta Land's board in 1907. Raphael Suarès died in 1902, before Delta Land was established.[60] Following these founders, another group of resident foreigners would become integral to building Maadi. Delta Land brought John "Jack" W. Williamson onto its board to fill Palmer's seat. His addition would mark a cultural and geographical shift for the company and its leadership. Rather than having a pedigree in Anglo-Indian imperial relations, Williamson spent his life in the port cities of the Levant and had recently moved to Cairo as the city's growing economy attracted more commercial expatriates. He and his family would become some of Maadi's first residents, establishing a strong link between the town, Delta Land, and a regional network of foreign merchants and entrepreneurs domiciled in Egypt.

2

PLACE OF PROFIT

S hortly after Delta Land's founding, Jack and Nan Williamson began construction on a new home in Maadi. The family took up residence there in 1908, shortly after the birth of their daughter Nancy.[1] The house, known as "The Grove," stood near Maadi's railway station. An early photograph of the house reveals elements of Maadi's initial development, when the large country houses stood out amid the surrounding agricultural landscape. In the picture, the photographer stands across the street from the home, exposing how carefully the new gravel road had been laid, with its border clearly defined and young trees planted along the adjacent pathway. Just past the row of fragile-looking trees stands one of the Williamson children, likely William, the eldest, who wears a white shirt, knickers, and a wide-brimmed hat as he looks off to his right. In the background, the Grove towers over its environs. The sky around the house looms large, without any additional features—man-made or otherwise—apparent in the distance.

While former colonial civil servants like Auckland Colvin and Elwin Palmer formed the initial business partnerships necessary for founding Delta Land, the actual construction of Maadi relied on the contributions of an additional contingent of foreign subjects in Egypt. Palmer's death in 1906 opened up a vacancy on the company's board, and rather than relying on another former imperialist, Delta Land brought in Williamson.[2] Although he was technically an English national, Williamson spent his life in the eastern Mediterranean, or Levant, and had only recently moved to Cairo.

Williamson represented a different kind of Briton within Delta Land's leadership. Often referred to by historians as European Levantines or simply Levantines, this sector of Ottoman society generally took up residence in the empire's port cities, where they could benefit from trade and gain a higher profit through the benefits of the Capitulations.[3] Utilizing the trade privileges granted within the sultanate, these Levantines lived in port cities like Smyrna (now Izmir) and Alexandria for centuries. As Cairo became increasingly important to the region's commerce, their influence extended southward. Williamson participated in the expansion of Levantine influence as it moved more deeply into Egypt, as he relocated from Smyrna to Cyprus and then to Cairo.[4] While less locally integrated than the Sephardic elite, Levantines like Williamson brought with them strong regional ties.

As a privatized development project that depended on the Capitulations, Delta Land's endeavor in Maadi became a meaningful residential space for Levantine businessmen and their families, who saw Egypt as an extension of regional networks of kinship and commerce. Their domicile was directly tied to Cairo's value as a site of capital investment. As the Egyptian capital became more commercially viable, it also became a location worth laying down roots. Before building Maadi, Delta Land had to become a fixture in regional networks of financial investment. The company's commercial success preceded Maadi's growth, even though the company would come to depend on the garden city. To become a viable investment, Delta Land would not only rely on the expertise of its Egyptian Jewish founders, but also on Cairo's Levantines, as well as investments managed by the Greek merchant houses that led much of the region's commerce.

Williamson was born and raised in the eastern Mediterranean. His father William Williamson first moved to Smyrna in 1840 and married Elizabeth Barker there in 1849. Jack was born seven years later, the third eldest in a family with sixteen children in all, although four died in infancy from diphtheria.[5] For many of these expatriate families, their sense of place came through their relationships with other similarly domiciled foreigners involved in trade. They and their neighbors balanced their lives between qualified assimilation and a defensive sense of national identity tied to their respective countries of citizenship. Levantines' dependence on good commercial relationships kept their interests and vision for future growth firmly planted in Ottoman territories. To carry out their affairs, for instance, the Williamsons spoke fluent Greek and Arabic, and could conduct business in a smattering of other languages. Elements of British and European culture, however, remained important signifiers of family distinction and prestige, no less because their foreign citizenship helped secure their profitability. The Williamson children attended school in Britain or Europe, which helped create an insulating, cultural buffer between their work in the Levant and the foreign traditions they preserved at home.[6]

Similar to Egypt's Sephardic elite, the Williamson family intermarried and formed business partnerships with other expatriates in Smyrna. These connections later grew into a regional network that spanned the Mediterranean. Jack's own pedigree exhibited generations of Levantine history. His mother Elizabeth was the granddaughter of William Barker, who first went into business in the region in 1760, when he purchased a share in the Levant Company. William's grandson Henry Barker, Elizabeth's father, extended the Levant Company into Alexandria in 1848. In marrying into the Barker family, William Williamson joined one of the most influential British families in the eastern Mediterranean. Descendants of Henry Barker remained in Alexandria until the 1960s, and other branches of the family intermarried with Britons and other Europeans in Smyrna and Istanbul, so that today much of the Barker line remains in Turkey.[7] Similar linkages formed with the Rees, Cumberbatch, Pengelley, and Lewis families.[8] Over the course of the nineteenth century, the geographic reach of these families spread throughout Turkey, Greece, Cyprus, Malta, Palestine, and North Africa.[9]

If Anglo-Indians like Colvin and Palmer provided the initial British face of Delta Land, regionally integrated Britons involved in Levantine commerce carried the company and Maadi into the future. Jack Williamson represented a new generation in the company's leadership—one that embraced the multinational qualities of Cairo's social and economic fabric, rather than interpreting them as regrettable impediments to British imperial hegemony. Like Egypt's Sephardic elites, these Levantine Europeans found a place in Egypt that did not exist in a binary of either local or foreign identification. In taking up residence in Maadi, Williamson and others like him made the town a space for long-term, deliberate domicile abroad. As they played an integral role in Maadi's early development, they also shaped the town as a place of foreign privilege and modern prestige.

Increased European imperial rivalries within Ottoman territories during the late nineteenth and early twentieth centuries made the sultanate's cities sites of growing social diversity because older policies, like the Capitulations, created openings for expanding trade relationships.[10] The same trends that saw the economic expansion of Istanbul, Smyrna, Salonika (now Thessaloniki), and Cyprus also affected Cairo and Alexandria. When Jack Williamson came to Cairo in the early years of the twentieth century, he brought deep regional connections with him. He first left Smyrna in the late 1870s to set up business in Cyprus with fellow Levantine William Rees.[11] Together, the two worked on a variety of ventures. They invested in mining and dabbled in archaeology, successfully extracting and trading valuable artifacts, which were later acquired by the British Museum. They also founded the *Cyprus Herald*, the island's first English-language newspaper. Williamson additionally joined the Cyprus Company Ltd., which traded wine and spirits. He even exhibited Cypriot wine at the Colonial and Indian Exhibition in London in 1886.[12]

In Cyprus, Williamson was among the first foreign nationals to take advantage of the island's growing significance to Mediterranean trade. Other European expatriates largely funded the expansion of real estate markets surrounding the island's ports, becoming locally engrained notables and helping develop the island's ports into increasingly metropolitan trade centers.[13] The location of the island nation made it easier not only to access trade in Greece and Turkey, but also to take advantage of the commercial opportunities opening up in Egypt.

In Egypt, Williamson already had family connections in Alexandria on his mother's side, but he strengthened those ties in his own right. When the British prepared to invade Egypt in 1882, Williamson and Rees gained a lucrative contract for supplying the British fleet from Cyprus.[14] The duo also made a profitable personal connection with Horatio Kitchener, who stayed with them while stationed on the island as a surveyor before transferring to Egypt. Indicative of how the growth of imperial influence in Egypt and North Africa fueled the expansion of regional financial networks, Williamson won a series of military supply contracts during Kitchener's campaign in the Sudan in 1883 and in his later position as sirdar of the Egyptian army under Cromer, when he secured British victory in the Sudan fifteen years later. Williamson additionally secured contracts for works in connection with the development of the Suez Canal.[15] As a resident foreigner, Williamson was not directly involved in the politics and policy of empire, but he still had a hand in constructing it through his investments. While we do not have the kind of personal source material that would attend to Williamson's feelings about British imperialism, his collaboration with Kitchener establishes the often personal ways that private commercial ventures became tied to empire-building.

The range of connections to Egypt Williamson generated from Cyprus eventually prompted him to move. He made a home in Cairo by at least 1902, when his young wife Amy Christine Black died in the Egyptian capital, only four years after their marriage in Syria.[16] Williamson remained in Cairo and married Hannah "Nan" Macredie in 1905. The couple had their first child, William Williamson, a year later—the same year Jack joined Delta Land's board of directors.[17] The Williamsons continued to move between Cairo and Smyrna in the early years of their family life. Just a year after William's birth in Cairo, their second child, Alithea Margaret, was born in Boudjah, an elite suburb of Smyrna. The family subsequently laid down firmer roots in Egypt, with Maadi becoming their most continuous place of residence. After moving to the Grove, they had another son, John Latimer, in 1913 and then a daughter, their youngest, Kathleen, in 1916.[18] The Williamson children grew up as Maadi itself developed, being among its first residents.

Williamson's trajectory across the Mediterranean, from Smyrna to Cyprus to Cairo, participated in broader regional trends, as the expansion of foreign commerce contributed to urban and suburban development. During the late nineteenth century, Smyrna similarly expanded to become not only the Ottoman empire's most valuable port for western European trade, but also into a significant urban cultural center. Smyrna's transportation infrastructure grew significantly in the late nineteenth and early twentieth centuries—the same years that saw the growth of a foreign merchant class who came to lead the city's export trade, as well as its banking, shipping, and maritime insurance economies.[19] A connection to a particular urban space, with the kinship ties that formed across generations through intermarriage and commercial ties, stood at the center of expatriate activities throughout the Levant. Maadi offers further evidence of not only these people's significance to the regional economy, but also their contribution to changes in the local built environments of the region's cities at the turn of the twentieth century.

The means of constructing and maintaining a Maadi home like the Grove relied on the wealth that the Williamsons derived from Jack's work in Levantine regional commerce, which secured the family's position in Cairo's upper middle class. The home embodied much of the town-and-country ideal that Ebenezer Howard's original scheme for the garden city was supposed to offer. Its location near the railway station offered easy access to downtown Cairo, yet it physically appeared to inhabit a space thoroughly in the countryside. The Grove's garden increasingly softened the home's stony exterior, presenting it as a place enmeshed in rustic environs. It served as an early marker of how Delta Land would repurpose the land outside the city as a signifier of bourgeois wealth and foreign commercial influence. Maadi's town-and-country features became a sustained brand for the town, defining it throughout the political upheavals of the first half of the twentieth century.

While Delta Land successfully constructed an idyllic garden city in Maadi, its creation did not exist apart from the social and economic inequalities of the time. Maadi was a place of privilege and relied heavily on the economic benefits granted to foreigners. Its country environs allowed residents to avoid extended exposure to urban poverty. That location did not mean residents were completely insulated, however, especially when it came to the people forced out of the village that the new garden city increasingly encroached upon.

Like central Cairo's European-styled city, the network of streets and *mayadin* in Maadi mimicked Haussmann's renovation a half-century earlier, and Delta Land intentionally looked to extend Cairo's affluent "European" city, thus exacerbating the capital's socioeconomic bifurcation. More than a small exclusive minority, Cairo's population of well-to-do foreigners grew in the early twentieth century, and Maadi and its garden city competitors worked diligently to attract their business. With the beginning of the British occupation, Egyptian cities saw an influx of foreign subjects looking to take advantage of growing commercial opportunities. The 1907 census reported that in the preceding ten years, Cairo's and Alexandria's urban populations had expanded at some of the fastest rates in the world, behind only Calcutta and Berlin. What is more, the growth was not attributed to industrialization or the movement of peasants into the city, but predominantly to the immigration of Europeans. The census reported:

> It is believed that in portions of many urban areas the native residents have actually been replaced by foreigners, and that in the many cases where the new arrivals are sharp-witted, pushing individuals on the look-out for employment, the result has been to actually drive a portion of the indigenous community, not to other quarters of the same town, but altogether out of the urban area.[20]

The strength of this incoming population to reshape urban demography made the development of elite-styled suburban spaces all the more profitable. It also indicated the social fissures that surrounded the growth of Maadi and other elite spaces from the very beginning.

As the movement and migration of Europeans led to displacement, Maadi's expansion hinged on the growth of the suburb into land formerly occupied by villagers who were increasingly pushed out of expansive agricultural spaces they called home. When Delta Land purchased the Suarès land in 1907, the company records do not attend to the lives of the villagers who inhabited the land. Maadi al-Khabiri remained, albeit in diminished form, throughout the first half of the century, and its residents would make themselves known throughout the various phases of Maadi's development. The lives of these villagers are only hinted at in the sale documents—in a section where the Suarès family secured the profits to one more harvest of berseem clover.[21] Those performing the labor of the harvest go unmentioned, yet they were essential to the agricultural life that preceded Delta Land's development. These villagers would maintain a life on the fringes of the garden city but were never incorporated into the company's vision for the area.

By the time that the Suarès land sale was complete, a different kind of movement had also taken place, for the company's leadership and Delta Land had officially relocated its headquarters from London to Cairo.[22] Plans to move began the summer after Williamson joined the board but did not take formal effect until May 1907. The geographic shift in the company's leadership was generational. When the company relocated, all of the board members residing in England resigned. By that time, both Felix and Raphael Suarès had passed away. As mentioned in Chapter One, Raphael died in 1902, before the company ever formed. His elder brother followed him in 1906.[23] In 1908, Colvin also passed away.[24] The broader relations between England and Egypt underwent their own generational turning point at this time. In 1907, Cromer retired from his position as consul-general and returned to England. He would be remembered as a paragon of British imperial dominance in Egypt, and none of his successors mustered the same level of control over Egyptian affairs.[25]

Once in Cairo, Delta Land's leadership was comprised of a different kind of partnership between Britons and Egypt's Jewish elite. Where the company had its start in the privatization of certain sectors of the Egyptian government, the company's new board maintained fewer direct ties to the colonial regime. The board of directors created in May 1907 had no designated chair. Instead, it was led jointly by its directors, who included Williamson, Baron Jacques de Menasce, Maurice (Moise) Cattaoui Bey, and Robert S. Rolo. Joining this cohort were Percy W. Carver, who had served on the board of Delta Railways since 1897, and Captain Alexander Adams, who was reappointed to the board after previously resigning from Delta Land in 1905.[26] One lone resident of England remained, Frederick James Horne, who continued in his position as the company secretary from London. His position secured the Delta Land's English registration, allowing it to preserve its Capitulations privileges.

Delta Land's move to Cairo proved fortuitous. In 1907, the global economy erupted into a worldwide panic. By that fall, the world's gold reserves were depleted, first by the Boer Wars and the Russo-Japanese War, and then by earthquakes in San Francisco on 18 April and in Valparaiso, Chile, on 16 August. All of these events worked together to destabilize global markets.[27] Agricultural economies like Egypt were especially hard hit by the global panic. Inflated land values plummeted, and the market subsequently bottomed out. The Egyptian economy faced further challenges following a significant decline in agricultural profits in 1908 and 1909, when a poor cotton harvest severely reduced the country's exports.[28] This economic downturn stunted Maadi's early growth. In 1906, the company's first year selling plots in Maadi, nine lots were purchased. By 1907—even as Delta Land acquired the Suarès land—the company moved only three plots. The board report that June stated flatly, "Property sales down due to severe worldwide economic recession and the financial crisis in Egypt."[29] Even worse, in 1908 they only sold a meager one plot. Sales rebounded in 1909, however, when total sales rose to thirteen plots.[30]

Arguably, the concentration of the Delta Land's leadership in Cairo allowed the company to respond adeptly to the financial crisis. Even with only gradual gains, the company weathered the financial crisis better than its competitor in Heliopolis. As mentioned in the Introduction, Baron Edouard Empain's Heliopolis Oasis Company responded to the 1907 panic by canceling the construction of the worker community included in the original design and focusing efforts on the more elite space centered on the Heliopolis Palace Hotel.[31] One year after the panic, the conflicts surrounding Empain's ambitions for Heliopolis led to the first major strike by Egyptian industrial workers. Early on the morning of October 17, 1908, sixteen hundred tramwaymen employed by Empain's Cairo Tramway Company lay down on the tracks throughout the city, refusing to move unless the company granted them higher wages, shorter hours, and benefits if injured on the job.[32] The strike, which was led by lower-skilled and lower-paid Egyptian drivers and conductors, lasted three days before the police broke it up. The workers' cause was not lost, however, and by the end of October they secured the better wages and hours.

Delta Land escaped the fallout from the major workers' strikes that accompanied Egypt's early twentieth-century economic instability. This was due in part to the company's corporate structure. While Delta Land's existence depended on transportation networks, Delta Railways managed those separately. What is more, the light rail used for the Cairo–Helwan line that would become Maadi's main thoroughfare was an entirely separate system from the tramway controlled by Empain. When the strike unfolded amid the construction of Heliopolis northeast of downtown, the light rail running south of Cairo to Maadi went largely unaffected.

The relationship between Delta Land and Delta Railways proved essential to sustaining the land company amid the economic uncertainties that unfolded shortly after the company was created. As the more substantial parent company, Delta Railways launched Delta Land to an existing network of investors who were integral to the new company's early success. While Maadi was the physical place that became most identified with Delta Land's ventures in Egypt, the town's development depended on the stability of the company as a place of global economic exchange. As a location of investment, the company had to gain visibility among networks of investors already heavily involved in the region. Because of the railway company, Delta Land was an object of investment well before Maadi's roads were laid or villas constructed.

Delta Railways shone a kind of spotlight on the new venture, promoting it to existing investors. For its part, Delta Land defined itself broadly to shareholders. When the company was incorporated in April 1904, its memorandum of association outlined a variety of possible development projects that it could undertake. These included managing residential, agricultural, commercial, industrial, and even archaeological land. Delta Land presented itself this way because its parent company possessed large portions of land throughout Cairo and northward into the Nile Delta where it already ran light rail. Because Delta Land was the scion of the railway company, its founders initially designed the company as a vehicle for developing any land adjacent to its many rail lines.[33]

For their part, Delta Railways' shareholders were apparently quick to jump on the new land development venture. Of Delta Land's initial hundred thousand shares, more than 85 percent were made available to railway company investors.[34] While it is not possible to tell how many of these shareholders invested in Delta Land, it is clear that the new company began with sufficient investor backing. Delta Land consistently raised its capital in its first four years. All of the initial shares made available were purchased at a cost of £1 each in 1904. Just a year later, Delta Land increased its capital from £100,000 to £250,000, creating another 150,000 shares. By 1907, that capital doubled to a total of £500,000.[35] The growing number of available shares helped sustain Delta Land following the panic of 1907. While early investors may have baulked at the diluted value of their initial shares, the changes also set up the company to make more long-term gains.

Delta Land's register of shareholders identifies the specific people and financial institutions involved in creating a place for the company in the market. Those investors included entities already affiliated with Delta Land's board members, like the Messers Suarès Frères and Compagnie and the Cattaoui Figlis and Co. Other investors had no apparent existing connection to the company. One of the single largest investors, for instance, was the French-born merchant banker Ernest Rüffer, who purchased 2,396 shares, but appears nowhere else in the company archive.[36] The investors also came from a range of backgrounds. The most common occupation was "gentleman," but they also included merchants, bankers, military personnel, widows, spinsters, and "married women." While speculation took place across a broad geography, many of these investments also grew out of existing networks of trade that were closely tied to kin relations. For these people, global networks of finance and commerce were familiar parts of ongoing family practices.[37]

The specific networks of investment behind Delta Land additionally grew out of the patterns of capital investment already at work in Levantine port cities. The company's participation in these connections further established it within a regional geography of financial investment and made the land company all the more dependent on the maintenance of the Capitulations.

While European financial investors were often identified with attempts to gain unilateral influence over the sultanate, their competition in the region made maintaining the Capitulations integral to the growth of Levantine and Egyptian economies—even as the existing system excluded the majority of locals from directly profiting from that growth. In Smyrna, for instance, French investment helped establish the Imperial Ottoman Bank, which stabilized Ottoman currency and made port cities more valuable sites for further speculation.[38] At the same time, German capitalists attempted to check French influence by working with Greek investors to found the Bank of the Orient.[39] British, American, and smaller European powers additionally attached themselves to the Smyrna Bank Ltd. and the British Oriental Bank.[40] Here, various foreign powers vied for influence through the banks. These financial institutions had an added regional impact. Delta Land's investors included, for instance, the Alexandria branch of the French-backed Imperial Ottoman Bank, which managed the purchase of more than three thousand of Delta Land's initial shares.[41]

Greek bankers and merchants throughout the region played an especially influential role in driving foreign competition.[42] They were instrumental in forming the Bank of Athens to capitalize on the opening of banks in Smyrna between 1904 and 1907.[43] Similar patterns of investment unfolded in Egypt. When Delta Land was created, for example, the Bank of Athens managed more than five hundred of the initial shares purchased.[44] Greek merchants and bankers were often more adaptable players within the Levantine economy than northern Europeans and Britons. Taking up long-term residence in the region's commercial hubs, they successfully incorporated themselves into local networks of business and finance. In Egypt, several Greek families, including the Zervudachis and Salvagos, worked closely with the country's leading Jewish financiers.[45]

It was, in fact, global networks of Greek merchants that made the launch of Delta Land a success. Greek merchants were among Egypt's largest body of resident foreigners. They, like Egypt's Sephardic elite, helped connect Delta Land to a broader network of capital investment that preceded the physical construction of Maadi and made it possible. These merchant connections grew out of household and kinship relationships that supported economic development throughout the region. The family connections embedded in Delta Land's list of investors is best exemplified by Ralli Bros. Ltd., a London merchant house responsible for the purchase of several thousand of Delta Land's initial shares. At least six different members of the Ralli family invested in Delta Land through a series of transactions, most of which were managed by the London merchant house. Additionally, Ralli Bros. managed the investments of three other Greek shareholders: Mary Rodocanachi, Pandely Argenti, and Julia Scaramanga. Their link to Delta Land grew out of a shared connection to Ralli Bros. that dated back to the families' diaspora from the island of Chios in the 1810s and 1820s.[46] While these Greeks suffered violence at the hands of the Ottomans, their displacement did not stop them from benefitting from the opportunities that the Ottoman financial system left open to foreigners.[47]

When Ralli Bros. purchased shares of Delta Land in 1904, the company was run by Lucas E. Ralli. The "brothers" in the firm's title referred to his father and uncle, Eustratios and John Ralli, who founded the London merchant house in 1826.[48] In connection with their family members in Liverpool, Manchester, Livorno, Marseilles, Istanbul, and Odessa, the Ralli family ran one of the nineteenth century's most profitable trade networks in the Black Sea and Mediterranean. By the time that Lucas took over leadership of the company in 1879, however, the merchant house had lost some of its earlier prominence. To expand the business, Lucas led a transition away from the Levant and increased its focus on South Asian and North American markets. He helped build the company's New York branch, moving to the United States in 1874 and only returning to England to take over the London merchant house after the death of his older brother John.[49] By the time that Ralli Bros. invested in Delta Land, their networks of investment and trade crisscrossed the Atlantic and maintained a strong footprint in the Mediterranean and Black Sea regions.

In their various trade endeavors, the Rallis worked in close connection with other prominent Greek families who similarly haled from Chios.[50] When the Ralli business shifted away from the Mediterranean, the Scaramangas took over their export/import business in the region, particularly in Marseilles.[51] The two families established one merchant house together in the Ukranian port city of Taganrog, called Ralli & Scaramanga, which they founded in the 1850s.[52] Even more prominent than the Scaramangas were the Rodocanachis. In the Black Sea and Baltic, the Rallis focused on exports from Western Europe, and the Rodocanachis imported those goods. As Stanley Chapman explains, by the mid-nineteenth century, the Rallis and Rodocanachis were London's wealthiest merchants, noting that "only Rothschilds were substantially richer, and they were now financiers rather than merchants."[53]

Similar to the interlocking financial and familial relationships formed among Egypt's Jews and Levantine Europeans, these Greek families' trade connections were inextricably linked to personal family relations formed through marriage. Their investment in Delta Land revealed global economic links that made the physical construction of greater Cairo possible. More than faceless pathways of financing, these connections were personal and familial.[54] Lucas's great-grandmother, for instance, was a Scaramanga. His wife Eugenia, "Jenny," was the daughter of Leonidas Argenti and Julia Ralli. Considering that Jenny was an Argenti, it is not surprising that Ralli Bros. managed the investments of Pandely Argenti, Jenny's brother, who purchased three shares of Delta Land.[55] Jenny likely proved especially beneficial to the business by connecting her husband Lucas with her cousin Pandely Ralli, a former member of parliament for Bridport, England.[56] When the merchant house invested in Delta Land, Pandely was Lucas's leading partner, and Delta Land listed their names together on most of the investments managed by Ralli Bros.[57]

Women like Jenny Ralli helped solidify ties between business partners and potential investors by informally extending the family's network of relationships. As an unofficial participant in Ralli Bros., she served the kind of semipublic role that had been integral to the growth of market capitalism and middle-class identity since the late seventeenth century.[58] When they invested in Delta Land, the Ralli women and their Chios relations were working beyond a supportive, strictly private role by purchasing shares out of their own means. Lucas's widowed younger sister Catherine Ralli, for instance, purchased 140 shares of Delta Land. Their merchant house also managed the investments of Julia John Scaramanga, who owned 140 shares, as well as that of Mary Rodocanachi, a "married woman," who purchased 120 shares. Overall, women represented about 10 percent of Delta Land shareholders. The company listed them as widows, spinsters, and married women, with a few named with their husbands as "Gentleman and Wife."[59] The majority of them were women of independent means who remained attached to their family's networks of capital. Women like Catherine Ralli, Julia John Scaramanga, and Mary Rodocanachi strengthened Ralli Bros. stake in Delta Land while also extending female involvement in the family business.

The family connection Jenny Ralli made to Pandely Ralli additionally buttressed some of the merchant house's closest ties to Egypt. Pandely, like Jack Williamson, was a close friend of Lord Kitchener. They also met in Cyprus, where Kitchener had stayed with Williamson before leaving for Egypt. When Kitchener would later visit England, he often stayed with Pandely.[60] Although it is not clear if Williamson and Pandely were personally connected, they certainly traveled in similar social and professional circles. Considering their shared interest in trade in Egypt and the eastern Mediterranean and the Ralli family's prominence in the region, it would not be surprising if they knew one another personally. If such a connection existed, it meant that an additional personal relationship tied Ralli Bros. to the merchant house's extensive investments in Delta Land.[61]

While the Ralli family represented only a fraction of the total body of Delta Land's shareholders, their patterns of investment indicated the specific connections that the company formed within the regional and global networks that shaped the Cairene economy during the early twentieth century. The involvement of these Greek merchant families, like that of Levantine Europeans and Egyptian Jews bearing foreign passports, undermined formal empire-building in Egypt, while also shoring up a range of multinational connections that supported Cairo's privileged class of foreign subjects.

The construction of the Williamsons' Maadi home lent a permanence to the garden city establishment. It meant carving out streets, planting a garden, and erecting walls. This was a location where children could play, where memories could form. This physical existence was not Delta Land's primary aim, however, but rather its secondary effect. Before Maadi could exist, Delta Land had to be a viable part of the global economy—a place of investment and exchange. That existence included the possibility of Maadi but relied more heavily on growing investment patterns that began with Delta Land as part of the global marketplace.

Maadi grew out of the broadly defined possible ventures Delta Land might undertake. And Delta Land had its own kind of population. Here, board members and shareholders populated its registers and moved money into its coffers. Their stories reveal how personal connections inform the histories of global capitalism. Networks of investment took shape, often in response to imperial expansion and diaspora. Those networks resulted in an interconnected economic world that supported Maadi's early growth.

In the years that followed, Delta Land slipped into the background and Maadi, as a physical place, moved to the fore. Over time, Delta Land would become known as the "Maadi Company."[62] The transition appeared natural to residents, who reveled in the seeming stability of their town-and-country lives. That idyllic existence, however, depended on the maintenance of the Capitulations. The economic and political inequalities tied to Delta Land's location in the market remained largely taken for granted—seemingly immovable, like the stone walls of the Grove.

PART TWO:
CONSTRUCTION, PHASE ONE

Delta Land was established in the networks of foreign investment capital that began guiding the Egyptian economy in the
mid-nineteenth century. The construction of Maadi that followed
would embed those global financial networks into the physical environment of greater Cairo. In the early years of building,
Maadi appealed to Cairo's growing body of resident foreigners,
who found a home for their cosmopolitan tastes in the semirural retreat. Just as development appeared to be thriving, however,
Maadi faced the fractures of the First World War. While the town
and much of its society successfully weathered the war, for Maadi
to continue it would have to appeal to Egypt's growing middle-
class intelligentsia.

3

VILLA SOCIETY

P assengers on the southbound light rail from Cairo to Helwan would have looked out on fields of berseem clover thriving in soil enriched by the silt deposits of the nearby Nile. Tenant farmers lived on and cultivated these fields and brought the crops to market. As Delta Land broke ground on its new venture, the company depended on these farmers to preserve the area's bucolic scenery.[1] Yet the company kept few records about these individuals and their families. When three adjoining plots were sold in 1910, the new owners scrambled to find the name of the tenant farmer already working the land, hoping to continue employing him as they built their homes on the property. Although anonymous to company officials, the tenant farmer, Amin Hassan, was known among Maadi's other workers—the cooks, gardeners, and laborers who brought the town into existence. His name only surfaced after Muhammad, a cook employed by a Delta Land manager, passed it along to the company leadership.[2] After the owners approached Hassan, he offered to continue working the land but only if a canal running through the middle of the land was removed, so that the crops were no longer damaged.[3]

While the growth of Maadi into a town-and-country suburb meant that domestic workers like Muhammad were increasingly in demand, Amin's agricultural labor became a temporary measure. The shift in land use from agricultural to residential was apparent, and he had no control over plot numbers and deeds of sale. As the modern Maadi expanded, his occupancy would become a thing of the past. Perhaps Amin saw the writing on the wall, for it appears that the new landowners were unable to meet his demands and secure his ongoing employment. A few months after Muhammad supplied

Amin's name, one company official wrote that the land had gone uncultivated and the purchasers needed to find someone to farm it, "so as to prevent its being made a dumping ground for rubbish and becoming a nuisance to the district."[4] As Maadi al-Khabiri gave way to Maadi garden city, the growth of a well-planned, orderly community was paramount.

As a business venture, Maadi was initially built for Cairo's population of elite cosmopolitans—resident foreigners who settled in the Egyptian capital as beneficiaries of the Capitulations. To maintain Maadi's appeal as a distinctive and planned community, it had to remain separate from Cairo, yet still be accessible to it. Modern transportation was essential because it allowed the area's resident foreigners to work easily in Cairo while living outside of it. This is why Delta Land's board enthusiastically reported in June 1909 that Delta Railways finished construction on Maadi's railway station, made completely convenient with kiosks and shelters.[5] This allowed the sale of land in Maadi to increase in earnest, and, as explained in the last chapter, sales in Maadi doubled that year.[6] To maintain its appeal, the construction of Maadi also had to fulfill the particulars of Delta Land's plans, which required that the company maintain autonomous authority over the area. To that end, the fulfillment of Delta Land's plans was overseen by the company's general manager, who became the central figure in executing the garden city scheme in Maadi. If that plan required the company's ability to operate as a separate municipality, then Delta Land's manager—who was always a resident foreigner and therefore beneficiary of the Capitulations and the protections of the Mixed Courts—filled that role.

If Delta Land defined itself broadly to its global network of investors, it played a much narrower, more focused role for those living and working in Maadi. The company took a distinct approach to its scheme for constructing a garden city, focusing the development of Maadi on a set of mutual obligations that made residents legally bound partners in the town's development. Where Garden City had its unique pattern of streets, and Heliopolis had its Euro-Egyptian building façades, Maadi had rules. Delta Land articulated specific guidelines for the construction and upkeep of Maadi by including a legally binding *Cahier des Charges* in every deed of sale. Within the *Cahier des Charges* residents found a list of specifications that outlined the obligations they and the company each had to the town. It stipulated that the company bore sole responsibility for developing roads, public utilities, and public garden spaces. At the same time, it bound residents to specific rules for the design, upkeep, and sanitation of their homes. The *Cahier des Charges* also set a socioeconomic border around the community. Adherence to the stipulations required the means to employ builders and a variety of domestic servants, and abiding by those regulations made Maadi into a villa community attractive to Cairo's upper middle-class consumers.

The stipulations included in the *Cahier des Charges* established that Delta Land sold all plots of land as residential space, and purchasers could not use the land for any commercial reason. When constructing a villa, it could not exceed fifteen meters in height or take up more than half of the plot's total area. Residents had to dedicate the remaining space to cultivating a garden with a lawn, and the whole property had to be bordered by a green hedge. The restrictions also set detailed guidelines for sanitation and waste disposal. If residents did not abide by these rules, Delta Land reserved the right to penalize them and take the resident to court. With the *Cahier des Charges* in place, the company could implement a complete and consistent plan for Maadi, which it maintained throughout the first half of the twentieth century.[7] Even as individual residents could develop their plots according to their own personal architectural and gardening tastes, they had to do so within Delta Land's constraints.

When enforcing the *Cahier des Charges*, Delta Land expressed that it acted in the interest of the community as a whole, making itself Maadi's legal arbiter of communal harmony. For their part, the residents embraced their obligations to the town. The *Cahier des Charges* provided a degree of local order and established a system of accountability between themselves and the company. As Geoffrey Dale, manager of Delta Land from 1948 to 1956, explained, "The rules were not onerous. They were not extensive and did not run to more than four pages, but they were sensible and in the interest of the community."[8] What is more, Delta Land used the *Cahier des Charges* to create a system of local, municipal authority and structure unavailable in other parts of Cairo. Delta Land offered Maadi residents their own local governing authority. In turn, property owners relied on and largely embraced the *Cahier des Charges* and Delta Land's management as the guarantors of a unique, carefully cultivated, garden city environment. For Delta Land, structuring the garden city according to specific rules became a profitable business model. In its Cairene context, these specifications became especially advantageous because they offered residents a stable, overt system of municipal governance that engrained exclusivity into the space while also making it into an attractive country residence, conveniently situated adjacent to the city center.

If any one person brought together the various strands of Maadi's early history—the personal and professional networks of investments, the partnership with the railway company, and the garden city design—it was Captain Alexander Adams. Adams started his career as a member of the Royal Engineers in Burma. He worked as the assistant manager of Burma Railways from 1893 to 1899, where, it is no coincidence, Sir Auckland Colvin directed the board. At the turn of the century, Adams left for Egypt to join Colvin's new venture, Delta Railways. In Egypt, he became the new company's managing director, handling the railway's day-to-day administration, which included everything from hiring clerks, engineers, and other staff to working with subcontractors to managing the company's legal affairs.[9] When the railway company expanded to form Delta Land five years later, the bylaws mandated several connections between the two ventures. Among them, the railway company's manager had to preside over the daily business of the land company, making Adams the bridge between Delta Land and Delta Railways.

Adams was among the town's earliest residents. Like Williamson, he purchased a large plot of land near the railway station soon after Delta Land was founded, and it was Adams's cook, Muhammad, who passed along information about Amin Hassan to the company.[10] One of Adams's successors, Tom Dale, who became manager in 1916, recalled that after Adams built his villa, it attracted other colleagues and friends who similarly built homes in Maadi. In Dale's telling, "Adams built his villa and Maadi Garden City, in miniature, had begun."[11] Adams was an owner of Maadi in every sense of the term—a resident, shareholder, and a Delta Land employee.[12] Yet, Adams did not remain in the managerial position for long. With both Delta companies growing quickly, having one person oversee both endeavors quickly proved cumbersome. By 1905, Delta Land amended its bylaws and no longer required that the companies share a manager. On 2 August of that year, Adams resigned from Delta Land, but continued with the railway company.[13] He rejoined Delta Land in 1907 as a board member at the same time that the company relocated its offices from London to Cairo.[14] While he did not serve as manager for long, Adams firmly established Delta Land's manager as Maadi's central authority figure.

Adams was replaced as manager by James Albert Wells "J.W." Peacock, who previously served as chief engineer at Delta Railways.[15] By January 1907, however, the company decided to change the nature of the position. They left Peacock as a manager, but in a role that focused on engineering and design. They added a general manager position, which was filled by Reginald Quixano Henriques, a former Cairo-based merchant with an interest in architecture.[16] Henriques took up residence in Maadi the same year he took over the managerial position.[17] Similar to Adams' task as the railway company's manager, Henriques handled day-to-day operations. He hired Delta Land's staff, which included engineers, architects, clerks, and gardeners. He contracted with builders, lawyers, and accountants. He also represented the legal face of Delta Land. In the nine years that he served as manager, Henriques helped Delta Land plant its roots in Maadi. Under his watch, Maadi increasingly became Delta Land's largest property. Its development into a fully planned town-and-country community became integral to the company's corporate identity, especially within Cairo, where it became known as the "Maadi Company."

Unlike the founders who came to Egypt from the Levant or South Asia, Henriques brought a background in trans-Atlantic trade to Delta Land.[18] His Portuguese surname indicates his descent from the Sephardic Jews of the Iberian Peninsula. Henriques' ancestors, like the Suarès family, fled Europe during the Inquisition. After being forcibly converted to Christianity, Jews in Portugal were among the first to emigrate to colonies in South America, particularly Brazil, in hopes of pursuing new opportunities in trade and escaping the Inquisition's oppressive gaze. Although they landed in Brazil, many of these "New Christian" families quickly moved out of Portuguese-controlled areas. Some left Brazil for Northern Europe, while others made permanent homes in Caribbean colonies ruled by Britain, Holland, and Denmark, where they enjoyed greater religious freedom.[19] The family relocated to Kingston, Jamaica, in the seventeenth century, where they formed Henriques Bros., a merchant house that expanded to form new branches in London and Manchester during the eighteenth and early nineteenth centuries. Reginald's father established a new merchant house in Manchester in the mid-nineteenth century, and Reginald was born there in 1869—the third child of what would be eight in all.[20] He and his younger brother Frank Quixano Henriques went on to manage the family business with their father.

Reginald was responsible for expanding the Henriques network into Egypt. In 1891, he moved to Cairo to establish the merchant house Henriques and Henriques, which focused on the textile trade.[21] He met initial success in Egypt and by 1898 added new offices in Tanta and Alexandria.[22] The Alexandria branch was among Delta Land's first investors, purchasing thirty-six shares in 1904. For his part, Henriques personally bought more than seven hundred shares. While the actual reason that Henriques left the family merchant house remains unknown, it is possible that his investment in Delta Land accompanied a relationship with the company's leaders and provided some of the impetus for hiring Henriques.[23] The move might have looked all the more attractive after the 1907 financial crisis. Like the Rallis, the Henriques family saw a boom in trade in the mid-nineteenth century, followed by a significant decline in the early twentieth century.[24] The market crash in the first decade of the new century likely provided the final push for Henriques to leave the family firm.

The combination of administrative experience and proficiency in design made him well-suited to oversee Delta Land's daily affairs as the company undertook the early stages of building Maadi.[25] Henriques hired a staff of architects and engineers to initiate the town's physical development and worked with local lawyers to help handle the administrative organization of the company's affairs. Several of these employees were, like himself, also Maadi residents and Delta Land investors. For instance, George Caruso, who purchased land in Maadi in 1907, was a lawyer and real estate broker, and worked with Henriques to manage some of Delta Land's legal affairs regarding land sales.[26] As the town's lead engineer, Peacock was responsible for building Maadi's first roads. He was also among Delta Land's first investors, purchasing 535 of the company's initial shares.[27] This layering of connections made both the company and the town necessarily collaborative. A variety of people from diverse backgrounds were responsible for the town's success, and their support for Delta Land's endeavor became increasingly personal as they built their homes and invested their finances into Maadi.

Like Henriques, the residents he managed were products of broadly construed global networks dependent on careers in commerce. The town's early populace included primarily Britons, Greeks, and Italians, along with a smaller contingent of French, Austrian, and German families. Between

1907 and 1913, Delta Land sold forty-one lots in Maadi to people with names like Angelo, de Cramer, Crawford, Whitman, MacDonald, Pilavachi, Bondi, Joanovitch, and Veloudakis.[28] The Williamsons, for instance, were not Maadi's only Levantine residents, and were joined by Erwin and Lucy de Cramer, who were of Austrian and Italian provenance, respectively, and had similar multigenerational connections to Smyrna on Erwin's side.[29]

The varied geographical backgrounds of Maadi's early residents were part of larger trends among Cairo's growing population of resident foreigners. According to the 1907 census records, the capital was home to 74,221 resident foreigners who hailed from twenty-eight different countries. The largest single foreign nationality resident group in Egypt were the Greeks, with 14,605 people. They were followed by the Sudanese and Syrians, both with more than 13,000 nationals in the Egyptian capital. Additionally, there were more than 9,000 from Turkey, and 6,642 from Italy. More than 5,000 of these Cairo residents originally came from the British Isles.[30] These larger contingents of resident foreigners were accompanied by smaller French, German, Russian, Austrian, and Armenian communities.[31]

Some of these residents came to Maadi after living elsewhere in Cairo. When the Crookshanks moved to Maadi in 1910, for instance, they had already raised a family in Cairo.[32] The couple would have been familiar with the project since its inception as it was Crookshank Pasha's report on the *da'ira saniya* that exposed Elwin Palmer to accusations of corruption.[33] When the couple moved to Maadi, Harry was sixty-one years old and Emma forty-one, and their two children—Harry Frederick Comfort and Helen Elizabeth "Bessie" Crookshank—were already at school in England.[34] The couple's new home became a countryside retreat after spending more than twenty years in metropolitan Cairo. They brought to Maadi a long history of international travel and residence. Harry first came to Egypt in 1883, when he was a surgeon in the Royal Navy, charged with treating victims of the cholera epidemic. He went on to serve in the Egyptian military campaign in the Sudan and then joined the Egyptian government as the director general of the prisons department—services for which the khedive made him a pasha. He married Emma in 1891 in Philadelphia, and the couple returned to Cairo. Shortly afterward, Harry moved from the prisons department to the Egyptian finance department, where he encountered Palmer.

Emma had an even more geographically complex past than her husband. She was born in Pennsylvania in the spring of 1869, the only child of Samuel and Elizabeth J. Comfort (née Barnsley). Her father was a major in the United States Army during the American Civil War, and went on to join Standard Oil, where he represented the company both nationally and internationally—work that included a six-year post in India. Because of her father's career, Emma had a global coming of age. She met Crookshank Pasha while vacationing in Cairo. Considering her own past, it is not necessarily surprising that she chose to live abroad, yet the move proved a painful detachment for her father. He wrote to her soon after the wedding, "Oh Emma dear, why did you go to Cairo, and fall in love, and have the great Dr. Crookshank Pasha carry you away from us all to Egypt." He continued that her parents did not begrudge her leaving their Philadelphia home, he only wished that "England had not taken so kindly to our American girl abroad."[35] The Comforts relocated to London in 1904, perhaps in part to be closer to their only child, who returned to England every summer. Comfort's letter offers a rare look into the personal strain that a life lived across a broad geography put on family relations. In Maadi, Emma and Harry found a community of people with similarly diverse geographical backgrounds.

For many of Maadi's resident foreigners, the town helped create some stability in otherwise peripatetic lives. A large number of them were highly mobile people, moving from one location abroad to another as they sought new opportunities. In the first fifteen years of the twentieth century, however, they planted themselves more firmly in Maadi. Both Adams and Henriques started their own families in Maadi. Adams married Catherine Mary Fox in London in July 1908, and the couple returned to Maadi soon afterward.[36] Similarly, Henriques married Annie Barnard in 1913, and the couple welcomed their daughter Margaret a year later.[37] As Maadi grew, these men went from globe-trotting bachelors to more established businessmen with families to support. In turn, they firmly located their families' interests in Delta Land's town-and-country development. This is not to say that they became sedentary. Many of Maadi's families continued to spend seasons abroad. The hot summer months, in particular, were usually spent in England or elsewhere in Europe. The developing garden city south of Cairo, however, became their home. Its verdant environment, as mandated by the *Cahier des Charges*, provided the setting for their social interactions, the first home that many of their children knew, and the place where their personal lives unfolded.

While Maadi became home to a portion of Cairo's British, Greek, and Italian populations, along with a smattering of other Europeans, there is a noticeable lack of Arabic-language surnames in the list of early landowners. People like 'Abd al-Malik Khatib and Armand Azeraoui appear to have owned land in Maadi before the company established the town, but they did not hold deeds associated with Delta Land. Theirs were among the only Arabic-language surnames in the company's registers until 1914.[38] While apparently few native-born Egyptians, Turkish Ottomans, or immigrants from elsewhere in the Arab world owned land in Maadi in the early years of its development, they were not absent from the town.

For Maadi's resident foreigners, the *Cahier des Charges* mandated accessible, secure, and well-maintained domestic spaces. Those terms created another Maadi that was a place of work rather than leisure. A great deal of labor went into constructing and maintaining not only Maadi's physical spaces but also the serene domestic life associated with the place. The town's villas generally included space either in the basement or in structures on the roof for live-in cooks and other servants. One Maadi resident recalled that her family's villa had a large basement with two bedrooms and a washroom near the kitchen for the servants.[39] The highly stratified society of early twentieth-century Cairo made for the creation of two Maadis—one for elite, cosmopolitan families like the Crookshanks and de Cramers and another for workers and servants.

The composition of the household staff added additional facets to the multiethnic complexity of Maadi society. Gardeners were generally Egyptian and considered of higher social rank than the indigenous North Africans and Nubians who were often employed as cooks.[40] Lower-class Europeans were also hired into household service. Both men and women worked as domestic servants in elite households, with European women often working as governesses. Through a careful examination of the Egyptian census records, Lanver Mak found a minority of British men and women who moved to Egypt from the British Isles to work as domestic servants.[41]

While Ebenezer Howard's original plan for the garden city promised to level social differences and allow all residents to access the town on equal terms, Maadi exhibited the town-and-country aesthetic without its social ideals. Rather than subverting the existing social hierarchy, Maadi relied on it. The town grew out of a stratified society that offered residents—most of whom generated their wealth through business dealings that benefitted from the Capitulations—a prestigious semirural retreat from the city. Their leisurely experience, however, also relied on the movement of labor into and within the town, which provided the work necessary for maintaining Maadi as a commodity of elite consumption.[42]

The *Cahier des Charges* further engrained Maadi's contrasting social experiences and meanings into the physical qualities of the place. For landowners, the *Cahier des Charges* offered a series of promises by requiring that all homes be held to the same standards in design, construction, and sanitation. While those guidelines required a significant financial commitment, the physical work involved in meeting the company's standards fell on lower-class builders and domestic servants.

For Delta Land, the rules outlined in the *Cahier des Charges* had the added dimension of setting the terms for the company's relationship to each segment of Maadi society. As a legally binding element within each deed of sale, the *Cahier des Charges* meant that any violation was a legal issue that would be addressed first in the consular court, and, if necessary, in the Mixed Courts of Appeal, making their ultimate enforcement well beyond Delta Land's sphere of influence.

Not long after Delta Land began developing Maadi, Henriques landed in court over a dispute about the company's responsibilities to its landowners. In 1913, two would-be residents accused Henriques of deliberately misleading them with regard to the construction of roads bordering their property. Considering the necessity that Maadi be accessible to Cairo, any challenge related to road access could have proven detrimental to the garden city as a whole. As British nationals, the landowners—Alexander J. Wakeman Long, a judge in the Egyptian Native Court of Appeal, and Samuel G. Brittain, a civil engineer in Helwan—brought their charges against the company before the British Consular Court in Cairo. In April 1910, the pair purchased land in Maadi with the intention of building homes for themselves and their families. Wakeman Long and his wife hired Cairo-based architect P. Rodeck to design their new home. The architect was already familiar with Maadi as a distinctive community, commenting in a 1910 letter to Mrs. Wakeman Long that the town was "beginning to look a very nice place indeed now and as a quarter promises to have a distinctive character of its own, which should make it impossible for people that have elected to live there ever to regret having done so."[43] The Wakeman Longs, however, were not as happy with their purchase as Rodeck predicted. The conflict arose not regarding the land itself, but the accessibility of the roads surrounding the property. The buyers claimed that Henriques deliberately misled them when he showed them a plan for proposed roads surrounding their plots of land. Henriques countered their accusations by invoking Article 12 of the *Cahier des Charges*, which stated that Delta Land had sole discretion over the development of roads. He additionally claimed that the roads were not obstructed as the prosecution claimed, that the British consul had no jurisdiction over real property, and that the matter should actually be tried in the Mixed Courts.[44]

Road construction proved challenging for Delta Land from the beginning. In June 1907, the company reported that negotiations with the government regarding building a road to Maadi had failed. While the government agreed to construct a road partway from Old Cairo, they expected the company to pay for the remainder of the road—far less than the board hoped the government would agree to.[45] The Wakeman Long and Brittain case was separate from Delta Land's negotiations with the Egyptian government, and actually exposed a conflict with Delta Railways. The railway company had apparently cut off public access to the roads that ran through Maadi, making it impossible for the new residents to have free and easy access to them, something they logically argued was "essential to the full enjoyment of the property."[46] When Wakeman Long and Brittain apparently attempted to respond by constructing their own roads, however, Henriques invoked the *Cahier des Charges*, successfully establishing that only the company had authority to build roads in Maadi and residents could not construct private ones. The arbitration finally resolved in the company's favor. On 29 April 1914, Wakeman Long and Brittain withdrew their charges and agreed to pay the balance of what they owed to the company for the land. They also agreed that Henriques and Delta Land had fulfilled their obligations as stipulated by the *Cahier des Charges*.[47]

The cause exposed the particulars of Delta Land's authority in Maadi. While unable to make demands of the Egyptian government, it remained in control of company-owned land. Even when residents purchased land, it remained under the authority of Delta Land's *Cahier des Charges*. Henriques successfully deployed the *Cahier des Charges* in his defense and exemplified the stability of the venture, proving that Delta Land was legally protected from accusations of negligence. The article that Henriques invoked in his defense stated that the roads outlined in the company's plan for the town were proposed but never guaranteed, and that the development of such roads was solely under the company's discretion—thus preventing residents from developing private roadways.[48] What is more, in making Delta Land's vision for Maadi central to the town's development, this same article of the *Cahier des Charges* preserved the rest of the community's stability, ensuring that an individual resident's desires could not reshape the company's town-and-country scheme.

Delta Land and Henriques survived the proceedings without any major losses. What is more, Maadi's budding reputation as a beautiful and carefully planned new community remained intact. The plaintiffs' lawyer Robert L. Devonshire moved to Maadi around the same time that Wakeman Long and Brittain made their land purchase. Two years later, Devonshire and his French wife Henriette went on to purchase the disputed land formerly owned by his clients. Henriette later became one of the town's most well-known residents.

As the berseem clover fields and their harvesters gave way to new villas and carefully planned gardens, Delta Land's directors and managers embedded their own lives more deeply in Maadi. The company's business interests and its leadership all converged on Maadi. By the time that Wakeman Long and Brittain withdrew their charges, Henriques, Adams, and Williamson all had homes in Maadi. By settling in Maadi, Delta Land's leadership and their expatriate neighbors participated in a commodification process that fulfilled the company's larger aim for the town. Through the garden city plan, Delta Land created a distinct and identifiable product on the outskirts of Cairo—one that the company could promote to both investors abroad as well as potential residents. The garden city they established fulfilled the aesthetic elements Howard first envisioned in the late nineteenth century. They successfully developed Cairo's rural environs into neatly planned villas and gardens, creating an attractive contrast to the congestion of the city center. Maadi's tree-lined boulevards and garden *mayadin* prevailed over the agricultural land and peasant life that previously subsisted on the land. Maadi became home to Cairo's elite cosmopolitan upper middle-class of resident foreigners and was maintained by its lower-class workers and servants. Having foregone any attempt at establishing a socially equitable space, Delta Land's board, its landowners, and its shareholders all embraced Maadi's association with affluence.

The establishment of Maadi engrained the networks of foreign capital behind Delta Land into the built environment surrounding Cairo. Maadi became a place heavily associated with the inequalities of foreign influence. In turn, Europeans and Levantines who benefitted from the Capitulations increasingly found a future in Egypt and a home in Maadi. So long as Cairo attracted both foreign investment and expatriate domicile, Maadi developed as both a business and a residential community.

When the privileges of foreign nationality were in peril, however, life in Maadi experienced a series of challenges. During the First World War, the town faced a serious threat to the seeming harmony of its early years. To survive, Delta Land had not only to continue making its product appealing to the foreigners who remained in Egypt, but also to attract the country's growing class of wealthy Egyptians.

4

BUILT FOR WAR

S oldiers began arriving in Maadi in December 1914, when the Australian Imperial Force (AIF) established a training camp northeast of the town. A month earlier, the British declared war on the Ottoman empire. While Lord Kitchener, then the British secretary of state for war, assured AIF troops that the plan was to deploy them in Europe and that they were only being held in North Africa because of scarce accommodations in Britain, imperial authorities had been anxious about protecting the Suez Canal since the conclusion of the Second Boer War in 1902. With the British rightly skeptical about Egyptians' willingness to fight for the empire, they instead deployed Australians to protect their interests in the Middle East.[1]

If the troops were disappointed to land in Egypt, British society there greeted them enthusiastically. The *Egyptian Gazette* observed the rapid alterations that the war brought to Maadi, reporting, "The change from the usual quiet of the little station at Meadi [sic] to the bustle and come and go of 'Our Australians' is not so bewildering as it would have been a few months ago."[2] Excitement about the war was pervasive. Australians and other British nationals already resident in Egypt and elsewhere in Africa made their way to the Maadi base to enlist.[3] Delta Land made its own contributions to the war effort, initially offering the AIF vacated homes of residents now deemed enemies and later opening up spaces for larger, more permanent installations.

Maadi's financial independence, under the aegis of Delta Land, did not offer shelter from the storm. On the contrary, the war's rapid expansion unleashed successive waves of nationalism that continued reverberating throughout the region for at least a half century. In Maadi, residents, business leaders, and workers all participated in and were impacted by various aspects of the war. In fact, Maadi's elite cosmopolitan society of resident foreigners, paired with its location outside the city, made the war's totalizing effects all the more profound.

The First World War has long been understood as a turning point in the history of the modern Middle East. The region suffered the war's highest casualties and was subsequently carved up into new nations with new imperial occupiers.[4] In Egypt, the war brought nationwide revolution and then only qualified independence. Within Cairo, not even profound wealth could offer full-scale protection from the war's destructive impact. And in Maadi, privileged foreign residents were among the war's first identifiable enemies. What is more, Maadi's location outside of the city center with easy railway access made it an attractive location for military establishments.

If Maadi was home to a range of foreigners before 1914, the war dramatically enhanced that demographic trend, but no longer in ways carefully monitored by Delta Land. Maadi became a temporary home to nurses and soldiers as well as prisoners of war. These new residents brought some of the region's most significant events of the war directly into Maadi—from the British tactical failure at Gallipoli to the fallout of the Armenian genocide to the ongoing conflict between the Turks and Greeks. Ultimately, Maadi's civilians felt the most lasting impact of the war. Neighbors saw themselves suddenly transformed into enemy aliens, and an entire reordering of Maadi society ensued. To secure Maadi's future, Delta Land would have to pivot its approach to the town, linking Maadi's future growth less and less to elite resident foreigners and instead to Egypt's upper-middle class.

Britain's declaration of war deeply entangled its far-flung empire, expanding the global scale of the fighting. For the white-settler colonies, or dominions, of Canada, Australia, New Zealand, and South Africa, Britain's declaration meant they too were instantly at war and soon deployed in Europe or other colonial theaters. For Egypt, the process was more varied. With the long-standing Ottoman alliance severed, Britain made Egypt a protectorate, and turned the khedive into a sultan and later a king.[5] This was Britain's most formal and imposing claim to imperial control over Egypt to date. As these assertions of British sovereignty intertwined, the Australian military set out for Egypt and, more specifically, for Maadi.

Egypt's influx of Australian troops indicated not only the magnitude of the war effort, but also the disintegration of Egypt's earlier economic and political ties to the rest of the Ottoman-controlled eastern Mediterranean. Here, Maadi played one small but significant role in the larger geographical reordering of the Middle East, as the AIF used the town as its staging ground for waging war against the Ottomans.

While the majority of Maadi's soldiers arrived directly from Australia, enthusiasm for the war effort drew a variety of British subjects to the town to enlist. It was rare for members of the AIF to enlist abroad, yet at least thirty-five men volunteered for the war effort in Maadi. The backgrounds of these local recruits varied widely. While the majority were born in Australia, nine were born in England, four in New Zealand, one in Scotland, and one other in the United States. It appears likely that several came to Egypt from South Africa, where they worked as farmers and miners. Several of them had previously fought in the Boer Wars.[6] Others, like John Alfred Rena, came from Egypt's elite class of cosmopolitan professionals. Rena was born in New York City and had been an apprentice at Edison's Electrical Works before he came to Egypt as an electrical engineer in 1909. He spoke fluent French, Italian, and Arabic, making him a valuable military recruit. Although fighting for the AIF, he had never set foot in Australia.[7] The war had the effect of collapsing the soldiers' social, economic, and geographical differences. Whatever their backgrounds, their shared enthusiasm for war drew them together into the unity and uniformity of military deployment.

The *Egyptian Gazette* took care to portray Maadi's new arrivals in heroic fashion, offering an idealized description of the soldiers at the town's train station:

> Stalwart khaki-clad forms with their broad-brimmed hats, sleeves rolled up revealing burnt brown arms stroll about awaiting the arrival of train-loads of baggage, food, etc, from Cairo, to be stacked on carts and hustled off to the camp. . . . A sharp "Keep off that," brings understanding of intention if not of words. These are the men "on duty;" on the opposite side of the line are seen the crowds of "off duty" men awaiting the train to Cairo and amusements.[8]

The newspaper's favorable depiction masked the often destructive effect that the new residents had not only on Maadi, but also throughout Egypt.

The soldiers arrived in preparation for the Gallipoli campaign, a joint Anglo-French attempt to capture Istanbul via the Dardanelles straits. Poorly planned from the start, the campaign began in April 1915 and soldiers on both sides soon found themselves mired in a bloody stalemate. When evacuations were completed by January 1916, there were a total of more than 392,000 casualties, which included more than 130,000 deaths. The Ottomans suffering the vast majority of the carnage (86,692 dead, 164,617 wounded), yet the battle had a profound impact on all sides.[9] The loss dealt a serious blow to Anglo-French confidence and galvanized a sense of national identity among Australians and New Zealanders as distinct from the British empire. It also made a national hero out of the young general Mustafa Kemal (later Atatürk), whose leadership stalled the Australian and New Zealand offensive and kept them from achieving their objective.

While trench warfare wreaked havoc in Gallipoli, the Australian deployment brought a different kind of conflict to Egypt. Contrary to the hopes of the imperial leadership, Maadi did not provide the kind of respite from conflict that officials intended for the space. During the campaign, Delta Land embraced Maadi's association with the AIF, extending the troops an enthusiastic welcome and making specific contributions to the AIF's military installment. In addition to allowing the imperial military to establish a base on the land just outside the perimeter of Maadi's main development, the company provided a nearby villa as a makeshift hospital. While the AIF quaintly referred to it as a "Bungalow Hospital," the house included an extensive front porch and two full stories with additional rooms in the attic, for a total of at least eight bedrooms.[10]

The makeshift hospital in Maadi became a site of the imperial conflict, as relations between Egyptians and British imperial authorities broke down. The hospital staff struggled to communicate with the Egyptian servants employed at the house and when the camp's medical officers were deployed, the nursing staff complained about difficulties with the house's staff. While the official report lacks a clear description of the specific conflict, L.E. White, the sister-in-charge at the hospital, requested increased oversight with daily inspections of the establishment. The inspection report further relayed that a man was required "to be put in charge of the Native servants."[11]

These kinds of disruptions and administrative weaknesses went on throughout the Australian medical installations in and around Cairo.

In Heliopolis, the Australians also set up a hospital in the requisitioned Heliopolis Palace Hotel. A breakdown in the hospital's administration took place because of a quarrel between the staff's lead doctor and matron. The political reverberations were significant enough to become a topic of discussion not only in the War Office, but also in the British House of Commons and Australian parliament.[12] Poor hospital administration was indicative of a mounting conflict between locals and the Australian war effort, which was increasingly seen by Egyptians as one of the most egregiously oppressive elements of the British occupation.

As hospital administration faltered, a more significant conflict grew between the Australian troops and the area's Egyptian peasants. While the *Egyptian Gazette* painted Maadi as a subdued and well-disciplined environment compared to Cairo's interior, Australian soldiers roughhoused in Maadi's restaurants and continually harassed and abused the Egyptian peasants in the area, whom they referred to pejoratively as "Gippos."[13] As a result of the soldiers' behavior, they found their disciplinary boundaries increased almost daily. On 10 June 1915, for instance, the military placed the Café du Nil, a popular Maadi restaurant along the eastern bank of the Nile, out of bounds to soldiers.[14] The following day, visits to neighboring Egyptian villages were likewise banned. The order stated, "Gambling with natives will in the future be considered a criminal offence [sic]. Men are warned against familiarity with the natives."[15] Yet the soldiers' damaging interactions with the villagers continued. Just two weeks after the ban, the brigade was warned against "molesting natives." Implying that the soldiers had damaged or possibly stolen villagers' property, the order continued, "It is to be clearly understood that any soldier interfering with their property will be court marshaled and is liable to a term of imprisonment with hard labour."[16]

Destructive interactions between soldiers and civilians fueled anti-British sentiment throughout Egypt. Within Cairo's central quarters, confrontations between Egyptians and the Australian and New Zealander soldiers (corporately known as ANZACs) were all the more common and often violent. In April 1915, a riot broke out because a group of drunken soldiers were enraged about the apparently low quality of alcohol served in Harit al-Wasa'a, the city's brothel district. The soldiers piled beds, pianos, mattresses, and cupboards in the street and set them on fire. When the British police arrived to break up the riot, the troops pelted them with stones and beer bottles. This kind of violent behavior in Cairo during the war deeply undermined the reputation and authority of the British empire. In response, Egyptians across the country supported a movement for national independence.[17]

Likely to the peasants' relief, the AIF vacated Maadi in March 1916, a few months after the Gallipoli campaign concluded in retreat and failure. Without the large contingent of Australians, the Maadi camp no longer needed the Bungalow Hospital, which they likewise closed in March, returning the villa to Delta Land.[18] The military sent the hospital's personnel and medical supplies to Alexandria, where the staff served at the Ras-el-Tin Convalescent Depot.[19] The camp subsequently shrank in size and became home to special British military details and their training.

After Gallipoli, Maadi proved attractive to the British war effort for other reasons. The town's most enduring wartime construction was a prisoner of war (POW) camp, located southeast of the town, in the rocky terrain of Tura. Known as Maadi-Tura, the prison made Maadi a site of the complex and violent rivalries at work between the war's belligerent powers.

Maadi-Tura served as the receiving station for all POWs in Egypt. For these prisoners, the Maadi they experienced had nothing to do with the town-and-country environs established by Delta Land. Upon arriving at Maadi-Tura, prisoners entered a large courtyard where they each came before a panel of British officers who confiscated their personal items and valuables, making a note of each prisoner's belongings. They were subsequently stripped of their military uniforms and possessions and given a towel. Then the prisoners entered a large bath, where they each washed in a cresol soap solution. One German prisoner, a medical sergeant named Lappe, complained that the process was "not very appetizing," an apt assessment considering that some nine hundred prisoners went through the baths at a time, some of whom had not bathed in weeks.[20] Following the bath, they received a new towel, thus ensuring the loss of any valuables stashed in the first towel. Finally, the British supplied them with prison clothes and inoculated them against typhoid, smallpox, and cholera.[21] Once processed at Maadi-Tura, prisoners were distributed among the network of eight POW detention centers in Egypt.[22] More than fifty-five hundred male prisoners remained at Maadi-Tura, the majority of whom were Ottoman subjects.[23]

An old government-run flour mill provided the original structure for the Maadi-Tura prison.[24] By 1917, the British added additional barracks, which were large, brick buildings with dirt floors. The buildings were left largely open, without completed windows or doors. Prisoners slept on platforms of beaten earth, which were raised about twenty-three centimeters above the ground and were just under two meters long. These platform beds were covered with woven mats, and each prisoner received three blankets, with extra blankets available on especially cold nights. According to the International Red Cross, which inspected the treatment of Ottoman-Turkish prisoners on 3 January 1917, the openness of Maadi-Tura's barracks provided optimal ventilation in the desert climate. The inspectors gave Maadi-Tura favorable reviews in all areas, including food, water, hygiene, accommodation, medical care, and religion. The prison guards granted the Muslim inmates the freedom to worship and provided them with a separate cemetery. On the Turkish prisoners' mentality, the Red Cross reported, "The many which we have asked show that there is no dissatisfaction among the prisoners with regard to the treatment they receive." The inspectors made a similarly favorable inspection of the other POW camps in Egypt, reporting that "our conviction, based upon careful investigations, is that the inspectors, commandants and officers of the camps treat the prisoners with humanity and do all in their power to soften their lot."[25]

To Sgt. Lappe, however, the conditions at Maadi-Tura were altogether inadequate. After the war, the returned prisoner issued his complaint to the German Foreign Office with the intention of exacting reparations from the British. Lappe gave the same physical description of the camp as the Red Cross inspectors. Where the Red Cross reported competence, however, Lappe emphasized deficiency and inhumanity. The openness of the barracks, for instance, rather than providing ample ventilation, allowed dust, sand, and rain to pour into the barracks. He complained that the blankets were too thin, especially when sleeping on what he described as wet and cold ground. In Lappe's opinion, the medical care was also unsatisfactory. When illness struck the prison, Lappe claimed that several prisoners died because "the English only had time for themselves."[26] Lappe's testimony indicates how national sentiment fueled wartime aggression and frustration.

In the same prison, Ottoman prisoners created arts and crafts, which they sold to civilians. The *Egyptian Gazette* reported that the camp authorities allowed the prisoners—mostly Syrians, Armenians, and Greeks—to purchase wood, glue, cotton, wire, and beads from the canteen and use the materials to make handicrafts, which they, in turn, sold.[27] Each prisoner priced the work and labeled it with his personal identification number, so that he could claim his profits. They made caps, handbags, rosaries, and stone-carved slabs, with the rosaries earning the smallest profit at PT 3 (Egyptian piasters) each, and snakeskin bags costing as much as PT 60.[28] The British military moved the goods from Maadi to downtown, where they were available for sale at the "emporium" near the Shepheard's Hotel.[29] The prisoners' access to raw materials and ability to earn some money contrasts with the inhumane treatment Lappe described. Taken together, these varied experiences of Maadi-Tura reveal how the prison itself was a site of war's competing visions for national supremacy.

The British soldiers and media in Egypt were similarly inclined to lean on nationalist caricatures and portrayed the Germans as particularly dramatic about their circumstances. One British guard at Maadi-Tura derided German prisoners as the "gentlemen of Maadi."[30] When Ottoman and some German prisoners were captured at Gallipoli and transported to Maadi, the *Egyptian Gazette* headline read, "Prisoners Arrive in Egypt: Histrionics of German Officers," yet most of the article discussed the majority of Ottoman troops involved.[31] These competing depictions of the prisoners and their treatment in the Maadi-Tura camp reflected the larger political and military battles waged during the war. The British, as they attempted to gain a tighter grip on Egypt's affairs, emphasized their generosity to Syrian, Armenian, and Greek subjects of the crumbling Ottoman empire. At the same time, German prisoners felt themselves particularly mistreated and victimized by their British enemies and additionally out of place in a prison in Egypt. The British, both civilians and military, appeared content to condescend to the Germans.

Maadi-Tura was not without its violent episodes, and there were times when the war's bloody rivalries became vivid features of prison life. On 25 February 1918, William T. Smith became a guard at the prison. On that first day, he recorded the demographics of the prison in his diary: "Start duty at Meade [sic] Compound as a warder with 1 Sgt and 5 other men to look after 4500 prisoners consisting of Germans 1482 Turks 1092 Arabs 900 Greeks 500 Armenians 526."[32] Smith began his war service at Gallipoli, where he was injured by an Ottoman shell. He convalesced in Egypt and was subsequently stationed in Cairo. The brief account of his first day at Maadi-Tura emphasizes the disproportionate nature of the task before him—seven men to manage forty-five hundred prisoners. It is no surprise, then, that his diary goes on to document his most difficult days on the job, when the prisoners escaped or turned violent.

Smith's initial reminisces feature more prison outbreaks than internal conflicts. After less than a month on the job, he wrote that one prisoner broke out on 12 March 1918. A large-scale manhunt ensued, and the prisoner was found within a sixteen-kilometer radius of Maadi in an unused pigsty, covered in straw. In April, a dozen German prisoners escaped sometime between midnight and five o'clock in the morning, and appeared to have gotten away. A month later, ten of them were returned from Port Said. The other two drowned after attempting to swim the Nile. One particularly violent outburst started in the summer of 1918, at the beginning of Ramadan. Arab prisoners captured in the Hijaz refused to work while fasting and then attacked the Armenians held with them. The warders had to guard the Armenians with fixed bayonets for the rest of the day. While Smith offers few details on the cause of the violence, Armenians had already been cruelly scapegoated during the war, and the Ottoman's targeted extermination of them could have helped drive the violent action. The day after the attack, ten Arabs were arrested as leaders of the mutiny. In response, the Arab prisoners increased the severity of their rebellion. Much to Smith and the other guards' frustration, elements of the Arab-Muslim population continued refusing to work until Ramadan concluded.[33]

As the war entered its final months, violent episodes appeared to increase. An especially bloody incident took place between Greek and Turkish prisoners on 12 September. Smith wrote in his diary:

> Between the hours of 6pm and 6am . . . a terrible fight took place between the Turks and Greeks . . . and when the warder arrived it was like entering a slaughter house blood everywhere and 4 dead Turks were found in the washhouse with their heads smashed to a pulp and 27 had to be taken to hospital and 7 outpatients.[34]

Smith and the other warders deduced that the Greek prisoners had used the canes of disabled inmates as weapons against the Turkish prisoners.[35] As a result, Maadi-Tura became an additional setting in the resurgent battle between combative Turkish and Greek factions within the Ottoman empire—a hostility that had its roots in Greece's declaration of independence in 1821, and had most recently erupted when Greece sided with the Allies against the Ottomans when it entered the war in 1917. The event illustrates how profoundly regional alliances had been reshaped by the war. Where Maadi initially grew out of the financial relationships Greeks worked out within the Ottoman empire, the war gave new meaning to national and ethic identities, violently highlighting old rivalries and making them appear like primordial differences.

One of the final episodes that Smith documented was a violent attack by Turkish prisoners against the British guards. On 15 October 1918, he wrote that Turkish prisoners attacked the guards after being told to clear up water pipes that had been torn up "for the purpose [of] causing terrible injuries to warders." The attack resulted in one guard losing his left eye and severe lacerations to two others. Six of the Turkish prisoners were subsequently executed on 24 October. Two weeks later, Smith recorded hearing "Rumours of Armistice," and fittingly concluded his diary a few days later, on 11 November. The events he recorded identify the shifting modes of national, ethnic, and religious identity that gained new significance because of the war experience. Violent outbursts among the POWs at Maadi-Tura highlighted the war's deadly divisiveness and how it moved well beyond the battlefront.

Among Maadi residents a different kind of battle unfolded—one less violent but still deeply connected to the very notion of what defines an enemy. When Austro-Hungarian Archduke Franz Ferdinand was assassinated in Sarajevo on 28 June 1914, Prof. Dr. Heinrich Herman Bruno "Henry" Bitter was employed as the director of the Egyptian government's Hygienic Institute in Cairo, a division within the Department of Public Health, created in 1896 as an avenue for European scientists to address the cholera outbreak in Egypt. A bacteriologist, Bitter first worked in Egypt as a sanitary inspector in Alexandria before he became the institute's founding director.[36] In the nearly twenty years he worked for the institute, Bitter also oversaw projects related to water purification and livestock health—all this at a time when international attention regarding Cairo's sanitary conditions grew because more Europeans made it a destination for tourism and domicile. As the *British Journal of Medicine* reported in 1910, "Cairo has become so popular a winter resort that on that ground alone every care should be taken by authorities to ensure that its sanitary arrangements are above suspicion."[37]

Over the course of Bitter's employment, his personal life exhibited the growth of elite cosmopolitan society among resident foreigners in Cairo. He married a Polish woman, Wanda, who was born in Cairo and grew up in Alexandria. She, like so many European families living in the country, was a foreigner by nationality but had always called Egypt home. The couple had two daughters—Gretel, born in 1904, and Hilda, born in 1906. The girls spent their childhoods in Maadi, where Henry purchased two plots of land and built a spacious five-bedroom villa.[38] While the family's prospects might have looked hopeful at the beginning of 1914, when Britain declared war on Germany that August, the Bitters' once promising Cairene life rapidly disintegrated.

After the declaration, the Bitters remained in Cairo for a few months. On 7 December 1914, as AIF soldiers arrived in Maadi, they left their garden city home and most of its contents and relocated to Koblenz, Germany. Eleven days later, on 18 December, the British declared Egypt a protectorate. In a place like Egypt, where Europeans made homes and found an economic haven, the beginning of the First World War meant the rapid hardening of the national identities that they previously found negotiable and even available for purchase.[39]

The British were especially quick to take charge of the legal affairs of German and Austro-Hungarian citizens in Egypt. Before making Egypt a protectorate, the British consulate created an administrative system for managing disputes with their now enemy populations. On 24 November, the consulate established a new court with jurisdiction over German and Austro-Hungarian subjects.[40] Called the Special Court for Germans and Austrians, it managed the legal affairs of former residents of Egypt well into the postwar years. Through the new court, the British carefully identified who among these populations continued to play integral roles in Egypt's economy. While some were quickly imprisoned or repatriated, others were permitted to stay in their homes and go about much of their usual business. Even Bitter's employment by a British-operated governmental institution proved insufficient protection against exile. Much of the difference in treatment followed ethnic lines. Where ethnic Europeans like the Bitters came to represent a rival foreign power, the British carefully monitored resident foreigners like Egypt's prominent Jews but allowed them to remain.

Soon after the war commenced, questions started about the true allegiances of the Menasces and Cattaouis—Egypt's two most prominent Jewish families with Austro-Hungarian citizenship. On May 26, 1915, the *Egyptian Gazette* reported on "Enemy Subjects in Egypt" and the Austro-Hungarian nationals on the board of the National Bank of Egypt (the same individuals on Delta Land's board). Quoting the "official view," the article reported:

> Apart from the question as to whether it would be in the interests of the shareholders to force men such as Baron Jacques de Menasce and Maurice Cattaui Pasha to resign their Egyptian directorships, holding the positions they do not only in the Jewish communities but also generally in commercial and financial circles in Egypt, and whose sympathies are above all Egyptian, it has to be remembered that such directors have been appointed by the shareholders for a term of years and probably not even the shareholders themselves can turn them out by a general meeting.[41]

The official view shrewdly emphasized the men's Egyptian sympathies and then invoked the bylaws for the bank's shareholders and its financial interests in order to avoid treating these influential men and their families as enemy subjects. Here, local circumstances trumped the larger events of the war and the official view reflected the economic situation in Egypt. Both families rose to prominence in Egypt's financial world during the second half of the nineteenth century, and their forced removal would have likely destabilized not only the bank, but also the whole of the Egyptian economy. If allowing these families to remain in Egypt compromised the official view of who constituted an enemy, it still served British imperial aims in Egypt by helping to stabilize the wartime economy. Exempting the Menasces and Cattaouis additionally ingratiated British authority with these powerful Jewish families, forging a valuable connection.

Yet these elite Jewish families were not as far removed from Austro-Hungarian interests as the official view reported in the *Gazette*. The British Public Custodian paid particular attention to Menasce and his seven children. While the British Residency continually claimed that "the family is unquestionably identified with Egypt," Menasce's offspring were dispersed throughout Europe during the war.[42] Two of his sons were in Austria: Rene, his second youngest, previously left Egypt for health reasons and spent the war in a sanitarium, and Henri, the second oldest, was conscripted into the Austrian army, only to be declared unfit. He served instead as a member of the Austrian Red Cross. Two of the baron's other sons spent the war in Switzerland, successfully avoiding conscription. Rather than viewing these European connections skeptically, officials considered Rene and Henri exceptional, and focused on Jacques Menasce's ongoing ties to the Jewish community in Alexandria as evidence of his true allegiance.[43]

British officials additionally looked for ways to link the Menasce family more closely with Britain. When the baron and baroness wanted to travel to France during the war, the Residency offered them *laissez-passers* and worked to get them British citizenship. Those in the Foreign Office viewed the family's nationality as more a product of the Capitulations than a form of genuine allegiance or identification. One message explained that "the members of this family . . . became Austrian like many others for their own convenience and in order to enjoy the advantages which have hitherto accrued in Egypt to subjects of the 1st Class European Powers; they are now suffering from certain disadvantages as a consequence of their choice of nationality."[44] British officials' negotiations with the Menasces indicated their willingness still to rely on the Capitulations as a means of expediency when attempting to shore up their higher priorities.[45]

Nationality took on a variety of meanings during the war. In some cases, it offered terms for the exclusion of foreigners and in others it provided means for maintaining an older, more flexible approach that allowed certain foreign subjects to remain in Egypt. For the Menasces, nationality remained a fluid category, which could be altered depending on the context. When Austrian citizenship became a problem, the baron and baroness garnered British *laissez-passers*. In the same way, two of their sons sought out Italian and Czecho-Slovakian nationality, respectively.[46] For ethnic Europeans like the Bitters, however, German nationality became inescapable. The British differentiated between these kinds of enemy subjects based on their own geopolitical priorities in Egypt as well as ideas of ethnicity and race. The official gaze concentrated on Menasce's social and economic ties to Egypt and largely ignored his arguably dubious connections to Austria-Hungary. The ethnicity of European "enemy" subjects, however, became a more insurmountable tie. As rival Europeans, rather than covert Egyptians, people like the Bitters had to be removed from Egypt despite their own lifelong social, economic, and political ties to the country. By allowing race and ethnicity to play a dominant role in who was considered an enemy alien, the British established a pattern where whiteness increasingly came to mean foreignness—a trend that would continue as the debate over Egyptian nationality took shape and minority populations were increasingly excluded from the national experience.[47]

The Bitters appear to have so closely linked their lives to Egypt, and specifically to Maadi, that even upon their departure for Germany in 1914 neither Henry nor Wanda understood how severe their break with Egypt would be. Based on correspondence included in the Special Court file related to the Bitter family's affairs, Henry anticipated that he and his family would resume life in Cairo soon after the war. He put Rose Kirby, Wanda's widowed sister, who also lived in Cairo, in charge of the upkeep of their Maadi home so that it might be spared total liquidation by the government. Initially, he also continued receiving his pension payments from the Hygienic Institute, which he assumed would continue throughout his absence. A year into their exile, however, the family's separation from Egypt appeared threateningly permanent. In January 1916, the Egyptian government stopped sending Henry his pension payments.[48] In the meantime, Kirby struggled to manage the Maadi property on her own. When the Bitters left Egypt, Henry agreed to pay her LE 5 (Egyptian pounds) per month to manage the house. With his pension cut off, however, he had no means to pay her, and she was forced to support herself and maintain the house on the salary she earned doing office work in downtown Cairo. In 1917, Henry wrote to the Public Custodian, asking that Kirby be allowed to stay in the villa as its caretaker, and that the cost of its upkeep be offset by a payment from his would-be pension payments, which he believed he would receive in bulk after the war. The Public Custodian allowed Kirby to reside in the villa, but there is no indication that she was compensated for her efforts.[49] To help make up some of the costs, Kirby managed to make some profit off of Maadi's newly arrived military residents. According to the register of accounts she supplied to the Special Court, she earned LE 25 in rent paid by billeted military personnel. Aside from selling a few household items, the catering she supplied to the house's new residents was one of the only sources of additional income she generated from her work managing her sister's villa.[50]

The Bitter family's situation grew all the more dire when Henry died in January 1918. Wanda and her daughters did not receive the same kind of careful, individual attention given to the Menasce family. British officials expended little energy on the specifics of her nationality, her Polish background, or her family's history in Egypt.[51] Instead, Wanda, feeling herself and her daughters stranded in Germany, made her own desperate appeals to the Public Custodian. Their situation grew increasingly dire because they owed money to Delta Land for the mortgage on the villa and had no means to pay it. To raise the LE 3,000 they owed the company, Wanda looked to sell her assets in Maadi. That October, Kirby auctioned off the family's furniture—enough to fill the five bedrooms, salon, hall, dining room, kitchen, and pantry. She raised almost LE 800, all of which went to Delta Land.[52]

When the armistice came in November, the Bitter family's problems were far from resolved. Because the furniture sale could not pay the full debt to Delta Land, Wanda looked for a way to sell the house, hoping that any leftover profit would be sent to her in Germany. Selling the villa, however, was more complicated than disposing of the furniture. Upon the family's departure from Egypt, their property technically belonged to the Public Custodian, which was charged with its liquidation. Up to this point, Kirby had been allowed to take care of the house at the agency's disposal. The request that the house be sold and some of the profits go to an exiled German national was unprecedented. As the debt on the mortgage continued to mount at 9 percent annually, Wanda, perhaps naively, still felt herself separate from the events of the war and wrote to the Special Court in November 1920, imploring them to grant her the pension payments that the Egyptian government would have otherwise paid Henry's widow. She also asked permission that the house be sold to pay her debts. She explained that she needed some return on their Maadi property because she had an opportunity to work abroad and needed the money to leave Germany. "I am a stranger in Germany," she wrote, "being born in Egypt, from Polish parents."[53] Kirby wrote a similarly beseeching letter to the Public Custodian, explaining that her sister's "health is so run down through all the hardships and privations she has to go through that she is quite unfit now to be a support to herself and her children. Is it possible that no sympathy shall be found for a widow and orphans in distress?" Their appeal apparently had some effect, likely because Delta Land simultaneously made a similar request that the house be sold and the profits used to pay the mortgage. By December 1920, the Special Court allowed Kirby to sell the house. It was purchased by Fouad Kamal on behalf of his sister Madame Zainab Gamal al-Francaoni for LE 4,000. More than a year later, in January 1922, Wanda Bitter received just over

LE 400 from her husband's estate in Egypt.[54] Whether the funds arrived in time or were sufficient for her to accept her position abroad is unknown.

The Bitter family's fate was of little consequence to British officials in Egypt. Even though, like the Menasce family, Wanda had only secondary connections to a Central Power before the war, she was easily labeled an enemy. Her nationality was absorbed into that of her husband, erasing from the official mind the more complex international networks that allowed her to be born and raised in Egypt—networks of privilege that the Residency and the Foreign Office carefully preserved for the more elite families considered Egyptianized.[55] The Bitters, like most white Europeans with German and Austro-Hungarian nationality, became targeted enemies of British imperial power. With the declaration of war, the Bitters' life in Maadi became untenable. Where the Menasces' and Cattaouis' contributions to Egypt's economy allowed them to remain in the country, debt became the Bitter family's most lasting tie to Egypt. Only well after the war and the subsequent Egyptian revolution—after British imperial power became significantly restrained—did Wanda receive a portion of her family's former estate.

As for the new owner of the Bitters' erstwhile Maadi villa, little exists in the archive about Madame Zainab Gamal al-Francaoni or her brother. In Maadi, they would have encountered a growing number of prominent women making homes for themselves among the town's villas and gardens. At the same time that they arranged for the purchase of the Maadi villa, an Egyptian scientist took over leadership of Cairo's Hygienic Institute. While the details of the transition are unclear, by 1923, bacteriologist Z. Khaled published new research on bacterial infections in Egypt's bovine population.[56] In the case of both Zainab Gamal al-Francaoni and Z. Khaled, their new positions and movement into Maadi participated in the growing influence of the Egyptian *effendiya*, or middle-class intelligentsia, during the war and in its immediate aftermath. The Bitter family's experience illuminates the war's disruptive effects on Maadi's civilian population. As it fractured the town's earlier elite cosmopolitanism, those breaks also opened up spaces for more Egyptians to move into the area.[57] This rising class of Egyptians provided the foundation for the town's postwar growth.

The *Egyptian Gazette* made a point of highlighting the contrast between the Maadi-Tura prison and Maadi's garden city environs, commenting that "it is strange to realise that here, in this peaceful spot so living and poignant a reminder of the realities of war existed, and that great numbers of Turkish prisoners were but a stone's throw away."[58] The war affected Maadi's residential population on different, more subtle terms than it impacted members of the military. These two spaces drew together the varied experiences of the First World War in Egypt. The arrival of the AIF brought the anxieties of British imperial power to a head. The troops' destructive behavior in Maadi's cafes and among its peasants drew the town into a national experience, which galvanized a revolutionary spirit that spread across Egypt during and after the war. The Australian soldiers were an affront to Egyptian honor, and their presence necessitated total independence from the British empire.

Maadi offers a fixed location for telling the many stories of the First World War in Egypt. The POW camp drew the larger events of the war into the small, suburban town. As the Central Powers weakened, the violence of the war unfolded among the prisoners, with targeted attacks against Armenians, Turks, and the British guards. While less dramatic, the wartime experiences of Maadi's civilian population had the most lasting effect on the town's future. While the AIF redeployed and the POWs returned to their countries of origin, the Maadi residents deemed "enemy aliens" could not return to their former homes, leaving significant holes in the town's social fabric. These people were not replaced, but the holes were filled. Former enemy property became the basis of the town's future growth, and Delta Land learned that to ensure future profitability, the town had to appeal to wealthy Egyptians who behaved in much the same way as the resident foreigners who remained in Maadi.

5

NATIONAL HOME

During their general meeting on 10 April 1919, Delta Land's board of directors had little good news to report from the previous year. Two repossessed houses had been sold, but, except for one 690 square-meter plot, Maadi sales were at a "standstill." Despite the high cost of materials, the board anticipated that demand for building sites would soon "increase drastically." Their optimism was based in part on a change in the company's land use policy. Following an agreement with the Traders & Growers Union, the company planned to begin using Maadi's arable land for more than simple agriculture, and the union workers would soon be cultivating fruit and forest trees on the company's lands.[1]

Delta Land was also in the process of acquiring property that the company had been trying to buy since the construction of Maadi began fifteen years earlier. A German couple, Willibald Luthy and his wife Maria Fredericke Zehnder, owned a large, forty-feddan estate that included a water pumping station adjacent to Delta Land's properties. While Luthy died in 1904 and never saw the company develop its garden city, Zehnder remained in the house and adamantly refused to sell to Delta Land. The changes wrought by the war turned Zehnder from an inconvenient neighbor into an enemy of British-occupied Egypt. In 1914, she was evicted from her home and departed Egypt for her native Germany.[2] Delta Land's subsequent acquisition of the farm became integral to Maadi's further development in the 1920s and 1930s—some of the town's most fruitful and profitable years.[3]

The board's optimism appears out of place considering the political climate of the time. Just a month earlier, a nationwide revolution broke out in opposition to the British imperial presence in the country. Four months after the armistice in November 1918, Egypt remained a protectorate of the British empire. To make matters worse, when the Wafd Party (Arabic for delegation) formed in November 1918 with the intention of bringing their demands for independence to the international community, the British refused their appeal.[4] Led by Sa'd Zaghlul, a prominent Egyptian lawyer, the Wafd's leadership was largely composed of educated, urban elites. In Egypt, the Wafd's appeal gained nationwide support. British attempts to squash the Wafd set the stage for ongoing uprisings and revolts until the British unilaterally granted Egypt qualified independence in 1922, maintaining control over imperial communications, national defense, the protection of foreign and minority interests, and the Sudan.[5] By 1923, Egypt had a new constitution, and over the decade that followed a complex mix of rivals—the British, King Fu'ad, the Wafd, and its competitors—all vied for control over the country's affairs.

For Delta Land, this nationalist turn and the gradual and uneven decline of British control that followed inadvertently contributed to the company's profitability. Nationalist leaders like Zaghlul and his wife Safiya were part of the *effendiya*—a class of educated professionals who identified their modern advancement and independence with global signifiers of bourgeois status like the abolition of the harem, single family households, athleticism, and consumerism.[6] Elite Egyptian women actively participated in revolutionary activities throughout this period, holding their own marches.[7] The *effendiya*'s politics opposed British imperialism, but their consumer habits and social practices were well suited to elite suburban spaces like Maadi, which also catered to foreigners. The town's villa and garden aesthetic, growing sporting culture, and promise of a quiet, semirural retreat complemented the symbols of the new Egyptian nation. Appealing to the *effendiya* would be the foundation of Maadi's sustained growth after the 1919 revolution.[8]

Maadi's history helps link the pre- and postwar periods of Egyptian history, where political transformation seemed possible but economic continuities—especially the maintenance of the Capitulations—made the events of 1919 less revolutionary than many had hoped. In ongoing negotiations with the British and other foreign powers, the Wafd permitted the continuation of the Capitulations and the Mixed Courts, utilizing them as checks on British power and prioritizing instead demands for political independence.[9] Because these institutions of foreign privilege persisted, foreigners continued to hold significant local influence, and, in turn, helped fashion the meaning of modern Egypt during the liberal era that followed the First World War.

Delta Land emerged from the war with a new manager. Unexpectedly, Reginald Q. Henriques passed away on 4 March 1916.[10] At the time, his daughter Margaret was only thirteen months old.[11] When Delta Land first hired Henriques in 1907, his most urgent and enduring charge was the growth of Maadi through either direct land sales or lending. Following his death, the company had to find someone who could quickly take up that mantle amid the challenges of the war. The ongoing conflict had put a number of financial strains on the company. Foremost among them were the properties left vacant because of wartime forced repatriations and imprisonments.[12] Less than a month after Henriques passed away, Delta Land hired Tom Dale to fill the position. Tall, thin, and clean shaven, with his thick hair neatly combed and parted to the side, Dale would become one of Maadi's most well-known and influential residents. He came to Delta Land with a background similar to Egypt's other resident foreigners. His father Jesse Dale first moved to Egypt in 1882 to work as an engineer on the canals of the Nile Delta, and Tom was born in the Upper Egyptian city of Mansoura six years later.[13] Tom subsequently received his education in engineering in England and returned to Egypt in 1911 to take a position with the Cairo branch of the Ganz Electric Company of Budapest. He joined Delta Land five years later.[14]

Dale's professional background in engineering sustained a connection between engineering expertise and the management of Maadi, which started with Alexander Adams, when he brought his training with the Royal Engineers and the Burma Railways to the establishment of Delta Railways and Delta Land. This pattern was more than a coincidence. The engineering knowhow required for infrastructure development has long been part of the construction of private roads, railways, and canals. Because these means of transportation often created exclusive methods for accessing marketplaces, they also led to the creation of upscale neighborhoods.[15] In many ways, then, it was Ebenezer Howard's idealism about infrastructure construction as something inherently democratic and his failure to see the exclusive potential of private investment in road and rail development that kept the more socially equitable elements of his garden city plan from being fully realized. In Maadi, Delta Land's various managers played critical roles in organizing the town and determining the terms on which different people could access it.

Like Henriques before him, Dale's job was to support and preserve Delta Land's vision for Maadi, maintain adherence to the *Cahier des Charges*, and make the town into an upper middle-class space that elite Cairenes— European and Egyptian alike—might come to see as home. Dale served as general manager until he retired in 1948, when his son Geoffrey took over the position. During his tenure, Tom was among Maadi's most recognizable residents. One prominent Maadi woman recalled how he "kept Maadi as a perfect residential area and was always ready to listen to suggestions and hear complaints, which were immediately remedied."[16] However idealized her recollection, the sentiment captured Dale's deep association with Maadi, especially as its overseer and protector.

Later in life, Tom penned his recollections of Maadi, giving some of the most personal records of the management of the town. He wrote about Maadi in a series of short, typed narratives that he deliberately put to paper as an act of preservation in 1970.[17] These "snippets" help illuminate the careful negotiations that went into Maadi's successful growth during years of revolution and liberal reform, as Egyptians vied for greater independence. Dale never explicitly mentions Egypt's political situation, or his own dependence on the Capitulations. Instead, he portrays himself as a contributor to Delta Land's larger vision, and his narratives hinge on the position of the company's sustained authority in Maadi despite the transformation of Egypt's political scene.

In one episode, Dale was inspecting some of Maadi's more remote parts when he found a herd of goats being led by "a small 'walad'" (Arabic for boy) as they were snacking on a resident's garden. He explained, "Residents were allowed to plant a portion of the 12 to 18 foot pathway outside their villa."[18] The grazing animals, however, were a direct violation of the *Cahier des Charges*, which stipulated that no farmyard animals could "disturb or trouble the tranquility or rest" of Maadi's inhabitants.[19] While Dale managed to get the boy and the goats to the police station, the effort left him battered. He fell down a steep set of stairs near the canal in an attempt to snag one of the goats. At the station, the boy explained to the police that the goats belonged to Nashid Bey, a prominent member of the governor of Cairo's staff, and Thomas Russell Pasha, the British head of the Cairo police. Dale later confronted Nashid Bey, who replied that the goats were Russell Pasha's and that he brought them to Maadi to feed. "Hardly likely, I thought to myself," Dale recalled. While Dale doubted Nashid Bey's defense, the story concluded in a stream of consciousness, where he related some of Nashid Bey's positive qualities. He made no further mention of the goats or the *walad*, and apparently never confronted Russell Pasha. The relationship between Nashid and Russell offers a telling indicator of the intricacies of Egypt's semiindependence and its bearing on Cairo's governance at the time—with the police force remaining under British control at the same time that Egyptians gained more authority over civilian affairs.

Although a comparatively minor incident, the Maadi goat episode points to a history of Russell's complex position within Cairene society. His supporters lauded him as a model civil servant. For example, in a review of Russell's 1949 memoir, Ibrahim al-Bakistuni celebrated Russell's work, saying,

> Russell sympathized with Egyptian nationalist aspirations though he disapproved of nationalist excesses and he tackled many a situation with firmness and tact where less experienced men would have rushed into disaster. But when violence or injustice had to be tackled he was ruthless and capable of meeting force with force, cunning with cunning.[20]

Those more ruthless qualities were on display in 1935, when he instructed the police to run down student protestors on horseback and beat them. After eight demonstrators were killed, he told the police to shoot buckshot into the crowds. The protestors, in turn, called on the support of Safiya Zaghlul, by then a widow, who initiated a boycott of all British goods.[21] The fallout brought about the end of Isma'il Sidqi's government and helped force the British to renegotiate their treaty with Egypt in 1936.[22] Yet, Russell remained the commandant of the police force until 1947, making him a key figure in the maintenance of British power in Egypt. To his critics, then, the goats in Maadi were a minor addition to an ongoing narrative of abuse of power.

The episode additionally reveals the limitations of Dale's authority in Maadi. For Delta Land's manager, the goat incident went unresolved because Dale had little recourse when faced with the commandant of the Cairo police. Dale does not tell the story cynically, however. Instead, he recalls the events with a sense of humor—the crux of the story being his fall near the canal. That his authority was upended because of the boy's connection to both British and Egyptian members of Cairo's government situated Dale's authority well below those with official governing authority, exposing the kinds of careful negotiations required for the maintenance of Delta Land's plan for Maadi after the war.

As state power increasingly centralized, Maadi's independent existence on the outskirts of Cairo under Delta Land's authority became more tenuous. To preserve the area's distinctive qualities, Dale needed a reputation for respectability and strong relationships with people in positions of power. In one recollection entitled "The Maadi–Cairo Road Lighting," Dale uses a small typed page to relate the resolution of a twenty-year dispute. He opens with his first impression of Maadi:

> In the year 1916 Maadi was a small village with the beginnings of a fashionable garden suburb, some 7 miles distant from Cairo. There was no street lighting for the residents loved the quiet, country life far from the noise and city lights. One solitary paraffin-pressure lamp in the midan near the railway station was considered sufficient just to show railway commuters to the beginnings of their way home.[23]

Dale goes on to relate Delta Land's ambitions to incorporate electric lighting along Maadi's streets and how the company's prerogatives were eventually achieved, despite residents' protests. Residents wanted to keep the community quite literally in the dark because of their desire to prevent late-night social gatherings common in Cairo's less affluent corners. Dale does not mention that the Australian Imperial Force camp made initial demands for increased electric lighting in 1917, after which Delta Land set in motion several changes that expanded the capacity of the Maadi power station.[24] Dale is explicit, however, about the socioeconomic dimensions of the conflict. He recalls in the next paragraph that after Delta Land constructed a power station for Maadi and road lighting was possible, residents' protest began in earnest. He explains that the objection took place "on the grounds that servants coming off duty would congregate under the light and enjoy what could be a noisy chatter far into the night."[25] The lack of street lighting helped create a certain perimeter around Maadi, determining who could use its open spaces, how they were to be used, and at what time. The town required servants for the upkeep and maintenance of its villa spaces, but if they socialized in Maadi's streets, their activity threatened the garden city's association with a quiet, semirural life. The episode is particularly revealing because it was not the residents who determined Maadi's perimeters, but the company. Ultimately, Delta Land's larger goal to create a modern space that retained an air of luxury triumphed. That kind of modern vision required certain technological advances, and electric street lighting was primary among them. Instead of detailing how the conflict with residents was mitigated, Dale simply states that the "object was eventually overcome"—emphasizing Delta Land's authority over Maadi.[26]

While the company lit the streets within Maadi, it could not make changes to the government-owned road connecting Maadi to Cairo. Like the challenge of constructing a road from Old Cairo to Maadi, the government likely resisted the lighting project because Maadi was south of Old Cairo, and thus distanced from some of the technological developments already present downtown. Cairo's European city had electric lighting in the early twentieth century, but there remained gross inequalities between the lighting and water works in the European city and what was available in the older, medieval city, which included the historically Coptic and Jewish quarters in Old Cairo.[27] Lighting the road to Maadi required building infrastructure that Cairo's Tanzim had neglected for decades. So, despite Delta Land's wishes, the road remained dark for several years. The situation changed, however, when a cohort of influential Egyptians moved to Maadi in the late 1920s and wanted to see the road lit. While Dale explains that the government refused the project, one particularly influential Egyptian resident, whom Dale does not identify by name, explained that he would host a luncheon at his villa and invite "certain important persons" to discuss the matter.[28]

At the luncheon, there were eight or nine guests, including Fahmi Karim, the undersecretary of public works, an unnamed "prominent newspaper proprietor" (likely Faris Nimr of *al-Muqattam*, a long-time Maadi resident), and Dale. Among this cohort of prominent men, the real arbiter of change during the meeting was the Egyptian hostess. Dale explains:

> After a sumptuous meal and adequate refreshments, Madame turned the conversation to the Maadi–Cairo road lighting which ended by Madame asking H.E. [His Excellency, aka the pasha] to grant her two

requests. One that he would receive Mr. Dale in his office without delay and secondly that he would do all in his power to persuade H.E. his Minister to give the Maadi Company the concession to illuminate the Maadi–Cairo road as far as Attar-el-Nebbi where the city street lighting began.[29]

After some persuasion, the pasha agreed to arrange the meeting, and Dale met with 'Uthman Muharram, the minister of public works, who granted Delta Land the concession to light the road. Dale concludes with the exclamation, "Magical! indeed and with no more effort than having to face a lengthy Egyptian feast presided over by a charming yet very capable Egyptian hostess!"[30] While it might have felt effortless for Dale, his narrative of Delta Land's ultimate success depended on a significant shift in Egyptian governing authority, as more Egyptians held positions of power and Maadi's Egyptian residents felt themselves empowered to exert their influence on Maadi's behalf. What is more, these negotiations required the continuation of the Capitulations, which granted Dale ongoing status within Egypt's economy and society, and the capacity to represent Delta Land as its own authority over Maadi.

Both the Arabic- and English-language press celebrated the new installation. *Al-Ahram* ran photos of the new light posts situated along the tree-lined street from *"Misr al-qadima"* to Maadi, reporting that the lights were unveiled at a celebration on 9 February 1933, by Lady Loraine, the wife of Sir Percy Loraine, British high commissioner to Egypt and the Sudan.[31] The *Egyptian Gazette* ran a descriptive article about the lighting, explaining how Lady Loraine received an "attractive" golden key from Delta Land's board, which she used to switch on the lights. The *Gazette* continued, "The drive back to Cairo under the new lights showed how extremely efficient they are, for the road was evenly lit, there being no pools of light intercepted by unlit spaces, which so often occurs."[32] The even and continuous pools of light emphasized the road's security, as these features of modern Cairo now extended southward to the suburbs.

While Dale makes no mention of the larger political events that served as the backdrop for his narratives, the street lighting episode was predicated on the 1919 revolution and the ongoing debate over Anglo-Egyptian relations that followed. He describes the kinds of informal negotiations that became integral to the development of Egypt, and more specifically

Cairo, during the interwar period. For the Delta Land manager, the company provided a larger continuity that appeared unaffected by the many political changes of the time. The company's ongoing authority, which was sustained by the Capitulations, was not as stable as Dale might have hoped or recalled. Delta Land's existence in Egypt remained largely contingent on the nationalists'—particularly the Wafd's—negotiated support for the Mixed Courts and Capitulations. For the Wafd, preserving the privileges of several foreign powers within Egypt offered protection from unilateral British action. As had been the case from 1882 until Egypt was declared a protectorate in 1914, the Capitulations and Mixed Courts granted other foreign powers an ongoing stake in Egypt's economic and legal affairs, thus checking British imperial intervention.[33] Even though the Ottoman empire was fully dissolved by 1923, the trade privileges that the sultan established centuries earlier remained in Egypt as an ongoing guard against direct imperial control by any one European power.

For Dale, the broader context of legal and economic privileges remain outside his memoirs of Maadi. His Maadi is closely tied to the authority of Delta Land, and he does not question the company's dependence on foreign privilege. Instead, a sense of nostalgia pervades Dale's Maadi recollections, which focus on the details of his work. For him, Maadi retrospectively appeared isolated from the larger political contests over Egypt's relationship to Britain and the rest of the world—a kind of oasis, removed from its political surroundings. Yet, the goat incident and especially the development of road lighting occurred in the context of significant political alterations and revealed some of the detailed ways that resident foreigners and the companies they worked for continued to utlize their Capitulations benefits and sustain a place in Egypt through careful negotiations with Egyptians and Britons in positions of power at a time when nationalists had gained greater but incomplete independence.

As described above, the revolutionary events of the spring of 1919 made only limited gains in securing Egyptian independence. After Britain declared proscribed independence in 1922, the 1923 constitution that followed enshrined elite authority, granting King Fu'ad expansive legislative and executive powers, restricting the Senate to the upper classes, and granting the Senate veto power over the Chamber of Deputies. Despite women's significant contributions to the nationalist struggle, the constitution denied their demands for suffrage.[34] Zaghlul, who returned to Egypt in March 1923, commanded a powerful victory in the elections of January 1924, but his term as prime minister was short lived. On 19 November, a group of radical nationalists assassinated Sir Lee Stack, the commander of the Egyptian army and governor-general of the Sudan. In response, Zaghlul resigned in the face of British threats of military intervention.[35] The years that followed would see Fu'ad, himself a relic of the Ottoman khedivate who only spoke broken Arabic, assert his enhanced authority under the 1923 constitution, and partner with the Wafd's rivals in a series of ongoing attempts to curtail Egyptians' freedoms.[36]

Where political rights were withheld, the social and cultural signifiers of a modern Egypt worthy of independence became all the more imperative. Often overlooking Egypt's social stratification, the Wafd identified the bourgeois habits of its leaders with a vision for an independent Egyptian nation.[37] While Zaghlul could not hold on to his position as prime minister, his home—a large villa south of downtown Cairo—became known as *Bayt al-Umma*, or house of the nation. This iconography made garden city establishments like Maadi, with its villas and verdant gardens, part of the nationalist iconography of Egypt's professional class. For Egyptian women, in particular, whose calls for suffrage fell on deaf ears, their role as *rabbat al-manzil*, or lady of the house, took on newfound profundity in these households. Dale's "very capable hostess" exhibited just this quality by using her authority within the home to exert significant influence over the development of greater Cairo.

Amid these complex political negotiations, the social life that developed in Cairo's suburbs preserved local space for resident foreigners to continue their lives near the Egyptian capital. If the villa and its surrounding garden were not only the idyllic homes for this privileged population, but also icons of the modern nation, then leisure time and consumer habits also became central to the meaning of modern Egypt in the 1920s and 1930s. Because the Wafd overlooked social differences in articulating its political platform, it often neglected the interests of the working class and peasantry.[38] In doing so, it eschewed a more radical politics. The party's moderation and even conservatism were reflected not only in policy, but also in how its leadership spent their money and free time. Popular athleticism, in particular, became central to displaying national strength and virility. Requiring leisure time and money, sporting activities, like domestic life in the villa, provided another overlapping place for nationalist and resident foreigner activity and socialization.

During the war, Maadi residents asked Delta Land to build a sporting club they could call their own. In response, the company introduced the Maadi Sporting Club in December 1920.[39] The club became the center of Maadi's social life. As Gabriel Josipovici would recall of his childhood in Maadi, the club "was very much a place of congregation for middle class Egyptian families and all the European families."[40]

Delta Land situated the club along the northern section of Maadi, where agricultural land gave way to the desert, directly south of the historically Jewish area of Basatin. They converted the northernmost reaches, nearest the desert, into a desert golf course. Closer to town, lawns were carefully manicured for a cricket pitch and tennis courts. The club's focal point was the white rectangular clubhouse. An open veranda wrapped around the structure, supported by white pillars that echoed many features of colonial architecture but with a streamlined, more block-like and modern aesthetic. Lush gardens surrounded the clubhouse, creating a verdant setting, neatly attuned to Maadi's town-and-country fashion. By placing sports and leisure at the heart of Maadi's social life, the club became foundational to the town's appeal to Egyptians and resident foreigners alike.

Even before it opened, anticipation concerning the new Maadi Sporting Club made the suburb more recognizable and significant. *The Sphinx*, a Cairo-based English-language weekly, reported on the upcoming opening, describing the club as Delta Land's gift to Maadi residents. The paper went on to articulate how sporting activities supported not only community life, but also upright morality. For young and old alike, the paper proclaimed, "The mental, moral, and physical stimulation which is the splendid advantage inherent in clean sport is one that is not availed of about this city as much as it might be."[41] Maadi's popular athleticism made it all the more attractive as an Egyptian space, where national prowess and physical skill could be put on display by both men and women. In the years following the 1919 revolution, physical strength and wellness served as indicators of the vitality of the new Egyptian nation. For Egyptian women, the club became a place of uninhibited modernity. Detached from the home and any stereotypes of the harem, activities like swimming and tennis allowed Egyptian girls and women to strengthen their bodies as individuals while also participating in a global culture of modern femininity.[42] Athleticism was equally significant for the postwar Egyptian man. Where the colonial regime previously portrayed Egyptian men as weak and deficient, the sporting club became an important space for showing the regeneration of Egyptian masculinity.[43]

A separate society column in *The Sphinx*, "The Epistles of Peggy," identified the new club as the future center of Maadi life. "Didn't know we had a garden city in Egypt, did you? Well, we have. And about the dinkiest little one ever," the author jested. If Delta Land's attempts to replicate Ebenezer Howard's model remained a work in progress, the Maadi Sporting Club stood out as particularly fashionable. The club, Peggy declared, "looks like being the attraction of that charmin' suburb."[44]

The club's success depended on how well it adapted to the complexities of postrevolutionary Cairene society. Opening in 1920 meant departing from the ethnic exclusivity of Cairo's other sporting clubs. The city's leading club was the Gezira Sporting Club, which became heavily associated with the most domineering forms of British imperialism in Egypt. Located on the island in the Nile west of downtown Cairo, Gezira was originally called the Khedivial Sporting Club and was leased by the British army in 1882. In 1912, Lord Kitchener forced the club to segregate, requiring that all Egyptian members resign.[45] In contrast, the Maadi Club was integrated, giving it a markedly different position in Cairene society and allowing Delta Land to distance itself from British imperial policy. The Maadi Club's integration marked a departure from norms in Egypt—all the more so in the larger colonial geography of British sporting clubs, which Mrinalini Sinha, in describing the clubs of India, describes as fostering a distinctive "colonial public sphere" that was instrumental in reproducing a class of European imperialists.[46] Maadi's leaders saw the club as constituting and reproducing a cosmopolitan class instead. This class remained elite, but these leaders distanced themselves from British imperial aims.

Egyptians' integration into the club life in Maadi was a process, however. The club's original board was predominantly British and required that all those applying for membership supply two—preferably British—recommendations, which made joining challenging not only for Egyptians, but also for some Europeans. Over the course of the 1920s, however, limitations on admission became less stringent, and the club developed into a shared, multinational space.[47] What is more, the integration of the club actively fostered more favorable social relationships between foreigners and Egyptians. As Dale recalls, "not until the Company built the club did residents really mix."[48] By the early 1930s, Peggy's predictions were largely fulfilled, and the club had become the center of Maadi society for Egyptians and Europeans alike. All of the club's members enjoyed the swimming pool, tennis courts, and cafe. Its existence further linked Maadi with attractive elements of bourgeois life in the suburbs—populated by individual families, who lived in villas and roamed the town on bicycles, free from the congestion of the city center.

As a place for families, perhaps the club's most significant patrons were the children who grew up splashing in its pools and competing on its fields. For those who grew up in Maadi after the First World War, the club was a fixture of their childhoods. As they played with other children, national, ethnic, and confessional differences seemed to disappear. In the politically turbulent years that followed, memories of formative years spent at the Maadi Sporting Club would become a potent rallying cry of a bygone era defined by tolerance and acceptance. Yet, Maadi's popular athleticism came, quite literally, at a cost. Club memberships, like villas, were not free, and Delta Land profited from the economic demands of participating in this particular form of Egyptian modernity. The company's board happily reported to investors that by April 1921, the club already had two hundred members "from both Maadi and Cairo."[49]

The athleticism on display at the Maadi Sporting Club echoed the signs, symbols, and personalities of the postwar Egyptian nation not by reversing the influence of resident foreigners, but by negotiating with it. The *effendiya*'s integration of global cultural influences as indicators of Egyptian modernity reflected the political climate of the time. The uprising in 1919 was nationwide, but the revolutionaries could only make limited claims to political independence and held even less control over the country's economy. This qualified independence was reflected in the culture, particularly in a place like Maadi, where foreigners functioned as locals.

Dale could not do his job as Delta Land's manager without carefully cooperating with Egyptian leaders inside and outside of the town. In his recollections, Dale articulates how Maadi depended not only on growing Egyptian independence, but also on the maintenance of older forms of foreign privilege that persisted in Egypt for as long as the Capitulations remained in place. The ethnic integration of the Maadi Sporting Club was one instance of this broader trend, but it became embedded in nearly every aspect of the town's development after the First World War—from the creation of electric light utilities to the relationship between Delta Land and the Cairo police.

The sustained control that Delta Land exerted over Maadi grew more tenuous after 1919, but it nonetheless remained intact. In 1924, the company's board enthusiastically reported to investors on ongoing development, with the construction of six new houses, all of which were already occupied. They also reported that the company decided to move its headquarters from downtown Cairo to Maadi, "the seat of the Company's most important activities."[50] As Delta Land physically relocated, it solidified its unofficial identity as the "Maadi Company." In the years that followed, Maadi's growth would be sustained not only by the company's ongoing leadership, but also by a growing body of Egyptian residents who identified the town's garden city plan with the best of modern Egypt. As more of the *effendiya* moved into Maadi, they were instrumental in transforming the garden city into a national space. Yet, the kind of nation many of these Egyptian residents envisioned never fully materialized.

PART THREE: CONSTRUCTION, PHASE TWO

Construction rarely goes according to plan, and while much of the garden city plan for Maadi was fulfilled in the 1920s, the town's founders could not have conceived of the critical role Egypt's *effendiya* would play in bringing their scheme to fruition. By the late 1920s, Egypt's political landscape was largely transformed as the nation's leaders claimed increasing independence from Britain. While independence can appear as a historical inevitability, this second phase of Maadi's construction reveals the negotiated aims, as well as the social, political, and economic compromises, which underpinned a liberal period that could be termed modern yet not wholly independent.

During the 1930s, Maadi's population of Egyptians continued to grow. They and the *mutamassir*, or Egyptianized resident foreigners, came to identify the area with a vision for an independent Egypt that still benefited from foreign investment and domicile. This plan for independence gained new urgency after the end of the Capitulations and Mixed Courts was secured at the Montreux Convention in 1937, which granted the European powers and resident foreigners a twelve-year transition period. With these international systems going away, Maadi's residents would look to the authority of Egypt's young King Faruq to sustain older forms of multinational harmony.

The events of the Second World War, however, would dash hopes of ushering in an independence where Egypt remained a hub of cosmopolitanism and foreign investment. Instead, the war heightened the significance of ethnic and racial differences, making Maadi's multinational society appear out of step with national feeling and Egypt's progress into the future. This discord would be etched into the town's postwar architecture, making Maadi appear increasingly like a figure of Egypt's past rather than its future.

6

AVENUE 'ABD AL-WAHHAB

On Friday, 22 January 1937, Wahib Doss Bey, a senator from Upper Egypt, gave a lecture on the Capitulations in Cairo.[1] The system, he explained, has created conditions where everyday Egyptians, the "man on the street, who is the majority of the population," had no expectation that a foreigner who committed a crime in Egypt would ever be brought to justice. The impact of this deep-seated sense of exploitation and unfairness, he continued, was twofold. First, it "is so detrimental to the national progress and so crushing to the national pride that the very foreigners of the criminal class have been instrumental in actually cowing the whole nation." The second was even more far reaching. Wahib Doss continued that distrust of foreigners was so ingrained in the Egyptian national consciousness that it would likely prevent favorable foreign relations from developing after the country secured independence from the British. A profound hatred for foreigners, he explained, "threatens to become insurmountable when the time comes for Egypt to collaborate in the world scheme of general brotherhood and united efforts for peace."[2]

Wahib Doss's lecture came shortly after a new Anglo-Egyptian Treaty in 1936 secured the country more substantial freedom, and Egypt prepared to join the League of Nations. Following the treaty, the Capitulations and the Mixed Courts that protected them posed the most immediate threat to Egyptian independence. Yet precisely what an independent Egypt looked like remained a matter of debate. Wahib Doss's lecture captures some of the anxiety among Egypt's *effendiya*, as they recognized their country's uncertain place in the world.

Where foreigners belonged in Egyptian society was more than a political or even an economic question and became deeply personal for Wahib Doss and other members of the *effendiya*. The Coptic notable lived in Maadi among the beneficiaries of the Capitulations, as did many of his Egyptian colleagues. The concerns he expressed to his audience reflected uncertainties not only about foreign policy, but also about a way of life for the *effendiya* that had developed since 1919, which accommodated persistent foreign influence at the same time that it demanded Egyptian independence. More than a contradiction, this existence participated in a particular vision of modern Egypt that eschewed the individual liberties promoted by the Wafd, and instead prioritized the country's economy. This vision allowed for sustained social and cultural connections to foreigners, and, in many ways, hoped to open up a path for ongoing foreign investment, but without the injustices of the Capitulations.

The leaders of this movement were deeply involved in the development of Maadi during some of the town's most profitable years. Rather than espousing the liberal nationalism of the Wafd's Mustafa al-Nahhas Pasha, who took over leadership after Sa'd Zaghlul died in 1927, they attached themselves to Isma'il Sidqi Pasha, his People's Party, and his vision for economic self-sufficiency. For them, Maadi was a realization of their vision for a rich and verdant Egypt. Yet, Sidqi's legacy of authoritarianism and corruption exposed the inequities of this idyllic Egypt. Likewise, the details of Maadi's history from the 1923 constitution until the renegotiation of Anglo-Egyptian relations in 1936 offer a vivid picture of how incomplete independence fostered a culture where a balance of foreign and national influences rested on the continuity of rigid socioeconomic divides.

In 1932, Wahib Doss moved with his family to Maadi and took up residence at the Grove, the former home of John W. Williamson. The Williamsons had left Maadi in December 1931, returning to White Plaines, John's beloved home in Cyprus near the village of Platres. Williamson passed away three months later, at the age of seventy-seven. His obituary in the *Egyptian Gazette* lauded him as a "Pioneer in Cyprus and Maadi," and stated that "he should be remembered with special gratitude by Maadi residents to-day for his continuous efforts to keep Maadi unspoiled by too commercial a development of its amenities."[3] His passing marked a larger generational shift in Maadi during the 1920s and 1930s. Upon his final departure for

Cyprus, Williamson was the only early founder of Maadi still living. When he joined Delta Land's board in 1906, he helped establish a regional identity for the company. In the twenty-five years that followed, the company remained a hybrid, connected to both national as well as foreign interests in Egypt. With his departure, more Egyptians would attempt to sustain that balance. Perhaps it is not surprising, then, that Avenue Williamson was renamed Avenue Wahib Doss in 1939.

Avenue Williamson was not the only street to get an update in nomenclature. That same year, Avenue Colvin was renamed after Ahmad 'Abd al-Wahhab Pasha and Maadi thus lost its most overt reference to British imperialism. Of Egypt's political leaders associated with opposition to the Capitulations, 'Abd al-Wahhab was among the most prominent. With a keen mind for numbers, 'Abd al-Wahhab entered the Egyptian government in 1919 when he began managing accounts for the Ministry of Education. He was later made the ministry's financial secretary.[4] He went on to serve in the Ministry of Finance under three different prime ministers—Isma'il Sidqi, Tawfiq Nissim Pasha, and the brief government of Ali Maher Pasha.[5] 'Abd al-Wahhab's varied career exposes the continuities forged between government administrations as economic policy connected party platforms rather than differentiating them. In the case of Sidqi and Tawfiq Nissim, the prime ministers distanced themselves from the Wafd's liberalism and instead associated their vision for Egypt with the ongoing authority of King Fu'ad.

The most prominent among these anti-Wafd leaders was Sidqi, who remains best known for abolishing the 1923 constitution and replacing it in 1930 with a new constitution that further reduced parliamentary powers and enhanced the authority of the crown. Sidqi had been part of the earliest formulations of Egypt's postwar claims to independence. He joined Zaghlul and the rest of the delegation in 1918 to appeal for Egyptian independence, but soon grew disenchanted with the Wafd Party.[6] His affiliation with Egypt's financial interests began early in his career, when he led the Ministry of Finance in 'Abd al-Khaliq Tharwat's 1922 government.[7] Perhaps most significantly, he served as an early president of the Egyptian Federation of Industries, which Belgian industrialist Henri Naus Bey founded in 1922.[8] Through the federation, Sidqi connected with some of Egypt's most prominent industrial endeavors and their leaders—most of whom were resident foreigners.[9]

When the People's Party came to power in 1930—after a short-lived Wafd government under Nahhas in 1929—Sidqi took a heavily centralized approach to governing in hopes of strengthening the national economy, expanding the country's industrial sector, and reducing dependency on cotton exports.[10] Sidqi's government lasted until 1933, when he resigned after a conflict with King Fu'ad. He remained in public life throughout much of the 1930s and 1940s, however, and served as prime minister again briefly in 1946. His 1930 constitution would leave an indelible mark on Egyptian politics, creating a governing crisis that ultimately required the renegotiation of Anglo-Egyptian relations, and, ultimately, led to a new treaty that substantially increased Egyptian independence.

When considering Sidqi in light of his economic approach, he is defined less in the negative—as an anti-Wafdist, anti-liberal dictator—and more as a nationalist fluent in the political and economic vocabulary of his time. As the global rise of demagoguery after the First World War indicated, nationalist leadership did not have to embrace liberalism, and often fared better when eschewing it. The People's Party embraced a platform that prioritized economic independence and self-sufficiency. This approach made Sidqi and members of his government like 'Abd al-Wahhab potent economic actors. Both men made strategic threats in public and private to unilaterally abolish the Capitulations. In doing so, they hoped to thwart foreign opposition to a protective tariff and new taxes. They followed these unofficial actions with the very public removal of Egypt's currency from the gold standard.[11] Had the move succeeded, the People's Party would have abolished one of the Egyptian economy's most distinguishing links to the British empire.[12] Foreign bondholders sued the Egyptian government in defense of their investment, however, and the Mixed Court of First Instance ruled in the bondholders' favor. The ruling triggered a nationwide call for the abolition of the Capitulations.[13] These tactics linked Sidqi and 'Abd al-Wahhab to the kind of anti-foreigner populism Wahib Doss described among the general Egyptian populace in his 1937 lecture.

While these actions would appear to mark the growth of a uniform anti-foreigner sentiment in Egyptian culture, the reality was far more complex. Sidqi's anti-liberalism and emphasis on economic self-sufficiency was certainly in line with some of the totalitarian political trends of his moment, especially after the stock market crash in 1929. Yet, Sidqi's nationalism accommodated cultural and ethnic differences in ways that became untenable among his fascist European contemporaries. Since his time at the Egyptian Federation of Industries, Sidqi's priorities had been more strictly economic, and he looked to work with rather than against existing resident foreigners. He believed his policies would ideally foster an Egyptian economy strong enough that foreigners, and their investments, would want to stay. This position gained Sidqi broad and varied support, especially as resident foreigners recognized the substantial popular and official threats to their Capitulations benefits.

'Abd al-Wahhab was not Sidqi's only supporter in Maadi. Elie Nissim Mosseri also backed Sidqi and his People's Party. Early in 1919, Mosseri joined Delta Land's board, filling a vacancy left after the death of D.P. McGillivray.[14] As a prominent member of Cairo's Jewish community, Mosseri was likely familiar with the company and its work in Maadi from early on. As mentioned in Chapter Two, Mosseri's wife Laura Suarès was the daughter of Felix Suarès, and she inherited a significant portion of her uncle Raphael's large estate.[15] Mosseri would go on to become one of the company's most influential and politically well-connected leaders. As Gudrun Krämer explains, he was affiliated with some of the world's biggest banking houses and served on the board or as manager of thirty businesses—several of which were among Egypt's largest commercial ventures—making him "one of the most influential figures in Egyptian business and a prototype of the local foreign minority member."[16] More than an economic actor, Mosseri actively participated in the politics of Egyptian independence and reform, contributing to a particular vision of modern Egypt that resident foreigners identified with and that was exemplified by Maadi.

A holder of Italian citizenship, and thus a beneficiary of the Capitulations, Mosseri's support for the People's Party might appear out of sync with his best interests. Yet, the stringent racist and xenophobic nationalism of Europe had far-reaching implications for Egypt's resident foreigners, especially the country's influential Jews. For Egyptian Jews with German and Italian citizenship, the growth of European antisemitism forced them to reconsider their multivalent, cosmopolitan affiliations. Mosseri, in particular, had been an avid contributor to Egypt's Italian community. When Benito Mussolini instituted antisemitic policies, however, he threatened to transfer his money out of Italy and reregister his business ventures in Egypt.[17] By catering to international business interests, the People's Party offered a platform for elite resident foreigners like Mosseri to identify their interests more strictly with Egypt.

A pathway to Egyptian identity was especially imperative for the People's Party after 1929, when the passage of the Egyptian Nationality Decree-Law defined Egyptian citizenship for the first time. The new law granted citizenship to former Ottoman subjects who were included in Egypt's majority ethnicity and religion, and additionally offered citizenship to assimilated *mutamassir* who had lived in Egypt for generations. It also granted Egyptian nationality to foreign women married to Egyptian men.[18] The law answered the question of whether former Ottomans could be considered Egyptian after the fall of the sultanate in 1923. It also responded to Britain's 1922 claims to authority over the interests of foreigners and minorities by aligning the Egyptian nation with the country's ethnic and religious majorities. The category of *mutamassir* would be imperative for elite resident foreigners who sought a future in Egypt. As Gianluca Paolo Parolin explains, "The 1929 Egyptian Nationality Decree-Law allowed for the absorption of foreign elements only if there was a common cultural, linguistic or religious background."[19] Likewise, Joel Beinin argues that the law established legal terms for the increased removal of ethnic and religious minorities from Egypt.[20] Significantly for Jews and Copts, the terms of Egyptian citizenship would be increasingly, but not exclusively, linked with Islam. When Sidqi came to power the year after the citizenship law passed, he would attempt to strengthen the economy in order to sustain ties between Egypt and the global economy. That same year, Sidqi appointed Mosseri to his Economic Council of Egypt.[21] Two years later, Mosseri would take over the chairmanship of Delta Land, following Williamson's departure. He would also oversee the "Egyptianization" of the town's street names in 1939.[22]

For his part, 'Abd al-Wahhab would go on to make a personal commitment to sustaining friendly relations with the British after the acceptance of a new Anglo-Egyptian Treaty in 1936. Following Sidqi's resignation in 1933, the 1930 constitution lacked a strong leader and political unrest mounted. After the student demonstrations in 1935 that Russell Pasha attempted violently to quell, King Fu'ad, whose health was failing, reinstated the 1923 constitution.[23] In turn, the Wafd successfully harnessed its popular base, winning an overwhelming victory in May 1936 and proceeding to renewed negotiations with the British. By August, they had secured a new treaty, in which the British recognized Egyptian independence, sponsored Egypt in the League of Nations, and decreased the number of British occupational troops to ten thousand, limiting their placement to the Suez Canal Zone, where they could remain for the next twenty years. The British also converted their imperial Residency into an embassy, and their once high commissioner Sir Miles Lampson became Britain's first ambassador to Egypt. The British sought these altered terms in response to popular unrest in Egypt as well as Mussolini's invasion of Libya, which threatened to garner Egyptian support.[24] The military provision allowed the British government to secure its highest priority—an ongoing military presence in the Canal Zone, which meant secure passage to India and a foothold against European rivals in the Middle East. The treaty served as a major victory for Egyptian nationalists, and created new impetus for Anglo-Egyptian cultural collaboration. A new organization, the Anglo-Egyptian Union, was formed in 1937 with a leadership made up of equal numbers of British and Egyptian men.[25] 'Abd al-Wahhab served as the organization's founding vice president.[26]

The Anglo-Egyptian Union was to form as an entity of binational friendship. Its premises included a lecture hall, reading room, and a library, where, the *Egyptian Gazette* explained, "it will be possible for the bonds of friendship between the two nations to be drawn tighter under the influence of joint interests and understanding."[27] The English newspaper's editorial board stated that they had lobbied for the creation of such an organization since the signing of the treaty, explaining, "That warm potential friendship did exist between Egyptians and ourselves, we did not for a moment doubt."[28] While it is possible to somewhat cynically read these statements as a thin veil for sustained imperialism, and see 'Abd al-Wahhab's participation in the organization as perhaps an instance of colonized consciousness, such an approach presumes a binary division between national and foreign interests. 'Abd al-Wahhab and an entire cadre of Egyptian nationalists were committed to a more complex vision for Egyptian independence that included ongoing ties, especially economic ones, to the British and other foreign powers. If that vision proved shortsighted, it remained real and potent in the mid-1930s.

For 'Abd al-Wahhab, 1937 included a number of landmarks. While he was no longer a member of the cabinet after the Wafd took over the government in 1936, he was a member of parliament, representing the Nikla district of Giza. He also saw the international community agree to the abolition of the Mixed Courts and Capitulations—a change he had pushed so earnestly for more than a decade earlier. That spring, the Montreux Convention in Switzerland agreed to the abolition of both institutions. As part of the agreement, however, Egypt had to concede to an extended, twelve-year transition period, and could not pass any anti-foreigner legislation in the meantime. The agreement offered a kind of stop-gap, where a tenuous status quo remained in place while a major shift in Egypt's economic relations became imminent.

On 16 April 1938, 'Abd al-Wahhab died unexpectedly of what was likely the flu. *Al-Ahram* celebrated 'Abd al-Wahhab for his service to the country, lauding him as one of the "great sons of the nation," and lamenting the timing of his passing because of the country's great need for his economic expertise. Upon announcing his death, the Egyptian parliament lamented that with 'Abd al-Wahhab's death, "so dies one of the great pillars of the economic renaissance."[29] Tellingly, the *Egyptian Gazette* remarked that Sidqi was now the only living Egyptian whose financial ability compared to that of the deceased.[30] That 'Abd al-Wahhab's name became explicitly linked to Maadi the following year is perhaps the clearest indicator of how the town's leaders identified Maadi with both Egyptian independence and sustained foreign influence. Had he lived, 'Abd al-Wahhab would have joined Delta Land's board that spring. He was elected one of the company's directors two days before his death.[31] The creation of Avenue 'Abd al-Wahhab was not the only indicator of a delicate balance between foreign and local influences, though. Domestic life in Maadi informally carried out these negotiations on a daily basis.

In 1935, Mary Kilgour Stout published *Gardening for Egypt and Allied Climates*, a handbook for garden planning and management. Stout moved to Maadi around 1910 with her husband Percy, a stockbroker by trade and former member of the Gloucester Rugby Football Club, where he played with his brother Frank.[32] The couple first relocated to Cairo after they were married in Mary's hometown of Cincinnati, Ohio, in November 1903. Mary was the daughter of the wealthy and influential Captain George Nelson Stone, the president of the Cincinnati Bell Telephone Company. Once in Cairo, Percy established a stock brokerage firm with Ernest Charles Hogg and his brother Frank Stout joined him a few years later.[33] Initially,

Percy and Frank were the more well-known Stouts of Cairo. It was not until the early 1920s that Mary made a more substantial name for herself. Her growing visibility was due in part to the changes wrought by the First World War. By the spring of 1915, Percy and Frank both departed Cairo for England to join the war effort and served together in the machine gun corps of the Royal Naval Air Service, fighting in France.[34] During Percy's deployment, Mary devoted herself more wholeheartedly to their villa garden in Maadi. The garden served as a kind of companion for Mary and her home became known as a particularly peaceful retreat—an ideal of the leisurely country space associated with town-and-country developments like Maadi. Sir Robert Greg, chairman of the Egyptian Horticultural Society, recalled Stout's wartime garden in the preface to her 1935 guide, writing that its flowers, creepers, and shrubs made it a "small earthly paradise on the edge of the desert as it then was."[35]

Gardening for Egypt and Allied Climates was Stout's second work on gardening in Egypt, as she coauthored an earlier, less substantial guide, *A Book of Gardening for the Subtropics: With a Calendar for Cairo*, with Madeline Agar in 1921.[36] By 1935, this first volume had outlived its usefulness, and Stout intentionally published her new work under the auspices of the Egyptian Horticultural Society in order to address it to the men and women of the gardening community. Several Maadi residents belonged to the society, reflecting both the organization's and the town's multinational society. These members included Taher al-Lozy Bey, the nephew of Safiya Zaghlul by marriage, Muhammad Aflatoun Pasha, *al-Muqattam* proprietor Faris Nimr, French archeologist Henriette Devonshire, Tom and Effie Dale, as well as Austrian Levantine Erwin de Cramer and his Anglo-Italian wife Lucy (Erwin contributed a chapter on cultivating roses to Stout's first book).[37] These Maadi residents were already well-known gardeners. In 1919, the society awarded Devonshire a bronze medal and certificate of merit for her roses, and that same year Aflatoun Pasha received a certificate of merit for presenting four distinct varieties of roses.[38] The society helped validate the shared habits of the Egyptian and resident foreign elite. Like the Maadi Sporting Club, it created space for shared interests.

Because Stout published her new guide through and for this body, her book offers a look into the construction of Maadi's verdant aesthetic, and, more significantly, how maintaining a clear class hierarchy was integral to fashioning the ideal Maadi villa and garden. It is worth noting that Stout also likely relied on the society for the publication of her book because by 1935 she no longer had a garden. In 1927, she and Percy left Maadi and moved to a *dahabiya*, or Egyptian houseboat, which they docked off of Gezira island. The couple sustained a connection to Maadi through Delta Land. Percy, who was known for having a daily delivery of two blocks of ice to keep himself cool, joined the company's board in 1922 and remained a member until his death in 1937.[39]

Stout opened *Gardening* with a series of guidelines for planning a garden, emphasizing the relationship between the house and the garden. "Do not forget that the house and garden belong to each other and that the garden is mostly seen from certain fixed points within the house," she instructed.[40] Her description for how a garden should be arranged additionally emphasized that ideally the plan for the garden would be taken into account while the house was under construction. Hedges, for instance, should be planted around the land's perimeter soon after its purchase, or, "if this is a year before the house is built, so much the better."[41] When builders completed construction on the house, then work on the rest of the garden could begin.

The actual garden could work in one of two ways: either a display of aesthetically pleasing flora or a botanical collection of interesting plants. Stout emphasized that "the two are incompatible."[42] She followed with an explanation of how to plan a garden for aesthetic purposes by planting trees near the perimeter, then shrubs, and finally flowers. Throughout she offered suggestions on how to consider particular color combinations with varying shapes and sizes, explaining that one should plan for either "contrast or harmony." She continued, "Merely to feel vaguely that certain plants 'will look nice together' is likely to lead to confusion."[43] Finally, the lawns were to be laid out, keeping in mind how they would be used—for either outdoor games or as a grassy space complementing the flower beds.

Throughout the book, Stout pointed to the labor behind the physical construction of Maadi's domestic spaces, mostly in terms of the traffic they represented across the would-be garden space. Because the villa's construction required people to walk across what would become the garden, it could only be laid down after the builders had done much of their work. Then flower beds could be constructed. Finally, she explained, "When the heavy traffic is done with, make the paths." The paths should be raised, she noted, because the nutrient-rich Nile water that irrigated the land would otherwise flood them and make the garden "useless."[44] Only after these sand or brick pathways were constructed could the actual botanical cultivation commence.

Amid all of this planning, construction, and finally planting, Stout also recommended a daily schedule of gardening tasks, such as "hoeing, watering, staking, spraying, removal of dead flowers, pruning and mowing."[45] The book's reader, however, did not perform this physical labor. The reader's primary task was planning the garden and managing the male Egyptian gardener. When discussing the gardener, Stout emphasized that the kind of garden she described required both expert horticultural knowledge and the gardener's less official, common knowledge.[46] After nearly forty pages of detailed instruction on how to create a suburban garden, Stout addressed the importance of the gardener, revealing the essential labor behind her previous directions.

Stout offered detailed instructions for filling the gardener's day with watering, overhauling a particular part of the garden, and general upkeep.[47] She advocated a relationship between her readers and their Egyptian gardeners that combined criticism and sympathy. *Gardening* included sections titled "An Indictment of the Gardener" and "A Plea for the Gardener." Her criticism was mostly a rant against presumed bad habits. In her estimation, the gardener overwatered, used only manure to fertilize, and lacked an appreciation for leaf mold. "He is propagation mad," Stout wrote, "and, unless frustrated, on all the paths will appear score of little pots, the watering of which will happily absorb his time." She sums up his faults as "largely those of delayed action, and a wish to save trouble."[48] Stout did not want the gardener to be viewed too harshly, however. To that point, she emphasized that employing a good gardener one could partner with was essential to the garden's success. She instructed, "If you have engaged a man of experience, pay him properly and trust him until he proves himself unworthy. Make him feel a pride in the garden, which he will if he knows he is responsible for it." Stout appreciated that gardeners had a community of their own in which they exchanged seeds and plants. Rather than lamenting these unsanctioned transactions, she explained their benefits to her readers. "Let him obtain any plants, seeds and accessories you want. Of course he will make something on the transaction, but direct purchase would only benefit the seller, not you, and your man will take greater interest in what he himself has bought."[49] Stout advocated that the gardener receive a degree of autonomy because his knowledge and connections could be advantageous to the garden. This independence had to strike a delicate balance, however, considering her earlier warning about the gardener's penchant for idleness.

In Stout's account, the garden's success required the homeowner's horticultural expertise and management skills, as well as the gardener's own local knowledge and methods. This arrangement also depended on a clear social hierarchy. Maadi's households had relied on the labor of lower-class servants since the town's founding. Yet, if the town was indicative of a particular kind of national community, then the question of who benefitted from that space and who primarily labored in it is critical.

In defining the national community, Egypt's *effendiya* often remained uncritical of their own bourgeois status. The more authoritarian position of the People's Party made this elitist stance perhaps less surprising, although the party had a vision for strengthening national industry. More significantly, this inattention to social class was true of the Wafd, which was considered the legitimate representative of the Egyptian people by the majority of the population throughout the 1920s and 1930s. For the Wafd—which had the support of most of Egypt's working class—until they secured full independence, other factional issues were to be subordinated to the larger interests of the nation.[50]

Eschewing social divisions offered wealthy resident foreigners a place in the nation, but it also failed to put forward a clear benefit for Egypt's working class and especially its peasant majority. Stout's 1935 guide indicates two significant continuities in Maadi's history: the town's ongoing association with a verdant domestic life, and that life's dependence on the labor of poorer Egyptians. When the Egyptian Horticultural Society published Stout's book, whether or not those continuities could sustain Egypt's transition to independence, and ultimately the end of the Capitulations, was still unknown.

Stout was not the only Maadi resident to offer a guide for navigating Cairo during the 1920s and 1930s. Where *Gardening for Egypt and Allied Climates* offered a picture of how to manage the villa household and maintain clear social ranks, Henriette Devonshire offered a more explicitly expatriate readership a method for interacting with the rest of Cairo, especially its Islamic spaces. More than a prize-winning gardener, Devonshire was far better known for her knowledge of medieval Cairo than for her roses. She first moved to Cairo in 1907 when her husband Robert took a position as a lawyer in the Mixed Courts. Henriette was forty-two years old at the time, and the couple's three children—Marie, Feray, and Antoinette—were already teenagers.[51] The couple soon became acquainted with Maadi when Robert served as a lawyer for Wakeman Long and Britton in their suit against Delta Land. As mentioned in Chapter Three, the Devonshires moved to Maadi by 1916, in the middle of the land dispute.[52] Over the course of Henriette's life in Egypt, she learned Arabic and wrote several monographs in French and English about the city's Islamic history. Her guidebooks were especially popular because they offered her expatriate readers a mode for participating in her ventures through the older parts of Cairo that were removed from the "European" half of the city that they inhabited.

Like Stout, the First World War was a critical period for Devonshire to fashion a stronger connection to Egypt. In 1916, the same year she moved to Maadi, she began writing a series of articles in *The Sphinx* from the perspective of a wounded soldier who ventured around Cairo, under the title, "A Convalescent in Cairo." Over time, Devonshire's scholarly interests became a personal comfort to her, especially after she faced a series of tragic losses. On 7 November 1919, Henriette and Robert's son Feray died while fighting with the Royal Air Force in the Third Afghan War.[53] Two years later, Robert died in their Maadi home after a prolonged illness.[54] Rather than repatriate to England or her native France, Henriette remained in Maadi and Cairo's medieval quarters came to fill her time and interests.

Following the success of her "Convalescent in Cairo" series, Devonshire compiled the articles into a guidebook called *Rambles in Cairo* in 1917. Written in epistolary form, *Rambles, as* Devonshire explained, was intended not for casual tourists but for people domiciled in Cairo for a longer term. Devonshire published a second edition of the book in 1931, explaining in her introduction that *Rambles* was "merely intended to add interest to the explorations of visitors whose curiosity is attracted by this fascinating and somewhat neglected branch of art."[55] In writing the book this way, Devonshire offered a kind of cultural history of Cairo's Islamic history, one where she hoped to make the places more relatable and meaningful through stories that gave some sense of the people who designed, built, and used them.[56]

Devonshire presented Cairo's medieval mosques as a personalized history lesson, explaining that it would "be very easy to acquire a few notions of [Cairo's history] by visiting, in chronological order and beginning by the earliest examples, the beautiful medieval monuments which still exist in Cairo."[57] To that end, she broke up the book into twelve chapters, opening with a description of the mosque of Ibn Tulun, which was built in ad 899, and concluding with Abu Dahab's 1774 mosque. Her concluding chapter looked at the surviving homes and palaces from the late eighteenth century. Throughout *Rambles*, Devonshire combined physical descriptions of the mosques with colorful stories. Upon entering Prince Ahmad ibn Tulun's mosque, for instance, she explained that the interior space was "a most impressive vista of cloisters formed by innumerable arches resting on massive triangular piers." The space was so impressive, she continued, that there "was nothing 'squat' about it." [58] She explained that, according to popular rumor, the mosque's pillars were stolen from churches, or, if not stolen, copied from pillars designed by a Christian architect whom Ibn Tulun freed from prison. The diplomatic prince, not wanting to offend Egyptian Christians, agreed to the architect's proposal that "he would gladly undertake to build him the finest mosque in the world without the use of any columns save two for the *mihrab* (prayer-niche)." After using these details to draw in readers, Devonshire switched to a more direct tone and contradicted the earlier narrative. "But there is no truth in this anecdote," she stated. As an alternative, she offered a "more scientific" explanation that the mosque was copied from a similar structure near Ibn Tulun's childhood home in Baghdad.[59] Although Devonshire disregarded personal anecdotes as empirically insignificant, she used them to populate the city's medieval past. She asked her readers to recreate these mythic scenes in their imaginations. Ibn Tulun was "one of the greatest rulers Egypt ever had," she explained.[60] He founded dispensaries, hospitals, and drinking troughs for cattle. Only the mosque, however, remained of his work. With her lively descriptions, Devonshire helped establish the mosque as a memorial to what she presented as one of Egypt's seemingly forgotten rulers.[61]

Devonshire's attempt to bring these medieval sites to life became more problematic, however, when she described places that remained relevant to contemporary Muslims. Devonshire's description of al-Azhar makes the mosque and university a kind of living history exhibit. In describing the school, she explained,

The lessons take place in the sanctuary, and with no class-room para-phernalia, desks or chairs; the students squat in a circle around the teacher who himself sits on his heels, with his back against a column, either on the floor or on a high-backed chair. It is truly admirable to see the attention with which they concentrate on their lessons, taking no heed of inquisitive visitors meandering between the circles; some-times, if a writing lesson is going on, a little interest shown in their calligraphy is received in a very friendly manner.[62]

While Devonshire remarked on the positive impression the students made—particularly as they studied without the accoutrements of a mod-ern classroom—her observations created a perceived parallel between al-Azhar's medieval past and the students' present practices, turning her contemporaries into historical illustrations. These Islamic scholars' debates about the role of Islamic education in opposing colonialism and Western influence did not figure in her description.[63] What is more, when Devon-shire reissued *Rambles*, al-Azhar's *ulama* were embroiled in a conflict with the burgeoning Muslim Brotherhood, which was founded just three years earlier. The Brotherhood identified a direct conflict with Egypt's resident foreigners, particularly missionaries, over orphan care.[64] Al-Azhar's *ulama* had their own conflicts with foreign missionaries, who ventured onto the campus in the same manner that Devonshire recommended in order to distribute missionary tracts.[65] These developments had no place in Devon-shire's account. If she provided a method for navigating and understanding the city, it upheld a bifurcated view of Cairo, where Egypt's past was located among the city's poorer population in the medieval and predominantly Islamic quarters and the present and future remained associated with the European city. The vibrant debates taking place in Cairo's medieval city over Egypt's future, as well as the articulation of new Islamist political ide-ologies, appears impossible in her telling.

In the years between the two editions of *Rambles*, Devonshire fashioned a deep connection to her life in Cairo. During the 1920s, she published an additional five monographs on Cairo's historical mosques.[66] These works were more scholarly in focus and written in French, the lingua franca of Egyptian academia at the time. She gave lectures in England and Egypt on her studies.[67] She also conducted regular tours of medieval Cairo and other archeological sites. The *Egyptian Gazette* published her comings and goings, so that its readers knew when the tours stopped during Henriette's summer holidays.[68] Her work later earned her the recognition of King Fu'ad and his son Faruq. In 1944, Faruq conferred on her the Order of al-Kamal—she was eighty years old at the time, and still giving weekly walking tours of Cairo's Islamic points of interest.[69]

Devonshire's work, like Stout's, made explicit how resident foreigners might fashion an ongoing life in Egypt—building a home and navigating the city. Their guidebooks reflected just how resident foreigners saw themselves as part of Egyptian life during the 1920s and 1930s. In both cases, that life required ongoing social stratification. Maadi fit into the Egypt they knew, which had become home for both women, especially for Devonshire. This same idyllic garden city symbolized the kind of international friendship that certain nationalist leaders hoped to foster apart from the Capitulations. If Maadi participated in this vision for an independent Egyptian nation, then how the Egyptian majority might see themselves as more than servants and workers remained an unresolved tension by the late 1930s. Ongoing political and cultural struggles, like the conflict over missionary activity that Devonshire overlooked, would make this version of the nation less and less sustainable.

When Elie Mosseri oversaw the renaming of Maadi's streets, he aligned the town with a version of modern Egypt that saw the garden city's verdant beauty as some of the best of what Egypt had to offer. This vision seemed to allow for both the abolition of the Capitulations as well as Anglo-Egyptian friendship. At the same time, it did not attend to the needs of the Egyptian majority. The "man on the street" that Wahib Doss described might work in Maadi's villas or even help construct them, but he did not call this piece of the nation his home.

Whatever class tensions remained under the surface, following the 1936 Anglo-Egyptian Treaty, Maadi appeared prime for ongoing growth. This was because of two important continuities. First, while the Montreux Treaty secured the end of the Capitulations, they would not be fully abolished until 1949. Second, the monarchy remained central to Egyptian governance. Egyptian nationalism and British imperialism were not the only two bases of political authority at this time. Until his death in April 1936, Fu'ad was an important defense against liberalism and popular sovereignty in Egypt. The ascension of Fu'ad's son Faruq promised to reinvigorate the crown. Optimism about Faruq affirmed the existing social structure, helping to secure the class hierarchy upon which Maadi's villas and gardens depended. Both Stout and Devonshire dedicated their books to Fu'ad during his reign.[70] Once Faruq was in power, Maadi's leaders would take more explicit measures to associate the town with the conservative authority of the royal family.

7

CONFESSIONAL INTERSECTION

The 1937–38 edition of *Egypt Today* lauds Maadi's beauty, opening with a rich description of the town's verdant aesthetic:

> "When one is in Meadi [sic] one has the environment of England and Switzerland," was the remark made by a recent visitor to this charming suburb of Cairo. Situated at a distance of about seven miles south of Cairo, Meadi is the one place in Egypt where such an assortment of sweet smelling and profusely flowering trees abound and thrive.

The article continues with a list of the various flowers and trees one might find in Maadi across the seasons—scarlet poincianas, blue jacarandas, yellow tecomas, mauve and white bauhinias, and pink and cream oleanders. "The Australian wattle and blue gums and picturesque casuarinas and cypress also revel in the joy of responding to the care bestowed on them." The publication—a yearbook "Published in the Interests of Egyptian Finance," as its subtitle explains—provides a portrait of Maadi in sync with the garden city ideals that its founders established. It notes, "The little township is chiefly composed of privately-owned villas where its residents escape from the City noises and enjoy the quiet, undisturbed existence denied to town dwellers."[1]

Egypt Today gives responsibility for Maadi's contemporary growth and beauty to Elie Mosseri, "under whose active guidance Meadi [sic] has taken on a new development, but always upon the lines originally laid down by its founders." By 1938, it reports, Maadi had more than three hundred villas and remained easily accessible from Cairo not only by rail but also by "well-lighted modern road." The article concludes, "Everything possible is being done for the comfort and enjoyment of Meadi's residents, and the attractions thus offered are greatly appreciated by that class of the public seeking a place in which to establish a real HOME."[2]

Egypt Today was designed to highlight Egypt's recent economic developments, emphasizing the talents of Egypt's local and *mutamassir* businessmen. The opening pages included portraits of "Prominent Financiers of Egypt," including Jewish notables like Mosseri, Aslan Cattaoui Bey, and Robert J. Rolo. The central image was Tal'at Harb Pasha, the founder of Bank Misr. Harb was the protege of Yusuf Cattaoui Pasha, and learned the intricacies of Egyptian finance as part of the larger Suarès network of business and banking interests.[3] By 1938, Harb was a powerful symbol of Egyptian economic nationalism and its potential to solicit sustained foreign investment. By working through Egypt's existing financial networks, Harb forged important alliances with resident foreigners and Egyptian officials. During the 1920s, Ahmad 'Abd al-Wahhab joined Bank Misr's board, and Harb served as an early board member for the Egyptian Federation of Industries when it was under Isma'il Sidqi's leadership.[4] These business leaders positioned themselves between local and foreign influence. With the Montreux Treaty securing the end of the Capitulations by 1949, they looked to use the intervening years to fashion continuity in Egypt's economy, not transformation and certainly not revolution.

As *Egypt Today* reflected, this vision for Egypt's future was more than economic. Culturally, these leaders looked to associate the modern parts of Cairo—which were previously seen as part of the capital's "European" city—with their plans. The yearbook highlighted the Egyptian capital's various advantages, including the Marconi Telegraph receiving station in Maadi, the modern shops and cafes in Midan Soliman Pasha, and the luxury apartment buildings in Heliopolis. Beyond Cairo, it featured images of agricultural advancements—ploughing in Lower Egypt and watering cotton fields in Upper Egypt.[5]

After 1937, Egypt entered a period of unstable continuities. For the next twelve years, resident foreigners and their investments remained protected. Egypt also had a new king, but Faruq was just sixteen years old when he ascended the throne and looked to stabilize the monarchy. Although the Wafd had the opportunity to push for a strengthened legislature in 1936, the British successfully negotiated for Faruq's smooth ascension, making

Faruq's authority under the 1923 constitution seemingly secure.[6] Maadi's growth from the 1920s until the beginning of the Second World War would depend on both the Capitulations and the king. For those who lived in Maadi at that time, it appears that Mosseri effectively planned for the future. If the end of the Capitulations was imminent, though, then a strong monarchy was essential for sustaining the community beyond 1949. The details of Maadi's physical construction during the 1930s expose the multinational and multiconfessional networks that the town continued to depend upon, as well as the gamble Delta Land and Maadi residents made on Faruq.

The particular form of Maadi's growth that Mosseri initiated in the 1930s was imperative for the town's garden city plan to continue. In the decade after 1937, Cairo grew at the rapid annual rate of 5.9 percent, from a total population of 1.3 million to more than two million. That growth rate was more than double the 2.3 percent annual increase experienced between 1927 and 1937.[7] While the city saw consistent growth after the government began taking a census at the outset of the British occupation in 1882, the population surge documented in 1947 represented the city's fastest and most significant increase to date.[8]

Egypt's mid-century growth indicated a different kind of expansion from what the country previously experienced. Where at the turn of the twentieth century an influx of foreigners made Cairo and Alexandria some of the world's fastest growing cities, the 1947 population numbers represented a reversal of these trends. After 1936, Cairo saw a significant decline in its population of foreigners. The Italian community saw the most substantial drop, losing roughly 20,000 of their 47,706 residents. The Greek population—the largest body of foreign nationals in Egypt—lost more than 10,000, going from 68,559 to 57,427. The French community experienced nearly as dramatic a decline, going from 18,821 to 9,717. The British community additionally lost nearly 3,000, going from 31,523 in 1937 to 28,246 in 1947.[9] As foreigners emigrated, Egypt's cities, especially Cairo, swelled in size because of internal migration. Poorer residents from rural areas increasingly moved to Egypt's urban centers in search of new opportunities. In Cairo, urban migration compounded the impact of rural-to-urban relocation, as Egypt's smaller cities saw their residents increasingly move to the capital.[10] The demographic trends that started in 1936 have continued to the present, with Cairo continuing to hold more and more of the country's population. Already by 1937, 27.5 percent of Egypt's overall population lived in cities. By 1966, Cairo absorbed some 80 percent of the country's internal migration.[11]

For Cairo's planned communities, these demographic trends significantly affected how residents related to one another and the town itself. Heliopolis had already experienced a significant population boom in the 1920s, going from 9,200 residents in 1921 to 224,000 by 1928. That rapid expansion meant that the town could no longer be managed according to the garden city perimeters that Baron Empain first established.[12] The subtle remark in *Egypt Today* regarding how Mosseri's plan to further develop Maadi remained true to the founders' plans reflected the pressure these communities increasingly felt as Cairo attracted more and more lower-income Egyptians. As resident foreigners began departing Cairo, Maadi did not yet see more of these rural and urban migrants move in, but instead continued welcoming a growing number of Egypt's *effendiya*, who remained committed to the town's garden city plan.

If Mosseri oversaw the plans for Maadi's development, Tom Dale remained responsible for the execution of those plans. To that end, he employed a team of engineers, architects, and gardeners for the maintenance and expansion of Maadi. Delta Land's chief engineer was John A. Clyma, a Canadian and former member of the Royal Engineers who came to Maadi at the end of the First World War.[13] He worked closely with engineer and architect Isaac Kipnis, a Russian Jew from Palestine who moved to Egypt in 1915 and joined Delta Land in 1927.[14] Together, Clyma and Kipnis oversaw the construction of the company's buildings. They worked closely with another prominent Jewish resident, Meyr Y. Biton, who used the company's property to cultivate the nurseries, orchards, and agricultural land. Biton grew bananas on the former Luthy-Zehnder farm that the company secured after the First World War. He also successfully cultivated mangos, guavas, and grapes, and continued growing berseem, which was used to feed mules. As Geoffrey Dale recalled, Biton was responsible for the growth of most of Maadi's trees, and his green thumb earned him the nickname "Mango and Banana."[15]

Kipnis, Clyma, and Biton coordinated their efforts with Ra'is Tantawi, Delta Land's head of road construction, irrigation, and house building, who moved to Maadi from the Delta town of Zagazig after previously working for Tom Dale's father Jesse.[16] In the mid-1930s, following Biton's death, the team added Ra'is Imam, to whom Geoffrey Dale attributed Maadi's horticultural growth throughout the late 1930s and 1940s, explaining that he was responsible for moving the trees cultivated in Maadi's nurseries out into the town's public spaces, successfully carrying on Biton's legacy.[17] This multinational and multiconfessional group managed the fulfillment of Delta Land's plans for Maadi throughout the 1930s and into the 1940s. They laid roads, designed villas and other buildings, and set the plans for cultivating the greenery along Maadi's streets, in its public gardens, and within its agricultural plots.

Kipnis's building designs subtly reflected the cultural changes at work during the complex transitions of the 1930s. In the middle of the decade, he designed villas for several prominent Egyptians who took up residence in Maadi. Where older villas like the Grove drew their design inspiration from the past, Kipnis's work emphasized modern clean lines and layered geometric shapes. Kipnis's own Maadi home had a rectangular, block-like structure. The northwest side of the house featured an open veranda leading out to the garden. The home's most striking features were the windows, which wrapped around the corners of the house.[18] The home's style emphasized a forward-looking aesthetic that maintained Maadi's town-and-country environs with modern flare.

Kipnis also designed a three-story villa for Hassan Mazlum Pasha. Mazlum Pasha served as Egypt's postmaster general in the 1920s and retired from his position in 1929.[19] Soon afterward, he joined Delta Land's board of directors, making him the first native-born Muslim Egyptian elected to the board.[20] (In 1927, Delta Land's board added Khalil Bulad, who was of Syrian origin and later became an Egyptian citizen.[21]) While working with Delta Land, Mazlum Pasha contributed to a number of other commercial ventures in Egypt, including the Egyptian and International Insurance Company, the Credit Agricole d'Egypte, and the Société Egyptienne de Constructions Modernes, also known as AL-CHAMS (Arabic for the sun).[22] If Mazlum Pasha did not move to Maadi when he joined Delta Land in 1931, he lived there by at least 1935, when Kipnis completed construction on the villa and initial landscaping. Like Kipnis's villa, the design of the pasha's new home was thoroughly modern. It sported art deco trimmings that joined the building's rectangular structure with circular embellishments. Each window was bordered by rounded molding, and the roof, which provided an attractive outdoor meeting space, was surrounded by a similarly round handrail.[23] Kipnis's photograph of Mazlum Pasha's villa captures the development of Maadi's environs in the mid-1930s, where new homes still stood high over their surrounding gardens. The sky figures large in the image, giving a sense of how far Maadi residents would have been able to see into the distance. It additionally captures the wealth, ease, and open space that Delta Land continued to associate with Maadi's garden city existence.[24] While neither Kipnis nor Mazlum Pasha necessarily perceived it at the time, this villa life would come under increased pressure because of the demographic trends already reshaping Cairo.

As part of their work, Clyma, Kipnis, and Biton collaborated on the construction of Maadi's various social spaces. Kipnis aided with the design and build of a new pool in Maadi, and Biton likely helped oversee the maintenance of the Maadi Sporting Club's various lawns and gardens.[25] The three were also involved in the development of Maadi's various houses of worship. During the 1930s, Maadi gained a church, synagogue, and mosque, in that order. While having a Jewish architect aid in designing a church might appear unusual, the cross-confessional linkages that became commonplace in Maadi's other construction projects did not cease when it came to religious spaces. Their collaboration perforated confessional boundaries to an extent, but the addition of these buildings also highlighted the religious differences within the community. Perhaps most significantly to Delta Land, the staff's ongoing collaboration ensured that the company's oversight remained central to all forms of the town's development. Each of Maadi's religious communities rented or leased land from Delta Land, and, they, like any other tenant, were responsible for adhering to the *Cahier des Charges.* For example, in Delta Land's rental agreement with Maadi's new church, the company reserved the right to inspect the building and retake the land if the building was destroyed.[26] These rules had a leveling effect that maintained Delta Land's authority over Maadi's growth, emphasizing its position above that of any one national or religious affiliation. So long as Delta Land could exist under the protection of the Capitulations and Cairo lacked a municipal authority of its own, the company could exert this kind of power.

While Maadi had long been home to a Coptic church, it gained a makeshift Anglican church during the First World War. The town's first church committee voted to bring a British "Church Army Hut" made of corrugated steel and wood from Ismailiya near the Suez Canal to Maadi in 1920. Delta

Land allowed the congregation to use a plot of land on Road 14 in the northeast corner of Maadi, near the desert, which earned the church the name "St. John's in the Wilderness." One history of the church, published as part of a fundraising initiative in the late 1940s, described St. John's as one of two necessary staples of Englishness in Maadi, explaining, "It is generally accepted that where two or three Anglo-Saxon families settle, it matters not in what isolated part of the world, that they at once strive for a Church and a Sporting Club." The year 1920, then, marked the birth of these two hallmarks of Englishness in Maadi, with the founding of the Maadi Sporting Club and the makeshift Anglican church both taking place.[27] Maadi's Anglicans made ready use of the "Church Army Hut" on the town's desert border for a decade. In those years, churchgoers donated funds for a harmonium, altar rails, and items necessary for communion services. Dale began making his own personal contribution in 1924 as St. John's organist. By 1929, however, Maadi's church committee decided to begin raising funds for a new, more permanent building.[28] The Anglican community also wanted to relocate the church to a more central place in Maadi. They, somewhat ironically, rented lot number 666 from Delta Land, which was located at the intersection of then-Avenue Colvin and Road 17—less than two kilometers from the Maadi rail station.[29] The congregation additionally simplified the church's name. Signifying its new location, they dropped the "wilderness" and called it the Church of St. John the Baptist.

The physical design of the church marked a final piece in the architectural lexicon of British imperialism throughout Africa. The initial drawings for St. John's exterior, altar, font steps, pulpit, doors, and electroliers were produced by Sir Herbert Baker, the architect to Cecil Rhodes. The church was Baker's last design in Africa and solidified the extension of his work from "Cape to Cairo." For their part, St. John's parishioners understood and promoted the church as the "Omega" of Baker's designs, with his church in South Africa serving as the "Alpha"—a reference to the beginning and end of the Greek alphabet and an appellation for Jesus Christ.[30]

While the choice of Baker as the building's designer seemed to confirm the church's imperial connections, a more complex network of workers from different confessional backgrounds actually constructed the building. Baker's drawings were not actual building plans and Kipnis had to convert them into a workable architectural scheme. Kipnis then worked with Clyma to oversee the construction of the church.[31] The church carried a number of possible meanings, as each stage of its construction gave the space significance to a different group of people.[32] Baker's initial drawings, particularly their symbolic importance as his last design in Africa, indicated lingering British imperial influence in Maadi. The execution of those designs, however, required Kipnis's translation. The movement from Baker's drawings to Kipnis's plans to the construction that Kipnis supervised with Clyma allowed the church to function as both a fixture in the built environment of empire in Africa and an instance of multiconfessional collaboration in Egypt. What is more, Kipnis's and Clyma's work subordinated the creation of the building to Delta Land's authority over land use and design, so that the church's construction, like that of so many other buildings in Maadi, relied on the company's sustained protection under the Capitulations.

After the establishment of St. John's, a similar chain of events unfolded with the construction of Maadi's synagogue. Delta Land's Jewish employees were more directly involved in the establishment of the synagogue, which opened in 1934. Biton donated the funds for the building's construction and Kipnis served as the architect. One of the entryways to the building was inscribed with the letters M.Y.B. after the building's benefactor. Geoffrey Dale recalled Biton joking that the initials were placed there "to show it was built by Mango and Banana."[33] One of the synagogue's founding documents exposed the more diverse support that led to the place's construction and opening, as it bore the signatures of a number of Christian residents and Delta Land employees. The signatures included those of Tom and Effie Dale, John and Sophia Clyma, and prominent Jews affiliated with Maadi like Felix Mosseri and a member of the Suarés family.[34] In his role as head of construction for the company, Ra'is Tantawi would have contributed to the building's construction, yet his signature is not included.

The sources on St. John's and the Biton Synagogue are largely silent about the contributions made by the country's Muslim Egyptian majority. Yet, Tantawi, in particular, would have been integral to Delta Land's construction projects. What is more, when Biton died soon after the synagogue opened and Delta Land replaced him with Ra'is Imam, Muslim Egyptians became more and more integral to the construction and landscaping of Maadi. The silence regarding Muslim Egyptians' work earlier in the decade is indicative of who exerted public authority in Maadi, particularly through the company, which remained largely identified with the majority of Britons and Egyptian Jews serving on the board. As mentioned earlier, by 1931 Delta Land's board included Khalil Bulad and Hassan Mazlum Pasha.[35] Their inclusion indicated the changes the company was undergoing, yet their influence apparently did not provide a more explicit context for Muslim Egyptian workers' recognition in the company records. Perhaps indicative of this lack of public recognition, it was another several years before Delta Land allotted space for a mosque. Yet, the ascension of Faruq in 1936 provided an important opportunity.

Soon after Faruq became king, Maadi's Muslim community began planning for a mosque named Masjid Faruq al-Awwal (Faruq I Mosque), after the new monarch. Tom Dale recalled working with the town's influential Muslim Egyptians, including Ahmad 'Abd al-Wahhab, Taher al-Lozy, and Fouad Kamal Bey to choose an appropriate site for the mosque.[36] The location was especially significant. The committee settled on a site on the Nile side of Road 9, which Delta Land was in the process of developing into residential space and which would become a gateway into Maadi. Upon its completion in February 1939, the mosque faced a large *midan*, which served as an entry point for all car and bus traffic flowing into Maadi. The location was a decisive contrast to the spaces given to Maadi's Anglican church and synagogue, both of which were tucked more deeply within the town. Unlike the church and synagogue, the mosque identified Maadi with the religion of Egypt's majority as well as with the new king. As Maadi's leaders looked to the future in 1939, King Faruq appeared to be the most stable authority for maintaining the town.

Maadi's Muslim residents used the mosque's opening as an opportunity to display the qualities of their town proudly to the king and other notables in attendance. The celebration marked Faruq's first visit to Maadi. As Dale recalled, the community received donations for the purchase of a large tent to be erected near the mosque's entrance. Inside, the subscribers placed oriental rugs and gold chairs.[37] The front page of *al-Ahram* included a picture of the king amid the pomp of the opening ceremony and described how Maadi's residents decorated the path that Faruq and his attendants followed from the town's entrance to the mosque. At the ceremony, the king greeted the building's architect Mahmud Riyyad and lead builder Ibrahim 'Askar—Muslim Egyptians whose work on the mosque broke from the earlier cross-confessional team involved in building the church and synagogue. The king also met members of Ittihad al-Maadi (the Maadi Union), a group of mostly Egyptian and *mutamassir* men who organized local support for Maadi's development and aided in the mosque's establishment.[38] Finally, Faruq shook hands with Delta Land's leadership, including Dale, Mazlum Pasha, and Hector de Cattaoui, offering his appreciation for the land that the company contributed for the mosque's construction.[39] The opening ceremony marked Maadi's most publicly visible event, with even more ceremonial display than the street lighting unveiling in 1933. In linking the town more explicitly to the Muslim community and giving Maadi's well-to-do Muslims a modern house of worship, the establishment of Masjid Faruq al-Awwal indicated Maadi's increased association with a particular version of Egypt's Muslim majority. The mosque's namesake clearly identified Maadi with the Ottoman-descended royal family, rather than an outwardly nationalist or significant Islamic figure. Like so many of Maadi's other physical, social, and cultural features constructed during the 1930s, it represented a conservative vision for Egypt's future that depended on the maintenance of existing forms of authority, especially the monarchy.

When Masjid Faruq al-Awwal opened in February 1939, Maadi's leaders were perhaps unaware of how delicate a balance the community continued to strike. The demographic trends that unfolded over the ensuing decade made a gradual and uneven impact. Maadi remained distinct from the capital at the time, and poorer Egyptian migrants found homes elsewhere. What soon became more concerning were the mounting racial and nationalist conflicts in Europe, which would come to blows by September with Germany's invasion of Poland. During and after the Second World War, attempts to sustain Maadi's earlier forms of elite cosmopolitanism would appear more and more out of place. If Egyptian Jews with Italian citizenship like Mosseri increasingly identified as *mutamassir*, or Egyptianized, could the larger way of life associated with resident foreigners in Cairo similarly become part of an independent Egypt? The reimposition of British military control during the war would stretch the *effendiya*'s European sensibilities to the breaking point, forcing a reconsideration of what it meant to be Egyptian.

Until the Second World War, Maadi fit into a conservative vision for what independence in Egypt might look like. Its leaders' careful incorporation of foreign influence into their nationalism meant that the town's planned streets, gardens, and villas might be part of a new modern Egypt. But, as the events of the fall of 1939 proved, Egypt remained more a part of the British empire than Egyptian nationalists might have supposed. As Britain again brought war to Egypt, and specifically Maadi, the understanding of what independence for Egypt really meant shifted. This time, Maadi's leaders would find it far more difficult to sustain the town's geographical distinctions and cosmopolitan society.

8

A WAR OF TWO VILLAS

On 2 April 1940, *al-Ahram* reported on Egypt's precarious position at the beginning of the Second World War. "Egypt is not at war, but prepares for war," the headline read. The newspaper went on to report that the Egyptian economy had thus far profited from the European conflict, with cotton prices on the rise and land values likewise increasing. As for whether or not Egypt would go to war, the paper reported that according to one political official, Egypt would not enter the war unless its borders were threatened, or its ally England was targeted. That last condition proved critical to Egypt's war experience, as alliance came to look more and more like the reimposition of imperial control.[1]

The *al-Ahram* story described how officials anticipated that the fire of war in Europe would "spark" a similar conflict in the Near East but had yet to do so.[2] Because of the particulars of its society, however, Maadi had already seen conflicts over European racial ideologies smoldering in Egypt. Beginning in 1933, a court battle over German antisemitism unfolded, indicating how the conflicts of the Second World War would fracture the town. That August, Umberto Jabes charged Wilhelm Van Meeteren, a Maadi resident and president of Cairo's German Club, with libel for publishing an inflammatory pamphlet based on Nazi antisemitism.[3] Van Meeteren was well connected to Egypt's elite, entertaining Dr. Hafiz 'Afifi Pasha, Ahmad Kamal Pasha, and Cairo's governor Shazli Pasha at his Maadi home.[4] Jabes's lawyer, Leon Castro, emphasized Egypt's identity as a cosmopolitan nation in his condemnation of the pamphlet, arguing, "If some Germans in this country were allowed to say, in effect, that Jews were bad people, it was a very serious thing because it might lead to some persecution of a minority, which in a country containing many minorities is very dangerous."[5] The pamphlet, titled "The Extension of Judaism in Germany," claimed that "Jews did not participate in productive work but preferred to make the work of others the object of their commerce."[6] In Van Meeteren's defense, his lawyer, German barrister Friedrich Grimm, claimed that the club published the pamphlet in response to growing anti-German demonstrations among Egypt's Jews following Adolf Hitler's appointment as German chancellor. Grimm additionally claimed that Cairo's German community "wished to be more moderate than their compatriots 'at home,' and wished to omit all matters of internal German policy."[7] Two days after the initial hearing, the Cairo Civil Chambers of the Mixed Tribunals tossed out the case and ordered Jabes to pay for the action.[8] The ruling served as an early indicator of the space Nazi antisemitism would find in Egypt, not only among the country's German community but also among some members of its ruling class.[9]

By 1938, this line of antisemitic reasoning specifically identified Maadi's founders on the floor of the Egyptian senate. An item addressed to the minister of the interior stated that "Jewish usurers" had acquired land on the outskirts of Cairo, Helwan, and Alexandria and, "by their well known ways and means," garnered the support of public officials to get the lands included in the borders of Egypt's cities. "In this way streets have been opened and water and electric light supplied with the result that the price of the land has been enhanced considerably." The statement drew from the Jewish stereotypes of laziness, dishonesty, and coordinated conspiracy—which were prominent in Van Meeteren's pamphlet—and beseeched the minister that such profits should be met with a tax "commensurate with the exorbitant profits gained without effort by these landlords."[10] Because of its multiconfessional and cosmopolitan society, Maadi was identified with both Jewish and Nazi experiences of the German Reich's antisemitism.

Questions about Van Meeteren's sentiments were resolved in April of the following year, when Joseph Goebbels, the Nazi minister of public enlightenment and propaganda, visited Cairo, meeting with Van Meeteren and his Maadi neighbor Baron Leonard von Richter, the president of the German Chamber of Commerce in Egypt.[11] What is more, by the fall of 1939, Maadi saw the return of British imperial troops, as New Zealand forces made their camp on the western outskirts of town.[12] When Italy invaded Egypt in June 1940, al-Ahram's prediction was fulfilled and Egypt was fully engulfed in the conflicts of the Second World War.

Where Maadi emerged from the First World War with its leadership intact and subsequently saw significant growth, this second global conflict would cause irreparable damage to the town's already strained society. Early events of the war quickly dashed the conservative *effendiya*'s hopes that King Faruq might maintain older forms of authority. His fragile position would have significant cultural and political ramifications. Cross-cultural friendship apart from the security of clearly defined political and economic systems like the Capitulations would prove less and less realistic. These changes were reflected in alterations to Maadi's built environment, as architects distanced themselves from art deco's global aesthetic and instead embraced a modern style that drew from more locally derived Islamic and Nubian influences. By the end of the war, Maadi's leaders attempted to resuscitate older methods for organizing the town, only to meet bureaucratic inefficiencies and unsatisfactory results.

Where the First World War swiftly redefined the meaning of "enemy" and "neighbor" among Egypt's population of resident foreigners, the Second World War clarified the meaning of "Egyptian," leaving far less space for foreigners' ability to act as locals. Because of its location on the perimeter of Cairo, and its associations with British and European influences, Maadi took on a somewhat precarious existence during the war. Its connections to the British empire, an influence previously on the decline, returned to prominence as Maadi saw the return of the telltale signs of its previous wartime geography. The former site of Australia's 2nd Light Horse Brigade had since been developed by Delta Land, so this time the 2nd New Zealand Expeditionary Force was located farther into the desert, near Wadi Digla, a dry valley cut into the rock and sand by flash flood waters finding their way to the Nile.[13] New Zealand sent an initial contingent of 110 troops to build a camp in the desert that would serve as the country's base of operations throughout the war. They rented the desert space from Delta Land as part of an agreement with the company to construct the camp's water and electric utilities. By the time that the First Echelon of the 2nd Expeditionary Force arrived in February 1940, the camp already had 150 huts built as mess rooms, cookhouses, washrooms, and storage facilities. Sleeping quarters, however, remained under construction, so the newly arrived troops spent their first nights at the Maadi camp in tents.[14]

Characteristic of military life, the daily camp activities emphasized structure and routine. The leadership carefully scheduled each day, beginning with the morning reveille at six o'clock, followed by a series of parades and inspections throughout the day, and concluding with the tattoo at half past ten o'clock at night.[15] Apart from routine drills, the New Zealanders made time for sport and for leave in Cairo and elsewhere in Egypt. For some enjoyment in the Maadi camp, they created an active rugby league. The commander of the 2nd New Zealand, British-born New Zealander Bernard Freyberg, ensured that the camp had access to a swimming pool. While the camp remained distinct from Maadi—its desert landscape standing in stark contrast to the town's greenery—one particular point of collaboration between the residents and the troops was the construction of a large new pool. Freyberg, once a competitive swimmer, wanted to locate the pool inside the camp, but, consistent with its emphasis on promoting Maadi as an active and sporting place, Delta Land successfully lobbied to have the pool built in the town so that Maadi residents could use it.[16]

By 1940, Maadi had a thirty-by-twelve-meter pool that Kipnis helped design and construct on Delta Land's behalf. On each side of the pool were large stands, making swimming competitions a spectator sport for community members. To that end, the pool had ample room for races and other fitness exercises, being two meters deep throughout and comprising six lanes.[17] Upon the pool's completion, Freyberg was the first to dive in, and, after an inaugural swim, he gave Kipnis a token of appreciation for his services in its construction.[18] The pool became a fixture in military life as well as an important contributor to the athleticism enjoyed in Maadi. One English soldier recalled it as a "marvelous affair," and as one of the few easily accessible places for a soldier to relax and enjoy himself without going all the way to Cairo.[19] Kipnis, for his part, proudly photographed Maadi's young people enjoying the pool he helped build, documenting it as a place where the garden city residents happily spent their time.[20] Before the war's end, the Maadi camp saw some seventy-six thousand New Zealanders move through its huts as they prepared for battle in northern Africa and southern Europe.

The 2nd New Zealand also saw action within Cairo in 1942, when they surrounded Abdin Palace. On 4 February, British Ambassador to Egypt Miles Lampson issued an ultimatum, demanding that the king peaceably abdicate or the New Zealand troops would forcibly depose him. In response, Faruq offered a compromise—he would remain king and call for a new government under the Wafd's Nahhas Pasha.[21] The event exposed the king's weakness and transformed the Egyptian political landscape. Not only did it debase the monarchy and its authority, it also discredited the Wafd. The political rumors that ensued somewhat distorted the actual events, and most people came to believe that Lampson had demanded abdication or the creation of a Wafd-led government under Nahhas. What the king did not know at the time was that Nahhas approached Lampson in June 1941, threatening, among other things, anti-British activity if the embassy did not aid in the Wafd's return to power. His actions reversed twenty years of anti-British activism by the party, which had promoted itself as the only true proponent of an independent Egyptian nation. For Lampson, while complete abdication was preferable, a weak monarch and a friendly Wafd-led government would still serve his interests in eliminating the threat of pro-Axis influences close to the king. Faruq's ensuing capitulation cowed his popular support, especially among the military.[22] Discrediting the Wafd, it fueled support for the Muslim Brotherhood and other anti-Wafdist popular movements.[23]

The Abdin Palace ultimatum marked the beginning of the Middle East's bloodiest year of the war. Before the end of February, the 2nd New Zealand was deployed in Lebanon and Syria. That summer, they saw further action in Egypt, when two battles unfolded in the western desert at al-Alamein. While the July battle ended in a stalemate, the fighting resumed in November and concluded with an Allied victory. By May 1943, the 2nd New Zealand returned to Maadi, where they remained for several months. They departed that fall to fight in Italy, where they remained until the war's end. As more New Zealanders joined the fight in Europe, their countrymen continued funneling through Maadi, and the camp remained active until 1946.[24]

The war brought a substantial challenge to the political allegiances of Maadi residents, many of whom had personal and professional lives that depended on the continuity of older forms of authority that preserved foreign privilege. As the European conflict drew the rest of the world into its violence, the war strained any hopes of maintaining an international community to the breaking point. In Egypt, an explicitly anti-British vision for the future took shape for many. Within Maadi, even with its connections to British cultural influence and the New Zealand military installation, the war created social and political divisions, sometimes within families. For some, Maadi became a site of wartime Anglophilia, but for others it was a space of subtle resistance.

Nadia Salem grew up in Maadi during the war. For her and those of her generation, Maadi's elite cosmopolitanism and town-and-country environs were a childhood fact of life. Her formative years were marked by a number of British influences at work in Egypt. Salem's father attended school in England and returned to Egypt with staunch pro-British convictions. In Maadi, he built a large villa for his family and some of his wife's relatives.[25] Salem and her siblings attended English and American schools. She was an early pupil at the Maadi English School, an elementary school for boys and girls between the ages of five and nine. The school used a villa on Road 82, across the street from Maadi's irrigation canal, and first opened its doors in the fall of 1932 as an extension of the English School–Cairo.[26] Its pupils largely reflected the diversity of Maadi's residents at the time, with a large number of English and Egyptian children, and a handful of students from elsewhere in Europe and the Middle East.[27] Salem's classmate Maggie Safwat recalled that the student body was composed of especially high numbers of European and Egyptian Christians, as well as large minorities of Egyptian Jews and Muslims.

Salem and Safwat were students at the English School and active in Maadi's branch of the Brownies, the Girl Guides' division for younger girls. During the war, they participated in a number of mandatory pro-British activities organized by the school and the Guides. Salem recalled rehearsing Christmas carols with her Brownie troop at friends' houses, in preparation for a performance before the troops. One December early in the war, they lit lanterns and walked to the Digla Camp. "It was lovely, because it was in the open air," Salem recalled with special fondness.[28] For both women, memories of the episode also carried a sense of entertaining irony because, as Muslims, the trip seemed wholly detached from their home lives. What is more, the activity's concrete display of religious and political sympathies appeared out of sync with Maadi's cross-confessional culture.[29]

As children during a time when foreign influence remained in place and the population of Egyptians in Maadi grew, the student body at the Maadi English School was aware of different cultural and religious practices, and largely took their coexistence for granted. Safwat recalled the

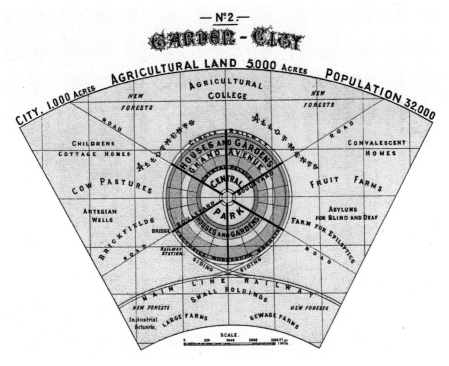

Diagram of Sir Ebenezer Howard's Garden City. Originally published by Ebenezer Howard in his *To-morrow: A Peaceful Path to Real Reform* (London: Swan Sonnenschein, 1898).

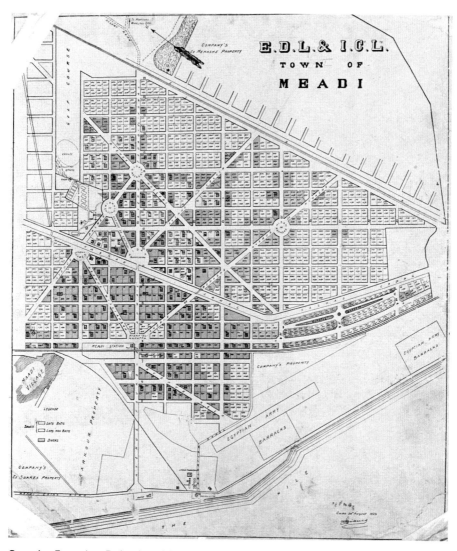

One the Egyptian Delta Land & Investment Company's first maps of Maadi. Courtesy of the Rare Books and Special Collections Library of the American University in Cairo.

A later, colorized image of the Grove after the garden had grown in. Courtesy of Alithea Lockie.

Three generations of the Dale family, with Tom standing next to his father Jesse, who holds his grandson Geoffrey. Courtesy of the Rare Books and Special Collections Library of the American University in Cairo.

The bowling lawn at the Maadi Sporting Club. Courtesy of the Rare Books and Special Collections Library of the American University in Cairo.

The clubhouse at the Maadi Sporting Club. Courtesy of the Rare Books and Special Collections Library of the American University in Cairo.

Children lined up at the Maadi Sporting Club pool, ready to race. Courtesy of the Rare Books and Special Collections Library of the American University in Cairo.

The villa that Kipnis designed for him and his family in Maadi. Courtesy of Nona Orbach.

The villa that Kipnis designed for Delta Land board member Mazlum Pasha. Courtesy of Nona Orbach.

A founding document for the Meyer Y. Biton Synagogue. Courtesy of Nona Orbach.

Young people at the Maadi pool built for the New Zealand troops stationed in the town. Courtesy of Nona Orbach.

Waters from the 1945 flood. Courtesy of the Rare Books and Special Collections Library of the American University in Cairo.

The damaged village at 'Izbit al-Basri. Courtesy of the Rare Books and Special Collections Library of the American University in Cairo.

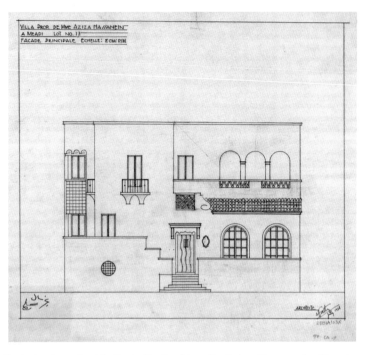

Hassan Fathy's plans for his first villa for his wife Aziza Hassanein. Courtesy of the Rare Books and Special Collections Library of the American University in Cairo.

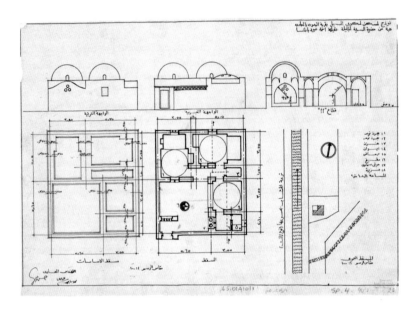

Fathy's designs for a 'Izbit al-Basri model home. Courtesy of the Rare Books and Special Collections Library of the American University in Cairo.

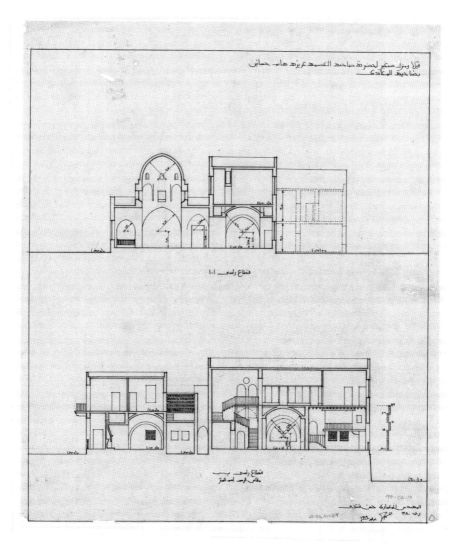

Fathy's second Maadi villa for Hassanein. Courtesy of the Rare Books and Special Collections Library of the American University in Cairo.

The new Victoria College-Cairo campus in Digla. Courtesy of the Rare Books and Special Collections Library of the American University in Cairo.

The Schuler villa. Courtesy of the Rare Books and Special Collections Library of the American University in Cairo.

The Wolff villa. Courtesy of the Rare Books and Special Collections Library of the American University in Cairo.

The dilapidated villa on Road 82. Photograph by the author.

sense of community among her and her classmates that was not subject to national or religious divisions, even while her family promoted the growth of Maadi's Muslim community. Her father Muhammad Safwat Bey was a member of Ittihad al-Maadi, the group that supported the construction of Masjid Faruq al-Awwal, and Maggie presented the king with flowers at the opening ceremonies.[30]

Similar to the way that Dale's recollections of Maadi placed Delta Land at the center of the town's affairs—removing Egypt's larger political negotiations from his narrative—these childhood memories focus on an internal social harmony that appears similarly distant from the more contested political issues that shaped Maadi's existence at the time. Their recollections point to Maadi as a place removed from the political turmoil of wartime Cairo. For them, Maadi remained a place of elite cosmopolitanism, where children of various faiths and ethnicities shared the same childhood experiences, attended the same schools, and felt themselves in close relationship with one another. In this context, certain events of the war stood out in their memories because they emphasized differences that previously remained in the background.

In Salem's home, the wartime caroling might have been at odds with her religious upbringing, but the more serious political tensions took shape among the household's adults. Salem recalled a particularly distinct disagreement between her father and maternal grandmother. While her father remained pro-British during the war, her grandmother supported the Germans. She spent her time knitting socks for the Germans in anticipation of their arrival in Cairo, so that she might greet them as liberators and supply them with fresh socks. While Salem recalled her grandmother's activities with amusement, the family's support for the Germans had significant implications. Two of Salem's maternal greatuncles overtly supported the Nazis, and following the Allied victory were forced into exile. Salem's family lost track of their whereabouts after the war, and she never saw them again. "They sent a card from Dusseldorf," she recalled.[31] The divided convictions within Salem's household indicated the kinds of political and social challenges that the war posed, as they clashed with the multinational harmony the town's young people previously took for granted.

Before the war ended, Maadi's natural environment brought the town's shifting culture and politics to the fore. On New Year's Eve 1944, a torrential downpour hit Egypt. The *Egyptian Gazette* reported that it was the "worst storm in 23 years." Outside of Cairo, Fayoum and the Suez were among the hardest hit, both taking on half a meter of water. Nearer the capital, the storm took the heaviest toll on Maadi.[32] During the night, an onslaught of rain poured down through Wadi Digla, overwhelming the dike and flooding the town as the water made its way to the Nile. Tom Dale received a call at five o'clock in the morning on New Year's Day with news that the dike had collapsed and the town was quickly flooding. The call came too late for Dale to be of much use. Upon opening his front door, he stepped into more than thirty centimeters of water, its muddy consistency soon flooding the first floor of his house. In the yard, he found the family's chickens neck-deep in the sludge-like water. Once the waters receded, the Dales had nearly thirty centimeters of soapy yellow clay in the garden that similarly cloaked the rest of Maadi.[33] The Dales were among the lucky ones.

The flood uprooted trees, took down telephone poles, and damaged homes, roads, and gardens throughout Maadi. The waters wreaked the worst damage outside the garden city development on 'Izbit al-Basri, the Arab village on the north side of town. Dale recalled, "The fragile, mud-built dwellings quickly collapsed with the destruction of most of their contents."[34] The *Egyptian Gazette* reported that more than two thousand men, women, and children were left homeless after the flood waters washed away their village homes.[35]

In the days following the tragedy, a joint public and private relief effort worked to meet the villagers' most pressing needs. As Dale recalled, "Maadi residents of all nationalities immediately got to work." They erected a large tent and installed drinking water and electricity for lighting. The police set up a mobile canteen, manned by some of the women of Maadi, who provided hot soup and other food for the villagers. The ladies' committee of the Red Crescent Society also brought in fabric to help make new clothing.[36] To aid in the recovery, the Ministry of Public Health donated tents and blankets. King Faruq donated LE 500 to the cause and the Muslim Charitable Society gave an additional LE 300. The most substantial donation came from Delta Land, which gave LE 2,000 to the stranded villagers.[37] While the community relief effort and charitable gifts helped meet the immediate needs to house, feed, and clothe the villagers, finding them permanent housing proved the largest challenge.

The Red Crescent Society formed a committee to plan a new village, and Dale was invited to join as Delta Land's representative. According to his recollections, the committee's initial meeting got off to a slow start of mixed Arabic and English dialogue, until Madame 'Abbud Pasha, the Scottish wife of wealthy industrialist Ahmad 'Abbud, asked if plans for any actual buildings were at hand.[38] The committee then asked two architects to submit proposals—one who proposed using mud brick and plaster to create a domed design, and another who proposed a stone construction. 'Abbud then offered each architect LE 100 to construct a prototype, which would allow the committee to make a more informed decision. On Delta Land's behalf, Dale offered a new space for the village's construction—one that would be further removed from the threat of future flooding.[39] What Dale did not explain, however, was that Hassan Fathy, one of Egypt's most prominent architects, proposed the domed, mud-brick design. The subsequent saga over the village's construction would make Maadi a fixture in one of Egypt's most significant architectural developments of the twentieth century. It would also indicate how Maadi's leadership fell out of step with Egyptian national culture during the war.

At the time of the flood, Maadi was already home to one of Fathy's designs. In 1938, he completed plans for a villa for his wife Aziza Hassanein. During this earlier part of his career, Fathy continued to draw largely from popular European styles that he learned as an engineering student at King Fuad I University (later Cairo University).[40] Fathy's first Maadi villa shows his early alterations of popular art deco styles as he incorporated elements of traditional Muslim Egyptian architecture. The design comprised a fairly modest block-like, two-story home, with servants' quarters on the roof and a swimming pool in the yard. For the interior, he created large, open spaces with high ceilings, allowing air to move easily through the house and keep it cool. The villa matched the design of other Maadi villas in size and dimension. As Kipnis did in his designs for Mazlum Pasha, Fathy included several rounded elements. The front of the house had five arched windows, and the east side included three porthole windows—indicative of the influence that airplane and ocean liner design had on domestic architecture at the time. Yet, Fathy also included features that identified the building with Cairo's Islamic quarters. He paired the porthole windows with the dark wood lattice work of the *mashrabiya*, which was traditionally used in Islamic architecture to ensure women's seclusion within the home.[41] The balcony on the second story, which was accompanied by a patio on the roof of the first story, was guarded by additional wooden latticework. In effect, Fathy's design participated in the global fashions of the time while also drawing in elements of Egypt's Islamic culture.

Like the development of Masjid Faruq al-Awwal, the construction of Aziza Hassanein's 1938 villa incorporated more Islamic design elements into Maadi's town-and-country aesthetic. The growing attention devoted to Muslim Egyptian design elements and institutions became all the more significant during the Second World War. By the mid-1940s, Fathy abandoned any reference to art deco style and drew strictly from locally derived influences, particularly the domed designs of Nubian villagers.

During a trip to the Upper Egyptian city of Aswan, he walked through a nearby Nubian village and observed how the peasants elegantly avoided using timber for the roofs of their homes—an expensive material that was subject to wartime shortages—by creating mud-brick domes. The structures were not only aesthetically pleasing, but also better for circulating air.[42] Inspired by the villagers, Fathy hired a Nubian mason and began incorporating the mud-brick materials and domed structures into all of his work, seeing no reason not to employ these materials and design motifs in the homes of wealthier clients.[43] Through the experience, Fathy formulated his concept of "architecture for the poor," which made him famous.[44]

Fathy remembered the events of the flood and the Red Crescent Society meeting somewhat differently from Dale. For Fathy, the Islamic influences featured in his architecture were also personal convictions, and, in this case, they affected his perspective on the villagers. To have experienced such a violent natural disaster, in Fathy's view, meant that they had done something to deserve God's punishment and the flood had been an act of divine justice. He later wrote, "This flood showed the hand of God quite plainly," describing the villagers as largely dishonest and deserving of the losses they experienced during the flood.[45] When it came to rebuilding the village, Fathy was invited to make a proposal by Madame Sirri Pasha, the president of the Red Crescent's ladies' committee and wife of the former prime minister Hussein Sirri Pasha.[46] After receiving the invitation, Fathy went to the village to survey its remains. He found that while the village had been built of mud brick, the construction was shoddy, and that similar materials—which he believed were the "sole hope of rural reconstruction"—could be used again in a more sustainable fashion. Fathy determined that if he used a thicker wall, and a stone foundation, "mud brick houses would survive even Noah's flood."[47]

The reestablishment of 'Izbit al-Basri offered Fathy his first opportunity to put his new architectural schemes to work before a large, influential audience. In advance of the Red Crescent meeting, Fathy prepared a detailed plan for the village. He estimated that by using mud bricks for the construction, the cost of building twenty houses would be only LE 3,000. Rather than receiving a positive reception from the committee upon submitting his plans, however, he encountered a series of tedious meetings. He recalled, "Meeting after meeting, resolution after resolution, objections, suggestions, evasions, bright ideas and serious doubts, until we could have built ten villages with our own hands in the time we wasted."[48] Fortuitously, Madame 'Abbud broke the pattern of indecision by asking him how much money he needed to build a prototype for one house. After he asked for LE 150, she wrote him a check. While most of the events Fathy recalled followed Dale's memory of the same slow decision-making process and 'Abbud's problem-solving gesture, Fathy made no mention of a competition between himself and another architect.

Fathy set about building the house, which included vaulted ceilings, two large rooms, sleeping alcoves, built-in cupboards, a large loggia, and courtyard, at a cost of LE 164. Upon completion, he anticipated that the committee would promptly grant him the commission and he could commence building the other nineteen houses. Madame Sirri Pasha regretfully informed him, however, that the committee had hired a different architect to complete the project—a man who proposed a village design that mimicked European cottages. His dome prototype was subsequently destroyed because it did not fit with the European aesthetic of the new village. Fathy remarked that the committee's architect actually built something more akin to wartime air raid shelters—concrete structures composed of two square rooms, no kitchen, and no sleeping recesses or cupboards. According to Fathy, the project cost LE 22,000.[49]

Even though Fathy's little house found no place in Maadi, the prototype helped launch the most influential period of his career. He quickly garnered the attention of a private company in the Suez that commissioned him and his masons to build housing for their workers. Most significantly, the Department of Antiquities took note of Fathy's design and asked him to help relocate the village of Gourna in Upper Egypt. The Gourna project allowed Fathy to articulate his vision for an accessible and aesthetically pleasing "architecture for the poor." Fathy hoped that the construction of New Gourna would spark a new movement in rural redevelopment that would change the Egyptian countryside. By showing the affordability of good housing, he envisioned peasants throughout Egypt constructing new domed residences for themselves. Later, he went on to propose a national program for rural reconstruction as a state-sponsored renewal project. Fathy's vision never came to fruition. The Gourna project was not completed—a failure Fathy attributed to "peasant obscurantism and bureaucratic hostility."[50] While the built environment that he hoped would transform Egypt never fully took shape, his philosophy for the establishment of locally sourced and sustainably constructed housing for Egypt's peasantry gained him worldwide renown.[51]

Similar to Howard's vision for the garden city as a cross-class community in a carefully planned satellite town, Fathy's plan was not carried out to perfection, but the idea held on. Maadi never fulfilled the social ideals of Howard's garden city, and it presented an awkward launching pad for Fathy's vision. In both instances, the town's leaders saw value in the design, but did not identify with the egalitarian ideology behind it. That Fathy was bested by a plan intended to mimic European cottages but in reality relied on concrete blocks, or the "stone" Dale described, is perhaps the most potent indicator of Maadi's precarious position by the end of the war. Fathy may have fallen short of reconstructing rural Egypt, but his vision for an Egyptian design that used Egyptian materials was increasingly identified with the future of the country. In contrast, Maadi's leaders attempted to blend European designs into the Egyptian landscape, and, in turn, found themselves out of step with the Egyptian nation taking shape during the war. That the actual village was in fact a completely utilitarian design, with few aesthetic qualities, was even more indicative of gradual slippage in Delta Land's control over the town's built environment. According to Dale, most of the villagers at 'Izbit al-Basri left Maadi. He left no description of the new village, but explained that financial mismanagement of the LE 15,000 the company raised to assist the peasants led most of them to move on. For those who remained, the company ensured that the village had proper drainage, drinking water, and electricity.[52] Acts of charity were not exactly Delta Land's strong suit. The company's priorities remained focused on the wealthier residents who lived within its garden city establishment. Ultimately, the company's emphasis on

Maadi's more privileged populace proved incompatible with the popular vision for Egypt's future that gained ascendancy after the war.

In 1949, Fathy built his third and final house in Maadi, another villa for Aziza Hassanein—this time a larger home that stood along the eastern bank of the Nile. The architectural design presented the same Nubian-styled motifs of his architecture for the poor.[53] Some eleven years after building Hassanein's first villa in Maadi, Fathy left no trace of the art deco features or other globally popularized trends that he previously used. Even the language of the new drawings stood in contrast to the 1938 house, using almost solely Arabic and discarding the French that had previously been the lingua franca of Egypt's business class. The new house included the arched doorways and corridors of Fathy's village homes. The house's exterior windows were covered in intricately designed *mashrabiya*—now a fully integrated part of the design. The new villa's most distinctive feature was a large, domed roof on the vestibule placed on the house's northwest corner. Fathy composed the house as a series of modern, interlocking blocks similar to Kipnis's villa, making the arches and especially the domed structure stand out in complementary contrast.[54]

The dome and *mashrabiya* employed in Fathy's 1949 design set the house apart from Maadi's other villas. Delta Land's architects had established a certain uniformity among most of the town's earlier homes, which were generally a combination of wood and stucco construction, rectangular in shape, and often shrouded by nearby trees. This new space, however, captured a different sense of place. Fathy wanted to create a home that he deemed appropriately set among its Egyptian environs. Where he believed the European cottage design proposed for the new 'Izbit al-Basri would sit awkwardly among the camels and palm trees of greater Cairo, he wanted his designs to blend in with the history and geography of their surroundings.[55] For them to look appropriate in their Egyptian setting, Fathy emphasized the use of Egyptian and Islamic influences. These elements represented the country's history and majority religion but had been largely absent from Maadi for the first thirty years of its existence.

The contrast between Fathy's 1949 villa and the 1938 house spoke of the cultural and political changes going on in Cairo and throughout Egypt during and after the Second World War. The war brought a reimposition of

British imperial power that broke earlier hopes of forging Anglo-Egyptian friendship. What is more, the population of the Egyptian capital swelled with an influx of peasants moving into Cairo. Even the establishment of Fathy's new villa proved vulnerable to the rapid changes permeating the city. Only three years after its completion, the Egyptian government demolished the house because it stood in the path of the new corniche road it built along the Nile. Where the house might have participated in a different kind of town-and-country aesthetic, one more locally derived but still indicative of the community's wealth and leisure, the structure could not withstand the changing dynamics of the city as a whole when Cairo's government looked to expand the capital. The war brought cultural, social, and political change on a scale not yet experienced, and even Maadi's most national elements could not survive untouched.

Egypt's multinational influences were not instantly erased after the Second World War, yet the older paths of cross-cultural, multiethnic accommodation and collaboration that Maadi depended upon were no longer stable. This was already clear in the conflicts over antisemitism in the 1930s, and only grew more apparent. The town became a place layered with rival meanings. It was still an orderly and aesthetically pleasing garden city to some. To others, however, it represented a holdout of socioeconomic inequalities, propped up by outdated forms of foreign privilege. New national ideologies of ethnic and racial purity only exacerbated these tensions.

While political uncertainty was nothing new to Maadi, Egypt's leaders looked to reorient their country's place in the world in the late 1940s and early 1950s. Faruq had lost his position of authority and entered the postwar years discredited and vulnerable. While his rule survived Lampson's ultimatum, no hope remained that he would somehow preserve the foreign political and economic ties that had provided much of the basis for Maadi's prewar existence. Without older systems of support, Maadi increasingly relied on its association with elite Egyptian society as a sign of its distinction and stability. Relying on Maadi's aesthetic and cultural qualities—the villas, gardens, quiet streets, and emphasis on athleticism and recreation—would prove far more tenuous than systems like the Capitulations, Mixed Courts, and monarchy, which previously supported the community.

PART FOUR: OVERHAUL

Since its founding, Maadi has been in an ongoing process of being made and remade. Yet the years following the Second World War were different. The abolition of the Capitulations in 1949 and the military coup in 1952 terminated the terms on which the town had previously prospered. What is more, the establishment of Israel in 1948 transformed political identities throughout the region. Maadi did not cease to exist, but its residents had to shift dramatically how they understood and related to the town. From 1945 until the dissolution of Delta Land in 1962, Maadi was redefined. Foreigners departed Egypt *en masse*, and Maadi's gardens, villas, and schools found new purposes amid regime change. Ultimately, Maadi lost its autonomy as an independent business venture, and instead became unevenly absorbed into a rapidly expanding capital city and vision for an Arab socialist republic.

9

BROKEN GROUND

In the months following the Allied victory in Europe, Gabriel Josipovici and his mother Sacha Rabinovitch made their way back to Cairo from war-torn France. Rabinovitch was descended from the same prominent Egyptian Jewish families who helped found Maadi, and she spent her childhood south of Delta Land's garden city in Helwan, where she was born in 1910.[1] While a desire to get out of Egypt drove many of the events of her adult life, the instability of Europe after the war and the harshness of its antisemitism made Cairo a haven. The mother and son moved to Maadi, where Sacha's sister Vera and her family had recently relocated. Their migration to Maadi as refugees reversed older modes for coming to the town—indicating the less privileged ways that more residents would take to Maadi during the second half of the twentieth century.

At first glance, the Second World War did not appear to significantly affect Maadi. Delta Land remained in charge of the town, and Tom Dale continued in his constabulary role as general manager. Its streets were lined with trees. The villas and their accompanying gardens—even amid changing architectural styles—leant a similar aesthetic and cohesive domestic shape to the town. For people like Rabinovitch and Josipovici, Maadi offered a refuge.

If Maadi appeared to offer stability and safety for families leaving Europe in the aftermath of the Second World War, it would not remain a long-term home for most of them. Three years after the armistice, Egypt's humiliating defeat in the Arab–Israeli War would fuel a military coup in 1952, heightening ethnic and religious tensions in the country. What is more, Egypt would become less hospitable to foreign business ventures—a development that began taking shape well before the war. Anticipating the end of the Capitulations, the Egyptian government passed a new Company Law in 1947, which instituted protective economic measures and reduced the number of foreigners a business could employ. This not only limited the population of Europeans in Egypt, but also the number of Jews, because so many—particularly those in business—continued to hold foreign nationality.[2] What is more, in October 1949, the terms of the Montreux Treaty were fulfilled and the Capitulations and Mixed Courts were abolished, ending more than four centuries of tax and legal privileges granted to foreign subjects in Egypt.[3] That same year, the government formed a municipality in Cairo, which began to shape its own initiatives for the city and eliminated Delta Land's earlier autonomy.[4]

This chapter and the following one work to unpack the near-simultaneity of the regional conflicts and policy changes that all unfolded at the close of the 1940s. Together, these events affected who could live and work in Maadi, and on what terms. This chapter addresses the impact of the Arab–Israeli War, and Chapter Ten examines the significance of domestic and international policy changes. Ultimately, the compounding effects of these events irreversibly altered the composition of the town's society, closing off older possibilities for multinational collaboration and marking the beginning of the end of Maadi's garden city existence.

For Maadi residents, the events of the Arab–Israeli War would come to represent the displacement and destruction that unfolded after 1948. Yet this transformative event occurred while the culture and society of the older garden city persisted. Those who recalled the impact of the Nakba also fondly remembered enjoying their time at the club and riding their bikes along tree-lined streets during the same years. Memories of the postwar years, especially from those who were children at the time, capture the tense continuity that unfolded at this time. The trappings of garden city life remained, but they hung in a delicate balance. Only gradually did Josipovici and other Maadi residents—not only Jews, but also resident foreigners, and Egyptian landowners—feel themselves unwelcome in Egypt and see the older modes of their shared, cosmopolitan society in Maadi disintegrate.[5] If the events of the mid-twentieth century established firm boundaries between foreigner and national, those borders were based on precedents set in the 1920s and 1930s. The establishment of Israel, however, would stand in for the ruptures of the period.

The experience of the immediate postwar years in Maadi exposed how major political events began transforming Egyptian society, even while certain cultural activities, especially athletic leisure, remained firmly in place. Ultimately, local economic interests broke from any association with resident foreigners, and changes in Egypt's economic and foreign policy reflected changes in national culture. While a previous generation of Egyptian nationalists envisioned an independence that maintained friendly relations with foreign cultural and economic interests, the Second World War and events of the late 1940s made that vision unsustainable. Maadi's history exposes how that political fracture came from more than the 1948 war while also revealing how the memories of major political events can overshadow deeper historical complexities.

"Is it possible to separate one's earliest memories from the stories one is later told about one's own childhood?" Josipovici asks in a biographical essay from 1988.[6] In it, he relates the events of his formative years in Maadi from October 1945 until September 1956. His recollections capture some of the complexities of Maadi's social, cultural, and political world during years of intense change. His reflection on how memories are shaped by the retelling of stories also identifies some of the challenges of relating a history that is touched by a mixture of often competing recollections. The memories of Maadi's postwar years included here—mostly gathered through personal interviews or written down in memoirs—not only address the town's past, but also explore how historical events are continually reinterpreted because of subsequent experiences. Josipovici shared his Maadi childhood with contemporaries whose lives charted very different trajectories into the remainder of the twentieth century. These divergent paths meant that Maadi came to carry different meanings for its various residents.

When Josipovici arrived in Maadi with his mother, the two set up house in a small apartment on Road 9, near the end of the commercial zone, just before the road turned back into desert. Every quarter-hour he could rely on the mechanical sound of the train as it bore passengers to and from Cairo. For Josipovici and his mother, the sound grew familiar, even comforting, but he recalls that guests found it continually surprising.[7] As the son of a single working mother, Josipovici's experience treaded some of the limits of Maadi's privileged and stable existence. His mother and father were both Egyptian Jews, and, on his mother's side, he descended from the country's more prominent Jewish families—his grandmother was a Cattaoui, related to the Rossi and Mosseri families.[8] Yet, "Egyptian Jew" was an incomplete label for describing Josipovici's identity, particularly considering his experiences during the war.

Sacha Rabinovitch was the daughter of a Jewish doctor from Odessa, who came to Egypt during a world tour. He later converted to Islam and passed away when his two daughters were young children. After being widowed, Sacha's mother became an Anglican, and had Sacha and her older sister Vera baptized.[9] Years later, in order to marry Jean Josipovici in a Jewish ceremony, Sacha underwent a ritual immersion at a Cairo synagogue, where Gabriel was told she was dipped into a "filthy pool, while someone chanted outside the window."[10] While Sacha returned to Judaism, Vera, affectionately known as "Chickie," later married Albert Bajocchi, an Italian Catholic, and converted. The family's multiconfessional trajectories participated in the social complexities of early twentieth-century Cairene life, as different religious identities took shape through personal negotiations with Egypt's interconnected confessional world. In the years following the Second World War, the Rabinovitch family's various religious affiliations gained more political significance and shaped each member's postwar experiences. Sacha and Chickie remained close, yet Egypt's changing political climate made it difficult for both of them to remain in Maadi.

For Sacha, moving to Europe during the 1930s made her Jewishness particularly personal and significant. She and Jean left for France in 1935, a year into their marriage, and both attended Aix-Marseilles University. Soon afterward, the turbulence that would characterize their life together set in. Sacha spent her time caring for the family's domestic needs, typing Jean's stories and thesis draft, and studying for her own master's degree. Jean, on the other hand, took to philandering, often with the couple's friends. They had Gabriel in October 1940, on the same day that they had booked tickets for Egypt, hoping to wait out the war abroad. His birth meant remaining in France. In the same years that France fell to the Axis powers, the couple's marriage crumbled. When Sacha was pregnant with the couple's second child, Jean departed for Paris with one of Sacha's closest friends. Now on their own, Sacha and Gabriel lived out much of the war in southeastern France under Italian occupation, finding a kind of haven in Nice. They avoided being rounded up by German forces through the protection of the French Resistance, which provided them with forged documents and train tickets to La Bourboule. On the train to La Bourboule, Gabriel's mother gave him one of his most significant introductions to his Jewishness. She made her young son ride separately from her, later explaining:

> I knew that if we were stopped and I was asked to account for myself I would most probably, despite my papers, say that I was Jewish. I felt that even though it would mean leaving you with strangers it was something I would have to do. There aren't many moments like that in life but I felt that this was one of them.[11]

Fortunately, she never faced the dilemma. In the eighteen hours that they rode from Nice to La Bourboule, German troops never boarded the train.[12] Once in La Bourboule, Gabriel's sister Elizabeth was born, providing the family with a brief reunion. Jean and Sacha's infant daughter died, however, only ten days later. After the loss, the couple split permanently, and Gabriel and Sacha remained in La Bourboule for the remainder of the war. Afterward, Chickie sent them tickets to Egypt, and they traveled on the English troopship Arundel Castle to Port Said.[13]

The pair moved to Maadi because Chickie lived there with her daughters Monica and Anna. During the war, the Bajocchis faced their own challenges. Because Albert was an Italian citizen, he was put in an internment camp early in the war. The family moved to Maadi from Zamalek to be closer to him during his imprisonment, and he joined them there after his release, roughly a year into the war. Chickie and Albert's daughter Anna (later Joannides) recalled that her father served a shorter stint than many of the other Italian prisoners, likely because of his connections to Cairo's British community.[14] Once in Maadi, Joannides was well aware of the military establishment in the town. She attended the Maadi English School, where she was childhood friends with Nadia Salem and Maggie Safwat. Joannides's first memories of Maadi fixated on the contrast between the beauty of the town's gardens and villas and the sparse military encampment. "There were quite a lot of military camps still," she recalled.[15] The contrast she recognized in those early memories resonated with a foreboding sense that the garden city establishment was not as stable or self-sufficient as some might have supposed.

While most Maadi residents recollected life in a villa comprising many rooms and accompanied by a large garden, Gabriel and Sacha's apartment

on Road 9 reflected a more spartan existence. While apartments never fig-
ured prominently in Delta Land's design for Maadi, the company began
constructing multiunit buildings in the 1910s.[16] Sacha and Gabriel's life
in the modest apartment did not rely on the labor of household servants,
gardeners, cooks, and nannies, who were ubiquitous in Maadi's wealthier
households. To support their new life and pay for Gabriel's enrollment
in one of Maadi's foreign schools, Sacha had to find work. More than an
idiosyncratic experience of postwar life, however, their cramped apartment became more typical as Maadi was increasingly incorporated into the
sprawl of greater Cairo.

Rather than establishing a seemingly permanent family home in
Maadi, as a wealthier nuclear family might, this single mother and her child
repeatedly moved. After the apartment on Road 9, they took up residence
in a basement apartment nearer the Nile on Road 6. Then they moved to
another apartment on Road 18. Finally, Sacha purchased one of the bunga-
lows that Delta Land built across the street from the Maadi Sporting Club.
The house had a wooden veranda along three sides and had the added
atmosphere of neighboring the verdant irrigation canal. Josipovici recalled
it as their little family's most cherished home in the garden city.[17]

Sacha had a number of different jobs in Maadi. Initially, she helped
deliver milk early in the morning, rising at five o'clock to make her rounds
and returning home in time to get Gabriel ready for school. Then she
would leave again for mid-morning rounds.[18] Because Gabriel arrived in
Maadi speaking only French, she initially enrolled him at the Lycée Fran-
çais. She soon withdrew him, however, because the school gave him so
much homework. "She was horrified that they were giving this little boy
who had been through the war homework," he recalled. She enrolled him
instead in the Maadi English School, which his cousins attended.[19] Later
she worked at the English-styled boys' school Victoria College to pay for
Gabriel's tuition. While Gabriel still recalled many of the hallmark features
of Maadi life—time spent at the club and cycling along its streets with
friends—he and Sacha did not experience the kind of leisurely, commodi-
fied Maadi life that appealed to early generations of resident foreigners
and the Egyptian *effendiya*. For them, the physical structures of the town's
garden city environment remained in place, but they confronted the severe
realities of the postwar world more directly, as social inequalities surfaced
and could not fit seamlessly into town-and-country life.

Josipovici did not have to sing Christmas carols to the British Common-wealth troops during the war, nor did he recall the Maadi English School presenting a significant academic challenge—sparing him the rigors of homework assigned at the lycée. Instead, he remembered the athleticism associated with Maadi, and all of the physical activities that comprised his daily life. "I got quite involved in a lot of sport, particularly in swimming and tennis and football [soccer]," he recalled. He played soccer at school and took up swimming and tennis at the Maadi Sporting Club. As men-tioned in Chapter Five, for Josipovici, like so many other Maadi children, the club was the center of his social world throughout his time in Egypt.

The club also had its boundaries and prejudices, which appeared to him as residue of earlier times. For instance, divorced women often faced trouble gaining membership. While Josipovici did not recall his mother dealing with any specific challenge, his cousin Anna remembered Chickie having an issue with the club when they first arrived in Maadi. With Albert still in the internment camp, Chickie confronted presumptuous discrimi-nation from the club's leadership because they believed she was divorced. While she cleared up the misunderstanding and the club became an impor-tant social space for her daughters, Anna continued to associate its environs with outdated patterns of exclusion.[20] Josipovici had similar memories of the remnants of racial and ethnic prejudices directed toward Egyptians. On one of his first visits to the club with his mother, he recalled overhear-ing a group of women making disparaging remarks as they watched an Egyptian man walk through the entrance. His mother turned to him and said, "These are old people," implying that the women's racism, though still present, was outdated and no longer prevailed over the place. Overall, Josipovici remembered the club as a place where middle-class Egyptian and European families in Maadi all congregated. "This was where you either played some sport, or you sat around drinking Coca-Cola, whistling at the girls, or you did both," he happily recollected of the boyhood he spent at the club. "I tried to do both," he said, with a laugh.[21]

While Josipovici and Joannides—who both later left Egypt—recalled specific instances of the club's social barriers, Egyptian residents who remained in Maadi throughout much of the rest of the twentieth century did not recall experiencing prejudiced or discriminatory treatment in my interviews. Neither Maggie Safwat nor Nadia Salem said they ever felt they were treated as lesser members of the community because they were Egyptian or Muslim. As it was for Josipovici and Joannides, the club existed as the center of Salem's and Safwat's lives. Salem played squash and swam at the club. Safwat, who was an accomplished swimmer, recalled fondly, "I was born practically in the pool." They remembered with particular affection the club's swimming coach "'Amm Ibrahim," who taught three generations of Maadi's young people to swim. "He was a character," recalled Ingy Safwat, who moved to Maadi in 1952.[22]

Instead of ethnic or religious division, these memories of Maadi's sporting culture identify the boundaries of social class that the club continued to reinforce after the war. In addition to swimming, tennis, and golf, Delta Land made water sports available on the Nile by adding a yacht club in 1946, which was incorporated into the Maadi Sporting Club in 1966.[23] Maggie Zaki (née Nimatallah) received several tennis trophies during her youth at the club and recalled that the yacht club made Maadi distinct in Cairo because it created space for sailing and water skiing. All of these sports carried an air of wealth and prestige at the time, especially because of the expensive equipment required. Zaki explained that tennis was among the most expensive and thus most prestigious sports at the club because families had to import the rackets, balls, and clothing.[24] The club's centrality to childhood memories from the 1940s and 1950s exposes how embedded active sporting culture became in Maadi, giving it an air of national health and wellness, but also engraining a marked elite social status that would prove problematic in the future.

Zaki's recollections, in particular, indicate the classed prestige associated with Maadi's athleticism. The club offered sports less accessible to the majority of Egyptians. While children could play soccer anywhere, tennis, swimming, golf, and water sports were distinctive, requiring special equipment and facilities. It is no surprise that Josipovici learned to play soccer at school but associated the rest of his sporting activities with the club. While many of Maadi's Egyptian residents did not remember personally experiencing racism at the club, they participated in the creation of enduring socioeconomic differences that prevented the majority of Egyptians from joining in club life. This social hierarchy weathered the political storms of the late 1940s, allowing the memories of sunny days at the club to coexist with the recollections of political fractures and the community's loss of stability.

The activities at the club indicated Maadi's separation from the rest of Cairo. Josipovici described his formative years in the garden city as part of his ongoing residence in rural or country places. He explained that he felt continually "un-streetwise" in large urban centers, in part because the dense metropolis stood in stark contrast to the tree-lined streets where he roamed freely on his bicycle. His Maadi compatriots had similar memories. For both Maggie Safwat and Ingy Safwat, trips to Cairo were special. They would go to the dressmaker, the cinema, or to Groppi's, a popular downtown cafe.[25] In contrast, Maadi offered familiarity and a sense of security, which made the place deeply valuable to its long-term residents. Maggie recalled that as a child in Maadi, she felt she knew almost everyone—from the gardeners to the displaced Turkish royalty who took up residence in the town. For Maggie and Ingy, this sense of childhood familiarity and social connectivity helped maintain a personal attachment to the town throughout adulthood. "When you grow up in a place, you feel that you belong to this place," Maggie related. "*Ya'ni*, it's your bigger home."[26] She recalled her former home with a deep sense of nostalgia, as though the older, familiar form of Maadi was a specter of the past, inaccessible in the present. Yet her recollections of Maadi's smaller, more familiar size during the mid-twentieth century relied on older forms of authority that were quickly dwindling, including Delta Land's ongoing control over the town and the privileged position of resident foreigners.

The emphasis these memories place on Maadi's physical and social distinctions—its small size, affluent sporting culture, and close neighborly relations—recall the town on pleasant, often idealized terms. Those pillars of Maadi's earlier existence were weakened by the Second World War and came under even more significant threat because of the events of 1948 and 1949. Residents recalled events like the Arab–Israeli War as having an especially deleterious effect on their former way of life, even as they still frequented the club, rode their bicycles, and attended international schools. The Arab–Israeli War and the end of the Capitulations would transform Egypt's place in the world, and, in turn, gradually dissolve older means for maintaining Maadi, chipping away at the stability that the town's children took for granted.

On 14 May 1948, Israel issued its Declaration of Independence and abolished the British Mandate in Palestine. While conflict had been occurring in Palestine since the United Nations Partition Resolution in November

1947, the abolition of the mandate sparked a war between Arabs and Israelis that would become known as Israel's War of Independence and al-Nakba, or the catastrophe, to its Arab neighbors. As a prominent member of the Arab League, Egypt's military played a critical role in the war, especially in the Gaza Strip, which it occupied after the armistice was declared on 24 February 1949.[27] The armistice marked the return of four thousand Egyptian troops, which included Gamal Abd al-Nasser, who had been surrounded by Israeli Defense Forces in the southern town of Faluja (now Kiryat Gat) since October.[28] The Nakba would be remembered as a singular turning point in shaping regional politics and identities. Yet, its impact on Egypt cannot be easily separated from the fulfillment of the Montreux Treaty in October 1949. Ultimately, the abolition of the Capitulations and Mixed Courts had a more immediate effect on Egyptian society, leading to the emigration of large numbers of Egypt's resident foreigners. Maadi's history captures how the near simultaneity of these two events caused a series of complex social disruptions that together dissolved older forms of cross-confessional and multinational harmony.

The political strife surrounding the partition of Palestine and the establishment of Israel compounded the rapid social and economic changes already at work after the Second World War. Before 1948, Egypt had a nuanced relationship to Palestine and the question of a Jewish state in part because of the country's large Jewish minority. As political Zionism grew, however, popular support for Arab opposition likewise increased in Egypt. However, Arab nationalism did not translate into a straightforward political ideology, particularly in the years when British power remained prominent in the country and King Faruq, an ethnic Albanian, sat on the throne. Into the late 1930s, this fragile balance of power meant that the Egyptian government took a more conciliatory stance toward the British and the Zionists than other Arab-majority countries, believing that such a position would aid the Egyptians in their negotiations with the British. Only after the Egyptian majority overwhelmingly associated Arabism and opposition to Zionism as integral to their national identity did the government change its stance on Palestine.[29]

Egypt's Jews also lacked a clear stance on Zionism. In the early 1930s, Yusuf Cattaoui took particular care to explain to the British Residency that he had no connection to Zionists, going so far as to note that he intentionally avoided visiting Palestine so that he was not mistakenly connected to the movement.[30] Baron Felix de Menasce, brother of Maadi founder Jacques de Menasce, corroborated Cattaoui's claim, confirming that he had no affiliation with Zionism or Palestine.[31] At the same time, members of the Mosseri family had been connected to Zionist organizations in Egypt since the end of the First World War.[32] Likewise, Delta Land's architect and engineer Isaac Kipnis quickly left Egypt for Israel after the armistice. Israeli independence meant a homecoming for him, and he returned to Tel Aviv to start a new life.[33] The majority of Egyptian Jews were ambivalent about Zionism, however. While many departed Egypt soon after the war, a large number remained in Egypt throughout the 1950s and 1960s, with some staying on even later.[34]

For Josipovici, Egypt's losses after 1949 set in motion events that continued a pattern of displacement and movement that he came to see as particularly Jewish. He identified his experiences in Maadi with those of a foreigner in Egypt, even though both of his parents were born in the country and his mother descended from a long line of the country's prominent Jewish families. In the memoir he wrote of his mother's life, he summarily described the narrative as a "very Jewish story."[35] In Egypt, he explained that even while Jewish families were part of the social fabric of the country, "no matter how assimilated or how Anglicised, there was the further sense that though this was the only country they could call their own they did not exactly belong to it."[36] This view broke with earlier notions of Egyptian Jewish identity—especially that of people like Elie N. Mosseri, who identified Egyptianization as a path of progress. Mosseri passed away in 1940, however, and by the end of the decade much of his understanding of Egyptian Jewish identity likewise became a thing of the past.[37]

Amid the varied sympathies of Egypt's Jews, elements of European antisemitism had already found a home in Egypt in the 1930s, and the popular political climate in Egypt turned sharply anti-Jewish after Egypt's military defeat by Israel in 1949. This resulted in attacks on Cairo's Jewish neighborhoods. The older Jewish *hara* was especially hard hit, with bombs killing twenty-two and wounding forty-one.[38] Because of Maadi's large Jewish population and the prominent Jews on the company's board, Delta Land's offices on Road 7 were also bombed. That bomb injured three people—an impact that paled in comparison to the disorder and violence that erupted elsewhere in Cairo.[39] Yet, the bombing was the first physically violent manifestation of Egypt's political instability within the bounds of the garden city and served as a direct attack on the town's older society and the company's multinational leadership.

The events of the war also saw popular backlash against Maadi's British community. As Geoffrey Dale recalled, "There was a time in the 1950s when certain people asked the British not to use the Club. This arose over events commonly known as the Israeli War. The Committee who were then mostly British was taken over by Egyptians."[40] It is possible that the presumed racism Josipovici recalled at the Maadi Sporting Club was actually a response to the club's new leadership. This turn of events, though less dire than the bombing on Road 7, heightened the significance of ethnic and national differences in local ways that differed from the exclusionary imperial policies put in place by the British.

Many of Maadi's Muslim Egyptians later recalled the establishment of Israel as a watershed moment in the town's history. Samia Zaytun reflected, "Our whole world was overturned with the creation of Israel." For her, the Jewish state created an unnatural fissure between Egypt's Muslims and Jews, which was especially felt in Maadi. She remembered saying goodbye to her good friend Carol Ades soon after 1948 and realizing the permanence of her Jewish friend's departure. Remarking on how unstable the world seemed at the time, Zaytun remembered telling Ades, "I'm never going to see you again. What is going to happen to us?"[41]

Remembering Muslim–Jewish harmony became especially important to the Egyptians who remained in Maadi throughout the second half of the twentieth century. Several of Maadi's long-term residents took special care to mention the large number of Jews who had lived in the town when they were children. When talking about her time at the Maadi English School, Maggie Safwat described the student body as heavily populated by Jews. Ingy Safwat additionally explained that the Egyptian government never forced the Jews to leave, a point she made to emphasize that the Muslim majority had not driven their Jewish neighbors out of the country. For Ingy, Maggie, and Samia Zaytun, Maadi's Jewish community was integral to the town's earlier social fabric.[42] "They messed it up," Zaytun said, referring broadly to the various governmental powers that allowed the events of 1948 to unfold.[43] For these Maadi residents, the establishment of Israel unnecessarily politicized an element of their lives that appeared retrospectively harmonious, creating a division that surprised and hurt them. These residents communicated a collective sense of losing their connection to a stable governing authority after 1949. Memories of 1948 describe a palpable sense of insecurity. Egypt's military losses broke what little support remained for King Faruq. Zaytun's feeling of profound uncertainty as her friend left Egypt echoed a national sentiment that increasingly supported revolutionary change.

Taken together, these memories expose the multiple modes of loss that unfolded in the mid-twentieth century. In his memoir *Out of Place*, literary scholar Edward Said, a Palestinian-American who spent much of his childhood in Maadi, describes a pervasive feeling of loss associated with the Nakba. As the founding of Israel severed Said's connection to Palestine, Maadi's Egyptians eventually lost their former home as well. Yet their losses unfolded more gradually and allowed them to remain connected to the place even as it irreversibly changed. While the experience of the Nakba carried different meanings, these varied memories share feelings of loss and insecurity that came with the end of clear and stable authority.

Said, who did not live in Maadi but went to school there and belonged to the club, most powerfully describes the pervasive feelings of insecurity after the Nakba.[44] He began making the trip to Maadi in 1945, when he started attending the Cairo School for American Children on Road 7.[45] His family moved to the fashionable Zamalek neighborhood of Cairo from West Jerusalem in 1937, when Said was two years old. While he resided more continuously in Egypt than in Palestine, Said recalls feeling like a perpetual outsider throughout his formative years. Said describes his ability to connect with his surroundings as perpetually encumbered by his parents' limited social circle and their strictly enforced household order. To him, his early life was comprised of many of the same hallmarks recalled by Maadi children. What others saw as benefits, however, Said recalls as a series of obstacles. He relates, "School, church, club, garden, house—a limited, carefully circumscribed segment of the city—was my world until I was well into my teens."[46]

When Said's family moved to Cairo, it had already been the central hub of his father Wadie's stationary business for five years. In Cairo, Wadie connected to a network of Syrians in the publishing industry, including long-time Maadi resident Faris Nimr of *al-Muqattam*, whose prominence in the city newspaper and publishing industry dated back to the late nineteenth century and who had lived in Maadi since 1921.[47] Additionally, the

Saids were American citizens because Wadie lived in the United States during the First World War and served in the army.[48] As Americans, the family remained beneficiaries of the Capitulations for the remainder of the system's existence. They, like so many generations of Levantines before them, moved to Egypt at a time when their foreign passports offered certain commercial and legal advantages. Yet, unlike other resident foreigners, the Saids remained in Egypt after 1949, living through a tumultuous period that deeply influenced how Said interpreted the world around him.

While the family lived nearer downtown, Maadi was an ongoing fixture in Said's childhood in Egypt. During the week, he rode to Maadi daily for school—first to the American elementary school and later at the British-run Victoria College, which opened in Maadi in 1950 (and is discussed at greater length in Chapter Ten). In each situation, he felt perpetually on the outside. After initially attending an English primary school in Zamalek, he thought the American school might give him the sense that he was surrounded by his own people. The informality of the American system, however, made him feel "evermore the stranger."[49] Things grew increasingly dire at Victoria College, where Said felt the school's British administration perpetuated a subtle yet ultimately domineering form of cultural imperialism.[50]

For Said, the events that unfolded from 1947 to 1949 crystalized a sense of perpetual displacement as integral to his identity as a Palestinian. In contrast to Cairo, Jerusalem carried a sense of belonging for him. It served as a foil to his privileged, multinational Cairene life. He recalled, "As we increasingly spent time in Cairo, Palestine acquired a languid, almost dreamlike aspect, for me. . . . I recall thinking that being in Jerusalem was pleasant but tantalizingly open, temporary, even transitory, as indeed it later was."[51] Said's recollections of Jerusalem became conflicted, carrying a sense of promise as well as foreboding. In the summers, he regularly returned to Palestine to visit family. As much as it offered a welcome alternative to Cairo, those visits also brought anxiety because upon arriving he knew that they would have to leave again. The impermanence Said associated with Palestine was so deeply embedded that he could not separate his pre-1948 experiences from the loss that came after the Nakba.

Those connected to Maadi did not experience the political transformations of 1948 and 1949 in a uniform way. Said recalled following the events of the Arab–Israeli War from Cairo, and sensing that "all of us seemed to have given up on Palestine as a place, never to be returned to, barely mentioned, missed silently and pathetically."[52] He remembered his father mournfully relating how a Palestinian family who had recently arrived in Cairo had lost everything, and then stating, "We lost everything too." When Said asked his father what he meant—since their family still had a successful business and a comfortable life in Cairo—his father bluntly responded "Palestine."[53] In Said's memory, the events surrounding the Nakba and Palestine became the central features of his memories of the entire region. Despite having spent far more time in Egypt, he identified Palestine as home, particularly after being cut off from it. The establishment of Israel heightened the significance of the Saids' Palestinian identity. He did not, however, connect his personal experiences with their impact on his Egyptian setting. For him, the memory of his family's severed connection with their homeland remained distinct from events in Egypt and the Egyptians around him.

Preemptory loss pervades Said's memoir, making it difficult to disentangle how he might have received and understood a particular event in the 1940s or 1950s from the meaning that his later commitment to the Palestinian cause attached to those memories. His Maadi contemporaries did not recall the same sense of disconnection and inevitable breakdown and loss. For people like Maggie Safwat, Ingy Safwat, and Samia Zaytun, the Maadi they remembered gave them a deep belief in cross-confessional community, making a conflict between Jews and Arabs appear unnecessary and unnatural.

All of the uncertainty embedded in the experiences of the late 1940s—from the waffling position of the Egyptian government, to the feelings of personal loss in Maadi, to Egyptian Jewish ambivalence—addressed the insecurities created by the shifting politics of the region, as Egypt moved away from its earlier association with European influence toward a regional, pan-Arab identity. The Nakba appeared to fix a date on the dissolution of older forms of authority. In the recollections of some, it destroyed the cosmopolitan social harmony of the past. For others, it solidified existing feelings of displacement and alienation—for Jews and Palestinians. Yet, the impact of the establishment of Israel cannot be separated from the other ways that political and economic stability were lost in Egypt.

Maadi's earlier success, like that of much of Egypt's economy at large, previously depended on strong regional ties to trade throughout the eastern Mediterranean, particularly the Ottoman port cities that were similar centers of foreign commercial privilege. While the Ottoman empire fell more than a generation earlier, the town remained attached to the Capitulations as well as the tenuous authority of the Ottoman-descended King Faruq. Before 1948, Faruq's authority was severely weakened by the events of the Second World War. After the Arab–Israeli War, he was wholly discredited, especially among the Egyptian military. The abolition of the Capitulations led to the most immediate social rupture of the late 1940s, as the majority of Egypt's resident foreigners emigrated. Those departures were compounded by the profoundly disruptive experiences of the Arab–Israeli War.

In contrast to resident foreigners, many of Egypt's Jews, especially those who considered themselves *mutamassir*, remained in Egypt. Josipovici and his mother continued living in the garden city until the mid-1950s. For them and others, Israel had no doubt heightened the significance of their Jewishness, but it had not cut them off from Egypt. Their continued residence in Maadi, like the ongoing social life at the Maadi Sporting Club, exposed the cultural continuities that lingered, despite the political crises of the period. Those cultural experiences would shape many residents' long-term commitments to the town.

Over the course of the 1950s, the various forms of authority that once supported Maadi and helped it thrive would simultaneously deteriorate. Without economic systems that disproportionately favored foreigners, a politically viable monarchy, or the leadership of an independent company, residents' personal commitment to Maadi would become the only remaining force promoting the town's older garden city existence.

10

RELOCATION

In 1948, Tom Dale resigned from his position as Delta Land's general manager. Soon afterward, he and Effie boarded a ship bound for England.[1] Tom's son Geoffrey, already a Delta Land employee, would take over his father's role as general manager. There would be little continuity, however, between the tenures of father and son. Of the many changes that occurred during the late 1940s, the departure of Maadi's many resident foreigners had the most immediate impact on the town. In anticipating that change, Delta Land profoundly altered the direction Maadi would take into the tumultuous 1950s.

For resident foreigners who had lived their adult lives in Maadi and now looked to retire, moving back to Britain or elsewhere in Europe appeared increasingly attractive. The same year that Tom and Effie left Egypt, so did John and Jean Crawford. John had been chairman of Delta Land from 1940 to 1945 and served as president of the Maadi Sporting Club from 1937 to 1948.[2] Maadi residents knew John as the stern "Duke of Maadi." He and Jean first moved to Maadi in 1909. Now, after nearly forty years there, they started over.[3] Most of the foreigners on Delta Land's board of directors also resigned and repatriated at that time, as did a large number of residents.[4] The Church of St. John reported that Maadi's British community dramatically declined from seventy families in regular attendance in 1948 to only ten in 1951. At that point, St. John's could no longer support its own chaplain and a priest at the Anglican cathedral downtown was placed in charge of the Maadi church.[5] In particular, those previously employed in the Mixed Courts had little reason to remain in Egypt, especially if they lacked fluency in Arabic, which became the only official language of the judiciary.[6] The repatriation of so many resident foreigners was not especially surprising. Since the Montreux Treaty was signed in 1937, resident foreigners knew the end of their privileged lives in Egypt was imminent. The addition of the 1947 Company Law helped define the meaning of those impending changes, designating resident foreigners as outsiders whose true homes lay abroad. The fallout from the Arab–Israeli War further entrenched a division between locals and foreigners, leaving less and less room for the cosmopolitanism of the previous generation.

Perhaps the symbolic end of Maadi's elite cosmopolitanism came with the passing of some of Maadi's most prominent and long-term residents. On 12 October 1949, Henriette Devonshire passed away in her Maadi home, having continued to conduct tours of Cairo's Islamic sites well into her eighties.[7] Two years later, Dr. Faris Nimr Pasha, the Syrian-born founder of *al-Muqattam*, died at the age of ninety-six. Both had been pillars of Maadi's older society. In many ways, their deaths marked the passing of an older form of home that existed for foreigners in Egypt. Nimr, in particular, whose newspaper had pushed for cross-national understanding and supported certain forms of British influence, would be largely remembered as a servant of imperial interests. *Al-Muqattam* would be labeled "the newspaper of the British occupation of Egypt" and close its doors in 1952.[8] By the late 1940s and early 1950s, home was increasingly defined by the nationality on one's passport.

The post-Capitulations departures indicated the ongoing reversal of older pathways into Egypt. Where legal and economic privileges once paved the way for foreigners' entry into and domicile in Egypt, the end of those policies set the terms of their departure. While some foreign nationals, like Geoffrey Dale, remained in Maadi despite the changes, most, perhaps understandably, did not exhibit the same kind of commitment to Egypt that withstood changes in economic policy, perceiving instead that their influence was no longer welcome.

While Delta Land's directors could not have fully anticipated the events of the Arab–Israeli War and the impact it would have on Egypt and the region as a whole, they could lay plans for a Maadi without the Capitulations. These plans departed heavily from the garden city of the past. In the late 1940s, the company set out to develop the rural green belt surrounding Maadi, which had previously created a deliberate buffer between Maadi's town-and-country environment and Cairo's urban center. As Delta

Land participated in the mid-century transformation of Maadi, residents became the most stalwart defenders of the town's earlier distinctions.

By expanding into the previously undeveloped rural and desert areas surrounding Maadi, Delta Land looked to preserve the company's commercial viability as resident foreigners departed and more Egyptian migrants moved to Cairo. This shifting vision occurred in connection with the creation of Cairo's municipality. The new governing body reoriented the organization of the city into a series of radiating rings. The center of Cairo included the old Islamic city, the "European" Cairo developed during the nineteenth century, and Shubra. Maadi was part of the first ring outside the city center, which also included Heliopolis, Basatin, and Giza.[9] While Maadi had previously been geographically and aesthetically distinct from Cairo, this new municipal approach would mean the suburb's absorption into the capital.[10] This took place not only because of changes in the city's governance but also because of the sheer weight of the rapidly growing population. Maadi had 42,944 residents in 1947. That number would more than sextuple over the next thirty years to a total of 267,056 residents in 1976. While central Cairo's population would actually decline during these years, Maadi and the rest of Cairo's "first ring" would see some of the city's most significant growth in the second half of the twentieth century.[11] Delta Land did not steer Maadi away from these changes, but instead began planning for them.

Delta Land's altered scheme for Maadi's future likely began in 1945. That year, the Bank of England authorized an increase in the company's capital, allowing it to issue registered shares in order to undertake two significant new development projects.[12] The first project, Hada'iq al-Maadi, or "Maadi Gardens," was located northwest of the original Maadi establishment, between the Nile and the electric rail line. This area became home to some of Egypt's internal migrants. The second endeavor, called Digla, looked to appeal to wealthier potential residents and stood southeast of Maadi, where the New Zealand military base stood during the Second World War.[13] With these developments, the original Maadi became known as Maadi al-Sarayat, or "Maadi of the Palaces," because of the large, older villas located there.[14] Delta Land constructed the new developments, particularly those in Hada'iq al-Maadi to be distinct from the original Maadi development.

Delta Land announced plans to develop Hada'iq al-Maadi in 1947, laying out a sixteen-hectare area along the Cairo–Helwan road in four ringed zones. The original plan was to develop the area as a second, more modern adaptation of Ebenezer Howard's original garden city scheme. The center would have large villas and gardens, which would be surrounded by apartments, houses of worship, hospitals, and more commercial spaces for hotels and cinemas. Rather than intentionally leaving the remainder of the land open, this was devoted to industrial endeavors, including an ice factory and public garages.[15] The construction that actually followed focused on the area between the Nile and the rail line, near what remained of the Maadi al-Khabiri village. While residents and the company remained hopeful that the area would become the "best part of Maadi," they encountered serious drainage problems because the area was even with the Nile during its flood season.[16] Where previously the company managed much of its own utility development, after 1949 the city of Cairo had to lay the necessary sewer drainage to make the expansion of Hada'iq possible. While development of the area began in 1947, the drainage issue remained a problem well into the mid-1950s.[17]

What Delta Land did develop in Hada'iq al-Maadi consisted of larger multiunit apartment buildings meant to offer state-of-the-art, modern housing to less affluent buyers and renters who could not afford a villa in the heart of Maadi.[18] The mass-produced modernity the company promoted in Hada'iq was a significant departure from the carefully controlled, town-and-country environs previously identified with Maadi's built environment. The area would go on to gain international notoriety at the dawn of the twenty-first century because of one of its most infamous former residents, Ayman al-Zawahiri, who was a founder of al-Qaeda. In 1960, Ayman's father, Dr. Muhammad Rabi al-Zawahiri, moved the family to Hada'iq. Journalist and author Lawrence Wright associates Ayman's upbringing in Hada'iq, as the poorer side of Maadi, with a sense of exclusion that would fuel his radical Islamist ideology. In particular, Wright identifies the Maadi Sporting Club and the town's Victoria College campus with elite spaces that al-Zawahiri could not access.[19] This sense of separateness in Hada'iq and the area's clear social distinction from the original development was driven by profit motives, as Delta Land looked to market to a new and growing market of potential residents. Hada'iq did not offer the classed distinctions of Maadi al-Sarayat.

Instead it presented the advantage of newness—an innovative establishment on the border of the city center. That it would become tied to radical Islamist violence, then, situates Delta Land's business calculations and Cairo's rapidly changing demographics within a larger history of how fractured suburban communities can fuel social and ideological dislocation, sometimes with devastatingly violent effects.[20]

In Digla, however, Delta Land departed from its original plans for Maadi in an altogether different fashion, looking instead to preserve whatever wealthy foreign footprint might remain in Egypt. The area took its name from the neighboring Wadi Digla, a valley that ran between the Nile and the nearby Muqattam hills—the same wadi that channeled devastating flood waters into Maadi in 1945. Development of Digla began in the 1950s, with plans for creating more capacity for the spacious villas like those of Maadi al-Sarayat. The area's higher elevation and distance from the Nile, however, made for an overall drier climate that was less hospitable to the trees and gardens traditionally associated with Maadi, although residents were promised that over time Digla would have the same pleasing aesthetic as the rest of Maadi.[21]

Maintaining strict control over how Digla would be developed proved more challenging for Delta Land, which by the 1950s no longer had the autonomy to enforce its own *Cahier des Charges* for the area. Geoffrey Dale recalled a meeting with Princess Fawzia, King Fu'ad's daughter and Faruq's sister, who already had a villa in Maadi al-Sarayat on Midan Menasce and wanted to build a larger residence in Digla. By this time, Fawzia, the former queen of Iran, had divorced the shah and was married to Egyptian diplomat Isma'il Shirin.[22] Ahead of the meeting, Dale recalled discussing with palace architect Mustafa Fahmy that they could not concede to the princess's many wishes. Yet, once Fawzia began discussing plans for her expansive home, her demands were agreed to, with only Dale telling her, "I do not agree with anything you have requested. They [the plans] do not conform to the company regulations." Yet Dale did not describe whether or not the princess could construct her home as she desired. She proceeded with a land purchase in Digla, and Dale did not mention whether or not the company's authority presided over the project. Where his father's recollections of Maadi revolved around Delta Land's priorities and his enforcement of them, Geoffrey's memories carried less certainty—indicative of the insecurities of the period.

As it turned out, Delta Land was not initially able to grow Digla as a space for additional villas and gardens. Instead, the company began attracting international schools to the area, which helped draw in more itinerant expatriates with families looking for rental properties. This trend began with the relocation of Cairo's Victoria College campus to Maadi in 1950.

The English-style boys' school was first established in the northern Cairo district of Shubra in 1940 because of the threat of Italian invasion in Alexandria, where the school was founded in 1901. Perhaps as an act of retribution, the Anglo-Egyptian Committee, which administered the school, established the new campus in a former Italian school sequestered by the British during the war. The Alexandria campus reopened in 1944, but the Cairo campus remained, having grown from 150 students to 450.[23]

By 1948, however, the Anglo-Egyptian Committee—like most organizations emphasizing multinational collaboration—found itself financially strained and looked to close the Cairo campus. To complicate matters, the Shubra campus proved too small for the growing student body.[24] Edward Said enrolled at the Shubra campus in 1949 and recalled, "The classrooms and assembly hall were dingy and cramped. A permanent cloud of dust seemed settled on the place, even though four tennis courts and several football fields gave us outdoor facilities of a lavishness I had not before encountered."[25] What is more, the campus could not be renovated because the property had to be returned to the Italians as part of the postwar agreement.[26] Moving the school or closing it appeared to be the committee's only options.

A group of Egyptian alumni, known as the Old Victorians, formed the Victoria College Cairo Committee to raise funds for the reestablishment of the campus in a more suitable locale. The Old Victorians saw their alma mater as an integral site of elite education for not only Egypt but also the whole region. Its alumni included Said and Michel Demitri Shalhoub (better known as Omar Sharif), as well as scions of the Sabbah and Ghanem clans in Kuwait, the brother of the sultan of Zanzibar, and the children of the Merghani, al-Mahdi, and Abu al-Ela families—some of the most prominent political families in Sudan. The school's most influential alumnus was likely Hussein ibn Talal, the king of Jordan from 1952 to 1999.[27] The Old Victorians had hoped to find a location nearer downtown but settled on Delta Land's proposal to build the campus in Digla. The company offered

Victoria College twenty feddans of land in Digla, five of which they offered for free. With land increasingly hard to sell, the new school provided a potentially profitable opportunity.[28]

The school's committee hired P.W. Poltock, a former member of the Royal Engineers, to design a state-of-the-art campus. He implemented a streamlined, modern design for the new school that emphasized straight lines and block-like structures. The design drew from the modernist architectural styles established by Le Corbusier in the interwar years. Like the other idealist designers affiliated with Maadi—Ebenezer Howard and Hassan Fathy—Le Corbusier looked to enforce certain social values through his work. He combined the intricate order of the machine age with urban life in hopes of creating a more unified and cohesive society that was less isolating. In contrast to his contemporary Frank Lloyd Wright, Le Corbusier's buildings were designed to stand out from their natural environs.[29] To that end, Poltock designed the school with block-like shapes surrounded by plentiful windows, all of which he elevated on rounded pillars. The clean, straight lines and overall unornamented design was thoroughly modernist.[30] The contrast with nature was perhaps especially fitting for Digla as it proved a difficult area for cultivation. Like the apartment buildings in Hada'iq al-Maadi, this new development in Digla broke from the town-and-country aesthetic of the original garden city and drew from a different vision for modern urban development.

Establishing the new Victoria College campus in Maadi might have appeared to preserve the elite cosmopolitanism of the town's past, but those international connections were far more strained by 1950, when the Maadi campus opened. Said describes the school as a "great distortion." He explains:

> The students were paying members of some putative colonial elite that was being schooled in the way of a British imperialism that had already expired, though we did not fully know it. We learned about English life and letters, the monarchy and Parliament, India and Africa, habits and idioms that we could never use in Egypt or, for that matter, anywhere else.

The students were not trained in Arabic, and, in turn, their native language became one of rebellion and opposition. Nor did they learn about the history or politics of Egypt or its surrounding countries.[31] Said did not complete a full academic year at the Digla campus. In the spring of 1951, his father enrolled him at an American boarding school. The move ended Said's long-term residence in the Middle East and meant his geographical removal from the revolutionary events that began in January 1952.

Not all students saw the new campus in such stark terms. For Gabriel Josipovici, Victoria College became a place to pursue new opportunities, albeit outside of Egypt. As mentioned in Chapter Nine, Josipovici's mother took a job at the college to offset the cost of tuition. He remembered Victoria College as a place that still reflected the multinational diversity of Cairo, where he joined a number of other minority students—Greeks, Armenians, Jews, and Copts—in addition to the Arab Muslim majority. Josipovici summarized much of his Victoria College experience in two short sentences: "I had a very happy time there. I don't think I learned very much." He did believe, however, that the students worked diligently despite the uninspired instruction.[32] The all-English faculty and the lack of Arabic-language instruction did not carry political and cultural overtones for him. Josipovici did not recall English faculty members treating Jewish and Arab students differently, nor did he get a sense that his teachers disparaged him.[33] Instead, Josipovici and the other non-native Arabic speakers at the school found themselves at a particular disadvantage after the revolutionary events of 1952, when Nasser's regime changed the language of education to Arabic in the mid-1950s. For him, his post-1952 experiences at the college heightened his sense of Jewishness and foreignness, fueling plans to leave Egypt for him and his mother.

The contrary meanings of Victoria College to its various students speak to the challenges that Delta Land faced when planning for Maadi's future. The school represented a kind of rehabilitation of the elite cosmopolitanism of the past. Yet the terms of multinational collaboration were altered and fraught with new political challenges. With its emphasis on English educational standards, Victoria College did not offer students a meaningful vision for Egypt's future. Instead, it appeared increasingly dated and out of place. Its establishment in Maadi was indicative of the company's own incoherence and short-term view of the area's future.

For Delta Land, locating Victoria College's campus in Digla established a new trend for Maadi's expansion. The town had long been home to smaller international schools housed in villas. The creation of more expansive, modern campuses in Digla and elsewhere on the outskirts of Maadi appealed to a growing number of American expatriate families who came to Egypt for shorter stints, seeing Cairo as a place of short-term opportunity rather than long-term domicile like previous generations. At St. John's, for instance, the largely vacant church grounds were repurposed by American evangelicals, many of whom worked for oil companies and used the grounds for a nondenominational community church.[34] Digla would later see the addition of the expansive Cairo American College campus, which catered to the American business community.[35]

With the additions of Hada'iq al-Maadi and Digla, Delta Land's vision for Maadi had clearly changed course from the original garden city plan from the early twentieth century. While this change came in conjunction with the creation of Cairo's new municipality in 1949, the company shifted direction internally before it ever had to react to new government oversight. Just after the Second World War, Joseph Kfoury, the managing director of Fayoum Light Railways, joined Delta Land's board and helped spearhead an initiative to turn greater and more immediate profits in Maadi.[36] He formed a smaller cadre of board members called the Committee of Directors, which met biweekly to organize profit-generating initiatives beyond the company's existing focus on land sales and rents. As a later board report explained, the committee "undertakes the every day affairs of the Company and their decisions are submitted to the Board of Directors for confirmation."[37] The group's first project: selling Maadi's trees for lumber at an estimated value of LE 500,000.[38] More than either of Maadi's new satellite communities, the lumber proposal was most indicative of a company leadership that no longer identified with the original vision for the town's development.

Preserving Maadi's trees would require the dedicated perseverance of the town's residents. When the committee brought the plan to the rest of the directors, Dale recalled, "No opposition was accepted." Instead, a group of residents raised a popular protest to defend Maadi's trees. Their activities included an anonymous letter to the *Egyptian Gazette* shaming the company. The letter opened, "Can anyone tell me by whose authority and for what purpose trees are being cut in Maadi?" It continued, "Maadi is a garden suburb and its trees are its chief pride." The letter went on to describe a rumor that the trees were being sold for timber, and appealed to anyone with authority "to have such vandalism stopped before serious damage is done," signing the letter "Suburban."[39] That residents had to appeal to an authority outside of Delta Land for Maadi's defense was a profound turning point in the town's history. Until this point, the company was the guiding force behind the town's distinct development. Residents had been accustomed to relying on Delta Land's authority as a guarantor of their way of life. If the board no longer identified with the particular town-and-country existence previously cultivated in Maadi, then the community's future was uncertain well before any of the revolutionary events of the 1950s.

A group of prominent Egyptian residents led by Mustafa Moyine al-'Arab, Khadr Gabr, and 'Abdu al-Shafi'i organized the defense of Maadi's trees.[40] Their activity in 1948 marked the beginning of a more organized effort on residents' part to maintain and preserve Maadi apart from Delta Land. Residents would find themselves playing an increasingly significant role in the wake of the events of 1952.

On Saturday, 26 January 1952, riots broke out throughout downtown Cairo, targeting foreign-owned businesses and cultural centers. Inspired by protests in the Suez Canal Zone and the previous day's stand taken by the auxiliary police forces against the British in Ismailiya, the Cairo protestors set fire to the signs and symbols of elite cosmopolitanism in the capital. They burned down department stores, car dealerships, the Cairo Opera House, Barclays Bank, and the all-British Turf Club, where several elderly members were killed.[41] Before the Cairo Fire, many Egyptians had looked to different branches of Egypt's existing political opposition—the Muslim Brotherhood, Young Egypt, and the communists—to topple the monarchy. But the events of 25 and 26 January emboldened the army's commissioned officers, who formed the Free Officers Movement, or al-Dubbat al-Ahrar.[42] Six months later, on the night of 22 July 1952, they staged a bloodless coup, and Faruq abdicated with little opposition, particularly because the United States and Britain refused to intervene on his behalf.[43]

If a new Egypt began taking shape in 1952, what the nation might look like remained unclear. The Free Officers lacked a coherent political ideology, with members carrying their own associations to nationalist, socialist, and Islamist movements.[44] Rather than unifying around a political ideology, they emphasized a set of goals—what Nasser called the "triple enemy" of imperialism, the monarchy, and feudalism.[45] Their more specific aims included ending the British military occupation of the Suez Canal Zone, reforming land ownership to ensure that peasants owned the land they farmed, stopping capitalism's substantiation of political power, achieving social equality, and building a strong popular army.[46] These goals allowed the revolutionary events of 1952 to appeal to Egypt's diverse and socially stratified society, taking on a number of political connotations without immediately generating alarm from any one sector of Egyptian society, except, of course, the royal family.

For all of its foreign influence, Maadi remained unscathed throughout 1952. That summer, most residents were optimistic about Egypt's future. Nadia Salem remembered her mother viewing Nasser as the "great emancipator."[47] Josipovici similarly recalled that he and his circle supported the social equality Nasser promised. "I had been very pro-Nasser," he said, "and, you know, we all felt Nasser was doing wonderful things. . . . [At] last . . . there were schools, and hospitals were being built, and unfortunately it all got swept away."[48] For Ingy Safwat much of the early support for Nasser and the Free Officers was rooted in their disaffection with the king, which became especially emphatic after 1948. "The last three or four years of Faruq," she recalled, "the people were fed up with his behaviors, so it was like everybody wanted something to happen."[49] In these early years, support for the Free Officers cut across social status and political conviction. Faruq's abdication meant change for a nation desperate for it.

Many residents were emboldened in these years to organize better for Maadi's defense. On 13 November 1953, a group of residents met in the home of Dr. Mustafa Musharafa to form the Rabatat Sukkan wa Mullak al-Maadi (Maadi Association of Residents and Landlords). The association aimed to defend the area's particular interests. Where in 1948, residents called for an outside authority to stop the destruction of Maadi's trees, they now asserted themselves as the community's leaders. They began their activities later that November with an appeal to the minister of town and country affairs that Maadi be granted a classification as a special municipality because of its history as a unique development under Delta Land's leadership.[50] Soon afterward, the Maadi association gained the support of an additional seventy-five members, all of whom looked to find a sustainable method for maintaining the garden city life they had known in Maadi.[51]

The creation of Rabatat al-Maadi defined the altered nature of Delta Land's leadership over Maadi. The company had already distanced itself from the earlier vision for the town, but after 1952, further changes to the company's board intersected with more revolutionary government policies, making the end of Maadi's earlier form all the more certain. By the time that the Free Officers deposed Faruq, Geoffrey Dale was the only Briton left on Delta Land's board and as general manager he had the least authority. Two years later, the company saw the retirement of its two remaining Jewish directors, Ernest Harari and Henri Mosseri, whose families had been affiliated with Delta Land since the company's founding. That same year, Taher al-Lozy, who had been on the board since 1949, became the company's new chairman.[52] Al-Lozy would guide the company through Nasser's rise to power, and ultimately oversee Delta Land's dissolution—something that took place due to events largely outside of his control.

Al-Lozy moved to Maadi in 1926, where he built a large villa on Road 11 for his family. As discussed in Chapter Six, he had strong ties to the Wafd Party when he first moved to Maadi, in part because his wife was the cousin of Safiya Zaghlul. In Maadi, he participated in the town's growing population of *effendiya*. Over the next twenty years, however, he became less and less invested in the Wafd's liberalism. During the Second World War, he was temporarily placed under house arrest because he supported the Germans in hopes that they would liberate Egypt from Britain. By the 1950s, al-Lozy identified with the new regime Nasser was building in Egypt. During the years of al-Lozy's leadership, he intensified Delta Land's commitment to interests outside the original garden city plan for Maadi.[53] Al-Lozy and Dale were regularly at odds with one another over how Delta Land should be run. Dale eventually left the company, moving his family from Egypt to Sudan on 16 June 1956—just three days before the British military made their final withdrawal from the Suez Canal Zone.[54]

Upon taking power, the Free Officers formed the Egyptian Revolutionary Command Council (RCC), which guided the new government's affairs. The RCC subsequently took aim at the country's government institutions, dissolving parliament in December 1952. The following June they abolished the monarchy and declared Egypt a republic. While Muhammad Naguib served as the new government's first prime minister, Nasser provided the real source of leadership. He became prime minister in April

1954 and was elected president by plebiscite in November.[55] As Nasser's policies became more socialist in nature, Maadi's social inequalities likewise became more obvious and problematic. That dissonance was initially felt when the country's new leadership targeted land ownership laws and British imperial influence. It was not until the end of the decade, however, when Nasser shifted the role of capitalism in Egypt's political economy, that Maadi ceased to exist in any form initially conceived by its founders.

Before the Free Officers abolished the monarchy or officially declared Egypt a republic, they set in motion radical land use reform policies. Their priority remained empowering the majority of Egyptians, particularly the peasantry. In September 1952, the government issued a decree that limited land ownership to no more than two hundred feddans (eighty-four hectares). The decree also redistributed royal lands to the peasantry, and abolished Islamic family estates.[56] Nadia Salem's family, who, in addition to their Maadi villa, owned a large farm in the eastern province of Sharqiya, was among those directly hit by the reform. The property they lost dramatically shifted their position in Egypt. Soon afterward, Nadia left Egypt for Berkeley, California, where her husband was attending graduate school.[57] The Salem family were among a minority of high-ranking Egyptians affected by these policies, but the event marked the early ways that the new regime exerted its power by targeting classed inequalities. These changes would see not only European and Egyptian Jews depart Egypt, but also many of the country's Muslim Egyptian elites.

The RCC's other major victory in the name of Egyptian independence came in October 1954, when it reached a new treaty agreement with the British, which secured the final departure of British troops from the Suez Canal Zone in the next twenty months.[58] The agreement was to mark the first time Egypt would be completely free from a British military presence in almost seventy-five years. In the two years since the coup, Nasser and the RCC had carved out a number of victories against Egypt's "triple enemy." By the mid-1950s, any remaining elements of feudalism were abolished, the monarchy dissolved, and a date for a final British withdrawal secured. The RCC had quickly taken action against the various forms of institutional and social inequality that had been at work in Egypt for generations. What that meant for the country's future, however, remained unclear.

More than a move to decolonize Egypt, Nasser's early policies demarcated who did and did not belong in the country. To do this, he worked culturally to promote an Egyptian nationalism that coexisted with a larger sense of a regional, Arab identity. His use of Pan-Arabism framed a sense of belonging that distanced Egyptians from a shared Mediterranean geography or the European connections previously associated with the Egyptian nation.[59]

While Nasser had yet to issue any explicitly exclusionary policies, some Maadi residents anticipated them. Sacha Rabinovitch, Gabriel Josipovici's mother, began looking for a way back out of Egypt not long after the 1952 coup. Josipovici recalled witnessing growing xenophobia in Cairo but did not remember experiencing any direct form of antisemitism. He believed his mother, because of her experience in France during the Second World War, had a keener sense of the kinds of challenges they might face in Egypt. She began appealing to Victoria College's headmaster Alan Guy Elliott-Smith to help her find a scholarship so that her son could attend Oxford. While the headmaster explained that Gabriel might attend a number of schools in England, Sacha insisted, "No, no, no, only Oxford." Elliott-Smith agreed to assist them and found Josipovici a place at Cheltenham College in Gloucester, where he had previously been a second master. By enrolling there, Josipovici could take his A-levels in England and then proceed to Oxford. Josipovici recalled Elliott-Smith's gesture as particularly hospitable. The opening at Cheltenham allowed Josipovici and his mother to leave Egypt in early September 1956, before Josipovici might have otherwise faced expulsion as a French citizen due to the fallout after the Suez Canal Crisis.[60]

Like Dale's departure for Sudan a few months earlier, Josipovici and his mother's move to England anticipated the profound changes that Maadi and the rest of Egypt would experience after the crisis. For Dale, the changing face of doing business in Egypt demarcated who did and did not belong in the country before the government issued any formal policy. With the end of the Capitulations and Mixed Courts, Egyptian business leaders had far less concern for the multinational networks of investment capital and personnel that had previously substantiated the Egyptian economy. While Dale could still legally remain in the country at the time of his departure, the space he once fondly called home had largely disappeared. Even more significantly, the company itself had a less clearly defined purpose, appearing to focus on short-term profits rather than a long-term plan for Maadi.

While it might appear as though one vision for Egypt's future was replaced by another because of the revolutionary events of 1952, earlier changes in Delta Land's aims for Maadi expose the precedents of mid-century political transformation. During the Second World War, long-term plans for Maadi's future profoundly shifted, as the company looked to develop Hada'iq al-Maadi and then Digla. The original plan for Maadi no longer appeared a worthwhile investment for the company, if the venture was going to remain viable in the future. The formation of the Committee of Directors affirmed this new direction, leading Delta Land to attempt the sale of Maadi's trees for lumber and turn far faster profits. This proposal marked the company's dissociation from any long-term plan for the older part of Maadi. Under al-Lozy's leadership, Delta Land would come into a more harmonious relationship with Nasser's government. By that time, however, most residents had already dismissed the company's authority over the town.

While many in Maadi were initially enthusiastic about Nasser, new land ownership laws were a harbinger of even more radical changes in the near future. Ultimately, most would come to grieve for the earlier years of life in Maadi. Many would become increasingly emboldened to defend Maadi on their own terms. After forming Rabatat al-Maadi in 1953, residents of Maadi al-Sarayat organized to defend not only the area's trees, gardens, and villas, but also the once harmonious town-and-country life they believed distinguished Maadi from anywhere else in Egypt.

11

DEMOLITION

Juliet Tabet moved to Maadi from Heliopolis in 1955 after marrying her husband Albert, who grew up in the garden city. For her, Maadi was a sought-after, verdant country retreat compared to the congested urban environment she recalled in Heliopolis. "It was like a giant garden," she said.[1] Just a year later, she saw a rift between foreigner and national tear through the seemingly idyllic Maadi she first encountered. On 26 July 1956—just over a month after British troops made their final withdrawal from the Suez Canal Zone—Nasser nationalized the French-owned Suez Canal Company. Tensions regarding the place of foreign businesses in relationship to the new regime had grown over the previous four years, and the war over the Suez Canal was as much a Cold War conflict as it was a battle over decolonization. Nasser nationalized the canal after United States Secretary of State John Foster Dulles withdrew his promise of Western support for construction of the Aswan High Dam. Dulles hoped to teach Nasser a lesson, reprimanding him for pursuing closer ties with the Soviets.

The nationalization of the canal, then, marked a definitive shift in the relationship between foreign capital and Egyptian development as Nasser determined that the independent state would be the arbiter of progress in Egypt.[2] Yet it was the British, French, and Israeli reaction to the nationalization of the canal that dealt the final blow to whatever influence foreign capital still had over the politics and economy of Egypt. The fallout from the ensuing crisis would mark the beginning of the end of Maadi as it had previously existed.[3]

In the months that followed Nasser's 26 July declaration, the British and French worked with Israel to reclaim the Suez by force. The joint invasion began with the arrival of Israeli paratroopers in the Sinai on 29 October. The British subsequently issued a ceasefire, and when the Egyptians refused, the Royal Air Force began bombing Egyptian military targets. By 5 November, a joint Anglo-French invasion began in the Suez. In response, both the United States and the Soviet Union demanded that the three invading militaries withdraw. In all, the British and French remained in the Suez Canal Zone for seven weeks. While the Egyptian military posed no significant threat to the invaders, the eventual retreat of Britain, France, and Israel, as well as their humiliation on the world stage, proved an enormous victory for Nasser, making him into a national hero and international champion of postcolonial independence.[4]

The Suez Canal Crisis, as it came to be known, had a direct impact on the population of Maadi. In the wake of the failed invasion, Nasser ordered all British and French passport holders to repatriate.[5] They were given two or three days to make arrangements and allowed to leave with only two pieces of luggage each. Anna Joannides, who was permitted to stay as an Italian national, recalled the period as especially sad because so many friends abruptly left. Like the forced repatriations that the British put in place during both world wars, Nasser's policy hardened national identities, singling out people who had spent their lives in Egypt as French or British outsiders. Joannides remembered watching people depart who had no particular connection to their country of supposed origin but had to leave because of their passports.[6]

At the same time that British and French families were forced to emigrate, Jewish families found it increasingly difficult to remain in Egypt.[7] In the winter of 1956–57, as many as twenty-five thousand Jews left Egypt, with two-thirds going to Israel and the remainder landing in Europe or the United States.[8] Albert Tabet was a lawyer to several Jewish families at the time, and Julia remembered trading furniture for his legal services because the emigrating families could no longer afford to pay him outright. For others, likely French and British nationals who were forced to leave more immediately, he managed their property, attempting to sell it so that they could get some return on sales they could not conduct in person.[9] The Tabets' daughter Mona still uses the kitchen table that Albert received from one of Maadi's Jewish families.[10] Mona recalled going on childhood walks through Maadi with her father, where he would stroll through the streets and refer to the villas by the names of their former Jewish owners.

"He would say that was the house of the Taynas, or house of the Golds, and these were the people he had grown up with," she remembered.[11] While Albert was sorry to see his friends leave, Juliet recalled the disruptive events with a sense of moving with the times—that these changes were regrettable to some, but represented the pain of progress. One had to accept them and move on, she explained.[12]

The fallout of the Suez Canal Crisis would define the end of Maadi's former existence. While the town had survived forced migrations before, the tranformational impact would come from the voluntary departure of Egypt's Jews. Jehan Sadat, wife of Anwar Sadat and herself the daughter of an English mother and an Egyptian father, recalled in her memoir the social impact of Jewish emigration following the crisis. "The war had taken a terrible toll. Anti-Jewish sentiment which started after the Palestine War in '48 now reached a fever pitch across Egypt. Thousands and thousands of Egyptian Jews with whom we had always lived peacefully either were expelled or fled."[13] In Maadi, their large-scale emigration would undo the last vestiges of the town's earlier elite cosmopolitanism. After the crisis, ethnicity and religion took on new and powerful political meanings. This time, Egyptians, not a foreign occupier, defined the enemy population. While Jews were never formally expelled from Egypt, their former sense of belonging to the nation—perhaps best embodied by former Delta Land chairman Elie N. Mosseri—evaporated in the face of the mounting regional conflict between Israel and its Arab-majority neighbors. What is more, the nationalization of the Suez Canal Company proved a precursor to the end of what little authority Delta Land still had in Maadi. The Cairo municipality had already circumscribed the company's governing role. The expansion of socialist reforms that began in 1956 would fully dissolve the company, drawing to a definitive close what little remained of Maadi as a distinctly governed part of greater Cairo. There would no longer be any growth of Maadi in the old ways. What remained would become a place that only the truly passionate hoped to defend.

Remembering how he observed the events of the Suez Canal Crisis from England, Gabriel Josipovici recalled his shock at the violent response to the canal's nationalization. While at school at Cheltenham that fall, he attended a lecture defending the British, French, and Israeli intervention. Josipovici stood up and questioned the speaker, arguing in support of the Egyptian government's right to nationalize the industries within its borders and pertaining to its natural resources. "I didn't feel detached," he said. "I felt horrified at what England and France and Israel were doing."[14] Had Josipovici still been in Egypt during the crisis, it might have proved more difficult for him to side with Egyptian nationalist interests. Already in England, however, his Jewishness and French citizenship carried less meaning, both politically and personally. Josipovici's convictions spoke to his awareness of Egypt's rights as a sovereign nation, and the complex nature of the Suez Canal Crisis as it marked a definitive path toward full decolonization. The crisis would become a turning point in postcolonial politics—a signal flare that European imperial power would not resuscitate itself on the global stage. It was also a deeply significant local event with a personal impact most felt in places like Maadi and Egypt's other cosmopolitan quarters.[15]

Following the Suez Canal Crisis and the forced migration of Egypt's French and British nationals, many residents elected to leave on their own accord.[16] Josipovici's cousin Anna Joannides departed for Italy in 1957 but returned a year later. "I loved Egypt," she explained, adding she missed the friends and family she left behind. When she came back to Maadi, she observed that it had "started over again," but in a different form. The Egyptian government was now in charge of the schools, and Jews were subsequently banned from the Maadi Sporting Club. "I think it was the first time they were *persona non grata*," she said. A year later, she married Aleco Joannides, a Greek journalist with Reuters. After their marriage, the couple left Egypt permanently.[17] The rest of Anna's family remained, however, allowing her to visit her former home regularly while most of those who left Maadi after 1956 never came back.

Anna's sister Monica, who married a Muslim Egyptian and converted to Islam, saw the changes in Egypt's political scene firsthand, as her husband served out his career in the Egyptian military.[18] Monica's husband had joined the military at a young age because, having entered the job market before the 1947 Company Law mandated that companies hire more Egyptians, he was unable to find a job as an engineer with a private company. Joannides, in contrast to her sister, remained both an Italian citizen and a devout Catholic. She moved to various cities around the world because of her husband's work before they settled in London. While her foreign citizenship and Christian beliefs might have previously found a place in

Cairene life, especially in the city's European half, those places closed after 1956. Anna instead became a visitor to Egypt.[19]

The various modes of migration that unfolded after 1956 directly affected institutions that had once thrived in Maadi. The town's synagogue lost its worshipers and stood empty for the majority of the year as a kind of monument to the town's Jewish roots. The Church of St. John likewise lost the remaining vestiges of the British community. The relocation of Victoria College to Digla in 1950 had somewhat resuscitated the church, but forced migration meant the departure of the majority of the school's faculty and the decline of St. John's as an Anglican space.[20]

One of the more symbolic events linking the Suez to Nasser as a post-colonial figure subsequently unfolded at Victoria College. Rather than closing the school, Nasser maintained the campus as a boys' school under a new banner of Egyptian nationalism. He renamed it Kulliyat al-Nasr, or Victory College. The name drew from a new nomenclature of power in Egypt. The Egyptian president's surname means "champion" in Arabic and is derived from the root word for "victory." The school's new name, then, not only poetically discarded Victoria for Victory but also established Nasser in the British empress's place. The symbolic name change clearly associated the nationalist triumphs of 1956 and the future of elite Egyptian education with the person of Nasser.

Changes to Maadi's religious and educational institutions spoke to the long-term effect of forced migration after 1956. The empty houses of worship became relics of an earlier period, while the transformed school spoke to new sources of power and influence in the Egyptian republic. Changes to these institutions indicated a break from the Maadi that was. Whatever the area became in the future would be directly tied to the new forms of authority that emerged during the mid-twentieth century.

Perhaps observing a void where the previous plan for Maadi had been, Rabatat al-Maadi began more widely publicizing its efforts to maintain the town's distinctive qualities amid Egypt's wave of revolutionary change during 1956. That year, it published the *Dalil al-Maadi/The Maadi Guide*, a bilingual directory that not only listed businesses and services in Maadi, but also explained in detail Maadi's history, geography, and the best practices for living there.[21] Before publishing the guidebook, the association had already attempted to make itself responsible for the ongoing observance of the *Cahier des Charges*. In 1954, it published a memo explaining to new residents the perimeters they were to leave around their homes in hopes of maintaining the town's distinctive aesthetic in the absence of Delta Land as a reliable authority.[22] The guide that followed two years later promoted the association's responsibility for the community and more explicitly outlined behaviors that were and were not acceptable in Maadi.

In explaining how residents should behave in Maadi, *The Maadi Guide* emphasized Arabic readers' more permanent commitment to the town, while English readers were assigned a more itinerant set of behaviors. Within the guide, the Maadi Association defined itself as the new arbiter of garden city maintenance. It explained that the association worked "for the preservation of the area's special reputation for being like a city of gardens" *(ka-madinat hada'iq)*. The English version, in contrast, did not make an overt statement about Maadi as a garden city, likely because it was targeting more American readers who would have identified less with the English planning movement or confused the language with the Garden City district near downtown. In English, the guide stated that the association intended to "preserve the stamp of Maadi and those special features which gave it its character."[23] To that end, Rabatat al-Maadi used the guide to make its role as the protector of the *Cahier des Charges* explicit. The guide explained that only designated parts of Maadi could be used for commercial space, that buildings could not exceed fifteen meters in height, and that green spaces had to be preserved between homes and in public areas.[24]

While the association could claim this authority, it had no means of enforcement. Nadia Salem recalled that when she and her siblings sold their family's villa, the buyers assured them that they would not tear it down. Yet, when the new owners demolished the house and erected a large high-rise apartment building in its place, Salem's family had no legal recourse.[25] Without a special court system to protect autonomous authority and a general manager on the ground to enforce that jurisdiction, Rabatat al-Maadi had no legal means to prevent other villas from meeting the same fate. What is more, they could not prevent an influx of new residents who did not identify with the older guidelines from moving into the town or purchasing property there. Where the company had previously been able legally to enforce the *Cahier des Charges* and identified its guidelines with residents' best interests, the association had no such power and there was no guarantee that Maadi's careful planning would mean anything to new residents.[26]

Because Rabatat al-Maadi could not prevent alterations to Maadi's built environment, it looked instead to create a shared civic consciousness by emphasizing each resident's personal obligation to the town. The guide included a list of residents' duties. In Arabic, the association titled the list, "*Man huwa al-muwatin al-salih fi al-Maadi*" (Who is the Upright Citizen of Maadi?), making the obligations of Maadi's Arabic-speaking population a civic responsibility. In English, the guide simplified the list into a series of "'Do's' and 'Don'ts' for Maadites." Both versions outlined the same rules for residents, focusing on preserving a quiet, peaceful, and clean atmosphere. *The Maadi Guide* stipulated that residents not drive around with a loud radio or honk their horns. They should also be careful to ensure that when guests left their homes, they departed quietly. Other rules included picking up litter and a ban on air guns, which boys used to shoot at birds.[27] In contrast to the Arabic rules, the guide's English version implied a more transitory existence, stating each rule as a polite but emphatic request. It made statements like, "Please DON'T damage any trees, flowers or any growing things" and "Please DO always observe the rules laid down for traffic."[28]

These requests were indicative of the changing face of Maadi's expatriate population. Where British and French residents had previously taken up long-term residence in the town, Maadi's new Americans generally resided in the town for three- or four-year stints and then either returned home or took a new international post. These rules gave a system of guidelines for itinerant expatriates without implying that they had to attach a sense of civic pride and obligation to the place. By emphasizing a sense of citizenship for the guide's Arabic readers, the association gave Egyptian residents the leading responsibility over Maadi's maintenance. This echoed the association's founding goal to develop "a spirit of cooperation among all Maadi residents."[29] Without Delta Land's authority and the legally binding *Cahier des Charges*, the association had to appeal to a more elevated sense of shared responsibility. In doing so, it hoped also to gain the support of new arrivals and existing residents.

Ultimately, the rules laid out in *The Maadi Guide*, like the design guidelines the association previously attempted to put in place, could not take hold in any permanent way. In turn, Rabatat al-Maadi faltered in its attempts to assert itself as a civic authority over Maadi. The association would dissolve in 1964 and its members would turn to more environmentally focused tactics for Maadi's preservation and conservation.[30] The association's disintegration would occur two years after Delta Land came to its final end.

While Rabatat al-Maadi attempted to establish a sense of continuity, its members soon found that Delta Land's older control, with its basis in the Capitulations and Mixed Courts, could not be replaced. After 1956, the company's power, like that of other companies and wealthy capitalists, further diminished. The nationalization of the Suez Canal Company established a new pattern for the Egyptian government's treatment of foreign-registered companies and their stakeholders. In the late 1950s, Nasser began nationalizing the other foreign companies that concentrated their affairs in Egypt. In July 1961, one headline in *al-Ahram* read, "New Procedures on the Road to Socialism," and reported that 399 companies had been added to the public sector.[31] The process of nationalization had a direct impact on some of Maadi's most prominent residents. The 'Abbud family saw the loss of much of their vast wealth. Madame 'Abbud had been instrumental in the Red Crescent Society's work to aid Maadi's villagers after the 1945 flood. Her husband Ahmad 'Abbud was among the country's wealthiest industrialists. In 1961, the family lost more than a $100 million in assets to the process of nationalization. They subsequently relocated to Switzerland, where, despite his significant setbacks in Egypt, Ahmad died in December 1963 as one of the ten richest men in the world.[32]

Delta Land joined the Egyptian government's roster of nationalized companies in 1962. Thus, what little remained of Maadi's garden city company ceased to exist.[33] The villas and gardens in Maadi remained as visible evidence of the town's earlier elite cosmopolitanism. But those spaces relied on regional and global networks of capital and culture that were now seen as antithetical to Egypt's progress. Without the economic and political protections of the past, Maadi appeared out of place, if not backward, in the new Egypt that emerged under Nasser. While residents attempted to preserve the town's culture, society, and unique built environment, their efforts proved insufficient. The Nasser regime explicitly opposed the kind of multinational culture that once thrived in Maadi, especially because of the foreign capital that supported it. By 1962, Maadi's former economic and political basis was fully abolished. Its earlier cosmopolitanism—with its emphasis on social hierarchies and affinity for

European tastes and habits—likewise appeared antiquated. Sustaining any of Maadi's remaining green spaces would require a different form of international support.

After the dissolution of Rabatat al-Maadi, one of its early leaders, Mustafa Moyine al-'Arab, and his wife Safeyyah (née Grace Weigall) reorganized the area's committed residents around a different set of values. They formed the Tree Lovers Association in 1973 and focused on the conservation of Maadi's trees, gardens, and villas, moving away from the association's emphasis on civic consciousness and garden city life.[34] Like so many Maadi residents before her, Safeyyah had a global upbringing. A British citizen, she spent the majority of her childhood in Brazil, where her father was the manager of the Bank of London and South America. She met Mustafa in London in 1937, after her aunt and sister became acquainted with the diplomat in Switzerland when he represented Egypt at the Montreux Convention.[35] After marrying in London, they returned to Egypt and moved to Maadi in 1947. Grace, now an Egyptian citizen, proceeded to change her name to Safeyyah, indicative of her identification with the Egyptian nation.[36] Together, the couple organized for Maadi's preservation through trash collection days, garden tours, and lectures on Maadi's horticulture, drawing on the rhetoric of the international environmentalist movement for Maadi's conservation.

In her 1991 memoir, Saffeyah used her early memories of Maadi to shore up support for its environmental preservation. Emphasizing the importance of living in harmony with the natural world, Saffeyah referenced the words of her contemporary Vivi Laurent-Täckholm, a botanist at Cairo University, writing, "If you know the name of a tree then it becomes your friend and then you care for and defend it."[37] Saffeyah hoped to use her past experiences as instructive tools, making older elements of Maadi's built and natural environment more meaningful to her late-twentieth-century readers. In one passage, she recalled returning to Maadi after a morning walk in the hills of Muqattam, writing, "Descending from the high desert ground into the green oasis, one was overwhelmed by the richness and diversity of trees. It was a dream land where cypress trees united with the sand and graceful eucalyptus trees swept the ground with their elegant branches."[38] In other parts of the memoir, she described in detail the orange and lemon blossoms, wisteria, beaumontia, grandiflora, honeysuckle, and jasmine that bloomed in residents' gardens and perfumed the town's air. She additionally praised Delta Land's work in Maadi's public spaces, having planted jacaranda trees and poinciana along the streets near the Maadi Sporting Club, and filled the park space of each midan with grass, palms, and a variety of other trees. Eucalyptus ran along the canal, which irrigated Maadi's gardens with silt-rich water from the Nile. Her account conjured up the image of a veritable paradise.[39]

The environmentalist initiative to preserve Maadi's garden city establishment never explicitly acknowledged the wealth on which the place relied. For those involved, the construction of high-rise buildings, destruction of villas, growth of heavy traffic, and the noise that came with it all betrayed the real Maadi. Certainly, these changes made the carefully controlled Maadi that long-term residents knew a thing of the past. Yet, these conservationists' silence also spoke to the overlooked social inequalities that made Maadi possible and later excluded it from the social radicalism of the Nasser regime. When reflecting on her life in Maadi during the 1940s and 1950s, Salem, who also became an ardent environmental defender of Maadi, acknowledged that growing up outside of Cairo isolated her from the urgency of national issues that she might have confronted nearer downtown.[40] The town's residents' physical removal from downtown often made the political and economic changes carried out after 1957 seem more alarming than hopeful. As residents confronted the democratization of space, and more lower-income people moved into and through Maadi, it became apparent how distinct the town stood from what Egypt was becoming. For the Egyptian majority, Maadi—despite its niceties—stood apart from the national whole.

To those who left Egypt, Maadi took on a different set of complex meanings. For Josipovici, the place had an illusory quality. He was not homesick for it, nor did he feel a sense of nostalgia for the childhood he spent there. He explained that after leaving Maadi, "it all felt unreal." Ever feeling himself a foreigner in Egypt, he described being continually cut off from the majority of Egypt's population, which made Maadi appear artificial and incomprehensible after his departure.[41] By the time Josipovici left Maadi in 1956, it was no longer the place where he and his mother had taken refuge after the Second World War. Josipovici saw his former home as part of a distant and unreclaimable past.

While Maadi's past appeared chimerical to some, for others the closure of its earlier world entrenched a deep sense of belonging. In recalling Maadi as her "bigger home," Maggie Safwat emphasized the personal significance that the place carried for her throughout her life.[42] Safwat could maintain this attachment to Maadi's older existence in part because while Nasser's rhetoric spoke to uprooting older social hierarchies and creating a new Egypt, the nation did not become the socially harmonious utopia he promised. Instead, other forms of inequality and corruption replaced the older social exclusivities and economic injustices. The Maadi that residents knew as children came to represent a more open society, a less secretive state, and a cosmopolitan existence that appeared almost impossible after 1962.

The real meaning of Maadi's past lies in the complex and interconnected human stories that informed the creation of its streets, the construction of its villas, and the planting of its gardens over the course of the first half of the twentieth century. Geographer Yi-Fu Tuan argues that a place becomes meaningful through the human experiences that make memories out of its various parts.[43] Understanding Maadi, then, requires sifting through the various experiences that unfolded at each stage of its development. For its founders, the benefits they mutually gleaned from the Capitulations and Mixed Courts set the groundwork for retired colonial civil servants and leading Egyptian Jewish bankers to join forces on this land development project south of Cairo. Delta Land, the company they founded, likewise relied on these institutions to set up the construction of Maadi according to a strict set of rules that all residents were subject to, regardless of their nationality, ethnicity, or confession. Through Maadi, the Capitulations and Mixed Courts became local institutions that shaped the city and the very meaning of modern Egypt to many. Egyptian nationalists, especially those focused on economic issues, saw Maadi as a model for the kind of international collaboration that might sustain Egyptian economic strength into an independent future. The events of the Second World War, however, made that vision untenable. Regional identities hardened along new fault lines after 1945 and especially after 1948. Where an earlier generation envisioned ongoing cooperation, popular demands for more radical change prevailed. After the revolutionary changes that began in 1952, Maadi garden city could not be maintained, despite residents' efforts.

The trees and villas that remain in Maadi have become the most lasting evidence of its former existence. The remnants of its aesthetic qualities point to a society and culture that lost its place of influence in the country.

The villas, now largely dilapidated, once required a great deal of wealth and labor to support. The gardens had to be tended. Ultimately, the social divisions that made Maadi possible also proved to be the community's weakness. Without a meaningful vision for cross-class participation, Maadi's once thriving life—with all of its ability to appeal to British imperialists, Ottoman notables, European expatriates, and Egyptian nationalists— would dissolve under the pressure of subsequent waves of mass migration that transformed not only Maadi but also the rest of the Egyptian capital. What Maadi had been could never be recreated for the Egyptian majority.

POSTSCRIPT

Short captions scribbled on the back of early photos of Maadi capture snippets of the town's former social life and the deep attachment residents formed to their homes. On the back of one photo, Edeltraut Schuler (née Wolff) wrote, "View of the Schuler house from the Wolff house."[1] While their German surnames might appear to indicate a shared European upbringing, Edeltraut and her Swiss husband Eduard (known as "Eddie") met across Maadi's Road 16 from one another. Her parents, Hermann and Hede Wolff, moved to Cairo early in the twentieth century as dentists and founded the Egyptian Odontological Society. Hede offered dental treatment to women in the khedival court, as well as to other elite households, including that of Huda Sha'rawi, the founder of the Egyptian Feminist Union—a connection that exposes how resident foreigners became enmeshed in the world of *effendiya* revolutionaries.[2] The pair of palatial villas feature the aesthetic hallmarks outlined in the *Cahier des Charges*. The Schuler villa, with its stucco exterior and tiled roof, is surrounded by a short and neatly trimmed hedge. The Wolff house sits back from the road, with a large lawn complete with a small pond. On the back of the photo, Edeltraut wrote, "My beloved home in Maadi, where I grew up."[3]

Other photos from the 1930s and 1940s show weddings, garden parties, and sporting events. One member of the Dale family took to painting some of the family's photos of Maadi's tree-lined streets to lend color to the black and white images. In these pictures, the bright reds and pinks of poincianas and Japanese mariposas come to life. Their vibrant hues stand in pleasant contrast to the soothing periwinkle blue of the nearby jacarandas. In one image, a resident rides a bicycle down a wide, unobstructed street, while others walk in the background. In the foreground, a woman in a bright blue dress stands holding a basket or tray. These colorized photos—like the snippet captions accompanying other Maadi images—capture pieces of the social and cultural life that made Maadi garden city possible.

The dilapidation that has unfolded since the 1960s and 1970s likewise tells the story of how Maadi profoundly changed over time. In some cases, Maadi's villas and gardens have been repurposed. In others, the homes have been torn down. And while some villas have been protected, many that remain have fallen into severe disrepair due to neglect. A 2011 picture of the villa on the corner of Roads 82 and 13 captures the deterioration that followed Maadi's nationalization and subsequent absorption into the rapid sprawl of greater Cairo. In the background, one can faintly see the rounded dome of the Meyer Y. Biton Synagogue, a site that lies empty most of the year and is protected by an armed Egyptian police guard.

The image exposes how features once erected in adherence to the *Cahier des Charges* have declined. The house stands at two stories, in line with Delta Land's stipulation that it could not exceed fifteen meters in height. All of the windows on the second story, however, are broken, leaving the house's interior exposed to the elements. One would have entered the property through a wrought-iron gate that remains in place. In line with the company's stipulations, the house lacks a boundary wall, and where a makeshift wire and grass fence has been erected there would have once been a waist-high hedge like the one surrounding the Schuler villa. Within the makeshift fence, the yard shows some of the most obvious signs of neglect. The land has little remaining greenery. Instead, the villa is surrounded by dirt and dust. It is littered with dead foliage and all manner of trash, including plastic wrappers, paper bags from fast food restaurants, and large pieces of styrofoam. Additional images of the yard give a more extensive picture, exposing not only rubbish, but also an overturned bathtub sitting haphazardly in the middle of the grounds. Seeming particularly out of place, prickly pear cacti, a desert plant native to sub-Saharan Africa and western North America, grow along the edge of the grounds—elements that generations earlier might have been exotic additions to the garden of a wealthy resident.[4] Behind the layers of litter, the depleted grounds, and the shattered upper-story windows is the banal observation that the house—whatever its former qualities—is now uninhabitable. While not all of Maadi underwent the kind of deterioration exemplified by this villa on

Road 82, its vacancy stands as physical evidence of how the social and cultural life that Maadi once relied on has largely emptied out of the place.

At the heart of Maadi's decline is a transformation of authority in Egypt. Maadi survived the turmoil of the First World War and the events of the 1919 revolution largely unscathed. In fact, Maadi thrived in the years following the 1923 constitution and the *effendiya's* rise to power. Those years between the wars, however, were characterized as much by continuity as by change. The British colonial order of the late nineteenth and early twentieth centuries increasingly fell away. What remained were older Ottoman systems—the khedivate (renamed a monarchy), the Capitulations, and the Mixed Courts. These residues preserved foreign domicile and economic privilege in Egypt. Likewise, the social and cultural tastes of resident foreigners from the Levant, Europe, and the United States influenced the meaning of Egyptian independence and national identity during this liberal era between the wars. When those Ottoman systems disintegrated after the Second World War—not with the flash of revolution, but with the more listless impact of international treaty fulfillment—this paved the way for the end of Maadi's former existence.

Some envisioned the continuation of Maadi despite the end of the Capitulations and Mixed Courts. Yet, the events of the Second World War and the Arab–Israeli War transformed national and regional identities, heightening the significance of race, ethnicity, and religion in ways that made Maadi's former elite cosmopolitanism appear outdated and backward. Even more significant, Maadi could not sustain the waves of migration that would see the population of Cairo swell from the mid-twentieth century onward. Changing demographics paired with a national identity rooted in Pan-Arabism and socialism set the context for Maadi's decline. In this new social and economic climate, Maadi garden city became unsustainable. European and Jewish residents largely departed. Maadi continues to bear the scars of their emigration. In this way, photos of Maadi—historical and contemporary—tell the same story. These former residents were once locals in Egypt and Maadi continues to bear their fingerprints.

NOTES

Introduction

1 André Raymond, *Cairo: City of History* (Cairo: American University in Cairo Press, 2007), 20.

2 Otto F.A. Meinardus, *The Historic Coptic Churches of Cairo* (Cairo: Philopatron, 1994), 82–83; Otto F.A. Meinardus, "The Church and Monastery of the Virgin Mary," Brochure, Binder 8, SRCARMPC.

3 Raymond, *Cairo*, 302; Michael Reimer, "Urban Government and Administration in Egypt, 1805–1914," *Die Welt des Islams* 39, no. 3 (1999): 289–318.

4 Raymond, *Cairo*, 308–309.

5 Raymond, *Cairo*, 312–318; Nezar AlSayyad, *Cairo: Histories of a City* (Cambridge, MA: Harvard University Press, 2011), 222–223.

6 Janet Abu-Lughod describes Maadi as the only true suburb of Cairo. Janet L. Abu-Lughod, *Cairo: 1001 Years of the City Victorious* (Princeton, NJ: Princeton University Press, 1971), 201.

7 Raymond, *Cairo*, 307.

8 Maurits H. van den Boogert, *Capitulations and the Ottoman Legal System: Qadis, Consuls and Beraths in the 18th Century* (Leiden: Brill, 2005), 7.

9 Nathan J. Brown, "The Precarious Life and Slow Death of the Mixed Courts of Egypt," *International Journal of Middle East Studies* 25, no. 1 (1993): 33–52.

10 Sir Richard Vaux, "Egyptian and Other Episodes: Personal, Political, and Legal," unpublished memoir (1941), GB165-0293, MECA.

11 Evelyn Baring, Earl of Cromer, *Modern Egypt*, vols. 1–2 (New York: Mac-Millan & Co., 1916), 125.

12 Bent Hansen, "Interest Rates and Foreign Capital in Egypt under British Occupation," *Journal of Economic History* 43, no. 4 (1983): 877.

13 Robert Tignor uses "foreign-resident bourgeoisie" to describe people who were foreign nationals but identified their economic interests with Egypt. Similarly, Marius Deeb uses "local foreign minorities" to describe people who did not necessarily assimilate into local society but "can be regarded as a major agent of change affecting the internal development of Egypt's social and economic history." Gudrun Krämer also uses "local foreign minority" in her extensive study of modern Egypt's Jews. See Robert Tignor, *State, Private Enterprise, and Economic Change in Egypt, 1918–1952* (Princeton, NJ: Princeton University Press, 1984), 3–5; Marius Deeb, "The Socioeconomic Role of Local Foreign Minorities in Modern Egypt, 1805–1961," *International Journal of Middle East Studies* 9, no. 1 (1978): 11; Gudrun Krämer, *The Jews of Modern Egypt, 1914–1952* (Seattle, WA: University of Washington Press, 1989), 31.

14 "Sharikat al-Delta," *al-Ahram*, January 9, 1904.

15 "Memorandum of Association of the Egyptian Delta Land & Investment Company, Limited," BT 31/43735, BNA.

16 No. 127, "Memorandum from Sir A. Colvin on state of affairs in Egypt," December 26, 1881, FO 407/19, BNA.

17 Joel Beinin, *The Dispersion of Egyptian Jewry: Culture, Politics, and the For-mation of a Modern Diaspora* (Berkeley, CA: University of California Press, 1998), 38.

18 Krämer, *The Jews of Modern Egypt*, 31–32.

19 Delta Land registered lists of the company's board members and man-agers, which included the nationality of each member, with the British Board of Trade from the company's founding in 1904 until 1955. "Mem-orandum," BT 31/43735; "Baron Jacques de Menasce and Baron Charles de Mensace," FO 141/655/6.

20 "'Ilan," *Al-Muqattam*, December 22, 1904.

21 "Memorandum," BT 31/43735.

22 "Meadi," in *Egypt Today, Published in the Interests of Egyptian Finance, Indus-try and Commerce, 1937–38*, 2nd ed. (London: Bemrose & Sons), 171, SRCARMPC.

23 Ebenezer Howard, *Garden Cities of To-morrow*, edited by F.J. Osborn (Cam-bridge, MA: Massachusetts Institute of Technology Press, 1965 [1902]).

24 Howard, *Garden Cities*, 48. Emphasis in original.

25 Howard's utopian vision drew from a variety of antecedents, including Thomas More's *Utopia*, Quaker spiritualism, Fabian socialism, and late

Victorian science fiction. He was particularly inspired by Edward Bellamy's *Looking Backward, 2000–1887*, published in 1888, which promoted similar ideals of basic human decency and progress through modern technology. Peter Batchelor, "The Origins of the Garden City Concept for Urban Reform," *Journal of the Society of Architectural Historians* 28, no. 3 (1969): 184–200.

26 Howard, *Garden Cities*, 61.

27 Dugald MacFadyen, *Sir Ebenezer Howard and the Town Planning Movement* (Manchester: Manchester University Press, 1970), 40.

28 Howard, *Garden Cities*, 92.

29 Howard, *Garden Cities*, 51.

30 Howard appealed to would-be residents' self-interest in articulating his plan. He argued that farmers, for instance, would benefit from the built-in, local market for their goods, which would be sold with little to no cost for transportation. Howard, *Garden Cities*, 50.

31 Howard, *Garden Cities*, 57.

32 Standish Meacham explains that while Howard's principles inspired the creation of many new townS and suburbs in the early-twentieth century, only Letchworth actually adhered to the whole of Howard's plan. Logistically, it was easier to build garden suburbs that were organized more like a company town than the cooperative environment Howard envisioned. Meacham, *Regaining Paradise: Englishness and the Early Garden City Movement* (New Haven and London: Yale University Press, 1999), 60.

33 Ken Tadashi Oshima, "Denenchōfu: Building the Garden City in Japan," *Journal of the Society of Architectural Historians* 55, no. 2 (1996): 140–151.

34 Alexandria became the first municipality in Egypt in 1890, inspiring similar local administrations throughout Egypt. Cairo did not become a municipality, however, until 1949, having only the Tanzim until then. See Reimer, "Urban Government."

35 William J. Hausman, *Global Electrification: Multinational Enterprise and International Finance in the History of Light and Power, 1878–2007* (Cambridge: Cambridge University Press, 2008), 103–104; Robert Ilbert, *Héliopolis, le Caire 1905–1922: Genèse d'une ville* (Marseille: Centre National de la Recherche Scientifique, 1981).

36 Samir W. Raafat, "Garden City: A Retrospective," parts I–III, Egy.com, http://www.egy.com/gardencity/98-08-06.php (accessed April 20, 2020).

37   On the architecture of Heliopolis, see, Agnieszka Dobrowolska and Jaroslaw Dobrowolski, *Heliopolis: Rebirth of the City of the Sun* (Cairo: American University in Cairo Press, 2006).

38   Robert Ilbert, "Heliopolis: Colonial Enterprise and Town Planning Success?" in *Coping with the Urban Growth of Cairo*, edited by Ahmet Evin (Singapore: Concept Media and Aga Khan Award for Architecture, 1985).

39   Joel Beinin and Zachary Lockman, *Workers on the Nile: Nationalism, Communism, Islam, and the Egyptian Working Class, 1882–1954* (Princeton, NJ: Princeton University Press, 1989), 60.

40   "Midan Simon Bolivar and South (Garden City)," Keeping Cairo (I'atni Balqahira), http://www.keepingcairo.org/items/show/186 (accessed June 11, 2012).

41   Ilbert, "Heliopolis," 37.

Chapter 1

1   Geographer Yi-Fu Tuan argues that a place becomes meaningful through the human experiences that make memories out of the different facets of the built environment, turning an unknown space into a known and significant place. Yi-Fu Tuan, *Space and Place: The Perspective of Experience* (Minneapolis, MN: University of Minneapolis Press, 1977), 10.

2   John Darwin describes the British empire as a complex and multifaceted "world-system" that looked to gain influence more than formal control. He presents Egypt as a central part of this nuanced arrangement, explaining that the British did not identify the country as a sovereign state but as a semiautonomous part of the Ottoman empire. As such, occupying Egypt with an aim to maintain its economic and political stability had the strategic value of not only securing passage to the Indian Ocean, but also of preventing another foreign power from taking its place of influence with the Ottoman sultanate. John Darwin, *The Empire Project: The Rise and Fall of the British World-System, 1830–1970* (Cambridge and New York: Cambridge University Press, 2009), 70–71.

3   André Raymond, *Cairo: City of History (Cairo: American University in Cairo Press, 2007)*, 317.

4   Juan R.I. Cole, *Colonialism and Revolution in the Middle East: Social and Cultural Origins of Egypt's 'Urabi Movement* (Cairo: American University in Cairo Press, 1999), 44.

5   Sir Auckland Colvin, KCSI, KCMG, CIE, *John Russell Colvin: The Last Lieutenant Governor of the Northwest Company* (Oxford: Clarendon Press, 1895), 15.

6   1901 England Census, Suffolk (East), Plomesgate, Earl Soham, col. 1, line 96, The Lodge, Auckland Colvin; database online, Ancestry.com, https://www.ancestry.com/ (accessed June 15, 2020).

7   Cole argues that "the forward party among the British hoped to replicate in Egypt the colonial enterprise accomplished in India." Cole, *Colonialism*, 47.

v8 Historians of Egypt argue that the Dual Control was evidence of European imperial coordination, rather than rivalry. Arguing against Ronald Robinson and John Gallagher's claim that European powers undertook a competitive 'scramble for Africa,' AbdelAziz EzzelArab argues that the British and French coordinated their policies to undermine the power of Sharif Pasha's cabinet in the late 1870s. AbdelAziz EzzelArab, "The Experiment of Sharif Pasha's Cabinet (1879): An Inquiry into the Historiography of Egypt's Elite Movement," *International Journal of Middle East Studies* 36, no. 4 (2004): 583–584.

9   In framing this East/West binary, Colvin took what Edward Said described as a thoroughly "Orientalist" approach, portraying both Egypt and India as thoroughly engrained in an "Eastern" mindset, which by nature of its geography was inferior to his own. Edward W. Said, *Orientalism* (New York: Vintage Books, 1994).

10 Colvin, *John Russell Colvin*, 44–45.

11 Cole's description of these revolutionary impulses emphasizes the role of the junior army officers. Cole, *Colonialism*, 234.

12 Cole, *Colonialism*, 235.

13 No. 127, "Memorandum from Sir A. Colvin," January 23, 1882, FO 407/19.

14 Sir Auckland Colvin, KCSI, KCMG, CIE, *The Making of Modern Egypt*, 4th ed. (London: Seeley & Co., 1906), 273–274.

15 *Dictionary of National Biography*, 67–68, photocopy, SRCARMPC.

16 "Death of Sir E. Palmer, Prominent Local Financier, Sketch of Successful Career," *Egyptian Gazette*, January 29, 1906.

17 Bent Hansen, "Interest Rates and Foreign Capital in Egypt under British Occupation," *Journal of Economic History* 43, no. 4 (1983): 877.

18 Cain and Hopkins identify Colvin with the spread of gentlemanly capitalism into Egypt because his argument for the British invasion looked

to support the financial investments largely centered in London. I would argue that the gentlemanly capitalism Cain and Hopkins describe only functions as one facet of the larger interests and negotiations tied up in empire and global relationships more broadly. Neither Palmer nor Colvin consistently represented the imperial priorities Cain and Hopkins describe as at the heart of British imperialism. Their compromises and subsequent involvement in local and regional networks of commerce and trade point to a much more complex geographical relationship than one created by the extended arm of the British empire. P.J. Cain and A.G. Hopkins, *British Imperialism, 1688–2000*, 2nd ed. (Harlow: Longman, Pearson Education, 2002), 314–315.

19 "Company No.: 58147; Daira Sanieh Company Ltd. Incorporated in 1898. Dissolved before 1916," BT 31/8066/58147, BNA; "Death of Sir E. Palmer," *Egyptian Gazette*, Jan. 30, 1906.

20 "Death of Sir E. Palmer," *Egyptian Gazette*, Jan. 30, 1906; Box 5, Folder 2, SCP.

21 The board also included Philippe Borelli Bey, F. Duseigner, William Willcocks, and 'Ali Sha'rawi Bey, whose wife Huda Sha'rawi went on to found the Egyptian feminist movement. Samir Raafat, "Familiar Ground: The 19th Century Privatization of Daira Sanieh," *Business Monthly Magazine*, July 1997, http://www.egy.com/historica/97-07-00.php (acessed January 26, 2012); Huda Shaarawi, *Harem Years: The Memoirs of an Egyptian Feminist, 1879–1924*, translated by Margot Badran (New York: Feminist Press of City University of New York, 1987).

22 A.B. de Guerville, *New Egypt* (London: William Heinemann, 1906), 54.

23 "Death of Sir E. Palmer," *Egyptian Gazette*, Jan. 30, 1906.

24 Autobiographical Notes, vol. 1, 38, quoted in Archie Hunter, *Power and Passion in Egypt: A Life of Sir Eldon Gorst, 1861–1911* (New York: I.B. Tauris, 2007), 43.

25 "Dossier Genl No. 14 of 1906, H.B.M. Consular Court–Cairo, In Probate: Estate No. 4 of 1906, Sir Elwin Palmer, KCB, KCMG," FO 841/87, BNA.

26 Stephenjh, "Elwin Palmer's Headstone, Freshwater, Isle of Wight, UK," July 21, 2010, http://en.wikipedia.org/wiki/File:Elwin_Palmer%27s_Headstone_.jpg (accessed January 12, 2012).

27 Colvin, *The Making of Modern Egypt*, 241.

28 De Guerville, *New Egypt*, 57.

29   De Guerville, *New Egypt*.

30   De Guerville, *New Egypt*, 52.

31   Robert Vitalis, *When Capitalists Collide: Business Conflicts and the End of Empire in Egypt* (Berkeley, CA: University of California Press, 1995), 37.

32   Gudrun Krämer, *The Jews of Modern Egypt, 1914–1952 (Seattle, WA: University of Washington Press, 1989)*, 95.

33   On the ongoing economic significance of the Suarès business group, see, Vitalis, *When Capitalists Collide*, 34–39.

34   Vitalis, *When Capitalists Collide*, 14–15.

35   Vitalis, *When Capitalists Collide*, 13.

36   Vitalis, *When Capitalists Collide*, 39.

37   Michael Laskier, "Cattaoui Family," in *Encyclopedia of Jews in the Islamic World*, edited by Norman A. Stillman (Leiden: Brill, 2012), http://brillonline.nl/subscriber/entry?entry=ejiw_SIM-0005120 (accessed January 24, 2012).

38   Laskier, "Cattaoui Family."

39   Krämer, *The Jews of Modern Egypt*, 88.

40   Krämer, *The Jews of Modern Egypt*, 31.

41   Hansen, "Interest Rates," 877.

42   Uri M. Kupferschmidt, "Suarès della Pegna Family," in *Encyclopedia of Jews in the Islamic World*, edited by Norman A. Stillman (Leiden: Brill, 2012), http://referenceworks.brillonline.com/entries/encyclopedia-of-jews-in-the-islamic-world/suares-della-pegna-family-SIM_0020610 (accessed January 23, 2012).

43   Krämer, *The Jews of Modern Egypt*, 36. This allegiance was not necessarily felt by all members of the Mosseri family. Travel records from 1910 indicate a multiplicity of nationalities within the family. When brothers Victor and Maurice Mosseri were traveling to New York, Jack presented a French passport while Maurice traveled as an Italian citizen. Both men were born in Egypt. "New York Passenger Lists, 1820–1957," 1910, Microfilm Serial T715, Microfilm Roll T715_1488, line 27, p. 14, database online, Ancestry.com, https://www.ancestry.com (accessed Feburary 25, 2011).

44   Krämer, *The Jews of Modern Egypt*, 42.

45   "Baron Jacques de Menasce and Baron Charles de Mensace," FO 141/655/6, gives detailed histories of the varied postwar trajectories of members of the Menasce family. The British attempted to grant Jaques de

Menasce and his wife British citizenship. At least one member of the family gained Italian nationality, and another Portuguese. Krämer describes them as becoming stateless. Krämer, *The Jews of Modern Egypt*, 75.

46 "Baron Jacques de Menasce," FO 141/655/6.

47 Adam Guerin, "Rolo Family," in *Encyclopedia of Jews in the Islamic World*, edited by Norman A. Stillman (Leiden: Brill, 2012), http://brillonline.nl/subscriber/entry?entry=ejiw_SIM-0018510 (accessed January 23, 2012).

48 This was not a particularly Jewish behavior. Marius Deeb associates these patterns with people he calls "local foreign minorities," and explains that Greeks, Armenians, and Italians who remained in Egypt for generations exhibited many of the same actions. Marius Deeb, "The Socioeconomic Role of Local Foreign Minorities in Modern Egypt, 1805–1961," *International Journal of Middle East Studies* 9, no. 1 (1978): 11.

49 "Abridged Prospectus . . . The Egyptian Delta Light Railways, Ltd.," *The Economist* 55, April 3, 1897.

50 "Abridged Prospectus."

51 Vitalis refers to these networks for local businessmen as "groups." Vitalis, *When Capitalists Collide*, 7.

52 Krämer, *The Jews of Modern Egypt*, 41.

53 Naguib Mahfouz, *Palace Walk* (New York: Random House, 1990), 17.

54 Krämer, *The Jews of Modern Egypt*, 39.

55 FO 141/480; "Abridged Prospectus," 522.

56 Colvin, *The Making of Modern Egypt*, 284.

57 "Daira Sanieh 4 per Cent, Bonds of 1890, Notice by the Controllers," *The Economist* 62, pt. 2, September 3, 1904.

58 Colvin, *The Making of Modern Egypt*, 284.

59 Krämer, *The Jews of Modern Egypt*, 41.

60 Vitalis, *When Capitalists Collide*, 33.

Chapter 2

1 Alithea Lockie (née Williamson), personal communication, November 25, 2011.

2 "Dossier Genl No. 14 of 1906, H.B.M. Consular Court–Cairo, In Probate: Estate No. 4 of 1906, Sir Elwin Palmer, KCB, KCMG," FO 841/87, BNA.

3 Marius Deeb describes Levantines as locally embedded beneficiaries of the Capitulations in the eastern Mediterranean who remained "local

foreign minorities." Marius Deeb, "The Socioeconomic Role of Local Foreign Minorities in Modern Egypt, 1805–1961," *International Journal of Middle East Studies 9, no. 1 (1978): 11.*

4   "Mr. John Williamson: A Pioneer in Cyprus and Maadi," *Egyptian Gazette*, March 29, 1932.

5   Levantine Heritage Foundation, "Descendants of Williamson and Pengelley Families of Izmir Tree," http://www.levantineheritage.com/wftree.htm (accessed April 20, 2020).

6   Alithea Lockie (née Williamson), personal communication, November 25, 2011.

7   "The Alexandria Barkers (Short) Tree" and "Introduction" to unpublished family history, papers of Henry Michael Barker, EUL MS 238, Archives and Rare Books, University of Exeter.

8   For more on the extent of these Levantine connections, see, Levantine Heritage Foundation, http://www.levantineheritage.com (accessed April 20, 2020).

9   The close-knit bonds within the Levantine community formed a 'third culture' in which they all could belong. Sociologists and anthropologists have described the children of diplomats, missionaries, and business-people who grow up abroad as existing between cultures at home and abroad, labeling them 'third culture kids.' The term 'third culture' was first coined by John and Ruth Useem while studying Americans domiciled in India. They went on to study expatriate communities in Asia, the Middle East, Europe, Africa, and the United States. See, Ruth H. Useem and Richard D. Downie, "Third Culture Kids," *Today's Education* 65, no. 3 (1976): 103–105; Warna D. Gillies, "Children on the Move: Third Culture Kids," *Childhood Education* 75, no. 1 (1998): 36–38.

10   Faruk Tabak, "Imperial Rivalry and Port-Cities: A View from the Top," *Mediterranean Historical Review* 24, no. 2 (2009): 79–81.

11   Rees went on to marry Ethelreda Barker. Levantine Heritage Foundation, "Barker Family Photo Archive Selection," http://www.levantineheritage.com/barker.htm (accessed January 4, 2012).

12   Thomas Kiely argues that Williamson's involvement in the artifact trade shows the thin line between exploitation and preservation. Thomas Kiely, "Poachers Turned Gatekeepers: The British Museum Archaeological Agents on Cyprus in the 1890s" (presentation, *The Tombs of Enkomi (British Museum Excavations)*, Nicosia, Cyprus, December 11, 2010).

13 Marc Aymes, "The Port-City in the Fields: Investigating an Improper Urbanity in Mid-Nineteenth-Century Cyprus," *Mediterranean Historical Review* 24, no. 2 (2009): 133–149.

14 Williamson continued working with Rees. Both served on the board of the Wardan Company, where Williamson was chairman until 1916, when the company was liquidated. "The Wardan Company," *Egyptian Gazette*, January 18, 1916; Levantine Heritage Foundation, "Descendants of Williamson."

15 G. Elliott Smith, "An Associate of Kitchener—Tribute to Mr. J.W. Williamson," *Times*, March 29, 1932.

16 Levantine Heritage Foundation, "Descendants of Williamson."

17 "Copy of the Register of Directors or Managers of the Egyptian Delta Land & Investment Co., Ltd.," March 28, 1906, BT 31/43735.

18 Alithea Lockie (née Williamson), personal communication, November 25, 2011.

19 See, Elena Frangakis-Syrett, "The Making of an Ottoman Port: The Quay of Izmir in the Nineteenth Century," *Journal of Transport History* 22, no. 1 (2001): 23–46; Maureen Jackson, "'Cosmopolitan' Smyrna: Illuminating or Obscuring Cultural Histories?" *Geographical Review* 102, no. 3 (2012): 337–349.

20 Ministry of Finance, "Movement of the Population," in *The Census of Egypt* (Cairo: National Printing Department, 1909), 28.

21 When the Suarès brothers sold the property to Delta Land, they reserved an extra two months before full control went to the company because of the impending berseem harvest. "Purchase of Land at Maadi al-Khabiri by the Delta Land Co. from Messrs. Suares Fréres & Cie," April 16, 1907, BT 31/43735 (originally in French, with notarized English translation).

22 "Purchase of Land at Maadi al-Khabiri."

23 "Purchase of Land at Maadi al-Khabiri"; Gudrun Krämer, *The Jews of Modern Egypt, 1914–1952 (Seattle, WA: University of Washington Press, 1989)*, 39.

24 "Obituary: Sir Auckland Colvin," *Sydney Morning Herald*, March 27, 1908, https://trove.nla.gov.au/newspaper/article/14953036 (accessed June 6, 2013).

25 See, Roger Owen, *Lord Cromer: Victorian Imperialist, Edwardian Proconsul* (Oxford: Oxford University Press, 2005), 61–182.

26 Adams also worked as the general manager of Delta Railways, a role further discussed in Chapter Four. "Copy of the Register of Directors or

Managers of the Egyptian Delta Land & Investment Co., Ltd.," June 4, 1907, BT 31/43735, BNA; Tom Dale Papers, GB165-0073, MECA.

27 See, Elwin Robert Anderson Seligman, *The Crisis of 1907 in the Light of History* (New York: Columbia University Press, 1908); E.R.J. Owen, "The Attitudes of British Officials to the Development of the Egyptian Economy, 1882–1922," in *Studies in the Economic History of the Middle East: From the Rise of Islam to the Present Day*, edited by M.A. Cook (Oxford: Oxford University Press, 1970), 485–500. On the impact of the San Francisco earthquake, see, Patricia Grossi and Robert Muir-Wood, *The 1906 San Francisco Earthquake and Fire: Perspectives on a Modern Super Cat* (Newark, NJ: Risk Management Solutions, 2006).

28 Owen, "The Attitudes of British Officials," 487.

29 See the transcripts of Egyptian Delta Land & Investment Company (EDLICO) Annual Shareholder and Board of Director Reports, "EDLICO Annual Shareholders and Directors Reports," SRCARMPC.

30 "Title and Deeds Maadi 1914–1940, Source: Notary Public Office— Giza," SRCARMPC.

31 Robert Ilbert, "Heliopolis: Colonial Enterprise and Town Planning Success?" in *Coping with the Urban Growth of Cairo*, edited by Ahmet Evin *(Singapore: Concept Media and Aga Khan Award for Architecture, 1985), 37.*

32 Joel Beinin and Zachary Lockman, *Workers on the Nile: Nationalism, Communism, Islam, and the Egyptian Working Class, 1882–1954 (Princeton, NJ: Princeton University Press, 1989), 60.*

33 "Egyptian Delta Land & Investment Co Ltd. v Todd (Insp.): Question of Residence of an English Company Abroad and Liability under Schedule D on Mortgage Interest and Rents," Stamps and Taxes Division: Registered Files, IR 40/2968, BNA.

34 "Memorandum of Association of the Egyptian Delta Land & Investment Company, Limited," BT 31/43735, BNA, 55.

35 "Egyptian Delta Land," IR 40/2968.

36 "List of Persons Holding Shares in the Egyptian Delta Land & Investment Co., Ltd. on the 9th of May 1904," BT 31/43736; Class RG11, Piece 51, Folio 105, p. 37, GSU Roll 1341011, *1881 England Census*, database online, Ancestry.com, https://www.ancestry.com (accessed December 10, 2019).

37 "List of Persons," BT 31/43736.

38 Elena Frangakis-Syrett, "Banking in Izmir in the Early Twentieth Century," *Mediterranean History Review* 24, no. 2 (2009): 117.

39   Frangakis-Syrett, "Banking in Izmir," 122.

40   Frangakis-Syrett, "Banking in Izmir," 126.

41   "List of Persons," BT 31/43736.

42   Alexander Kitroeff thoroughly examines the significance of Greek merchants to modernization in Egypt, with a detailed look at the Choremi,
Benachi, and Salvago families. Alexander Kitroeff, *The Greeks and the
Making of Modern Egypt* (Cairo: American University in Cairo Press,
2019).

43   Frangakis-Syrett, "Banking in Izmir," 123.

44   "List of Persons," BT 31/43736.

45   Deeb, "The Socioeconomic Role," 16.

46   In the spring of 1822—before the Greek revolt and subsequent Ottoman
massacre—between a hundred thousand and a hundred and twenty thousand Greeks lived on the island of Chios. By the end of it, only twenty
thousand remained. Those who were not killed fled or were enslaved by
the Ottomans. Davide Rodogno, *Against Massacre: Humanitarian Interventions in the Ottoman Empire, 1815–1914* (Princeton, NJ: Princeton
University Press, 2011), 67–68.

47   On the profitable networks that grew out of the Greek diaspora following
the Chios massacre, see, Gelina Harlaftis, "Mapping the Greek Maritime
Diaspora from the Early Eighteenth to the Late Twentieth Centuries,"
in *Diaspora Entrepreneurial Networks: Four Centuries of History*, edited by
Ina Baghdiantz McCabe, Gelina Harlaftis, and Ioanna Pepelasis Minoglou (Oxford: Berg Publishers, 2005), 147–172. The collection argues
that people in diaspora are at the root of the modern global economy,
and includes scholarly essays on the entrepreneurial activities of people
displaced by the Jewish, Arab, Chinese, Japanese, Indian, Maltese, Greek,
and Armenian diasporas.

48   Eustratios also helped found Ralli & Petrocochino in 1818 and Ralli
Brothers Manchester in 1827. Christopher A. Long, "Family Group Sheet:
Eustratios Stephanos (Stephanos) Ralli," http://www.christopherlong.
co.uk/gen/rallichaviaragen/fg03/fg03_263.html (accessed April 20, 2020).

49   "Passenger Lists of Vessels Arriving at New York, New York, 1820–1897,"
Records of the United States Customs Service, Record Group 36, Microfilm Serial M237, Microfilm Roll M237 393, line 38, list 985, National
Archives, Washington, DC, database online, Ancestry.com, https://www.
ancestry.com (accessed February 25, 2011).

50 The Scaramanga name was additionally immortalized by English writer Ian Fleming, when, in his final book in the James Bond series, 007 faced off with the infamous Francisco Scaramanga, aka "The Man with the Golden Gun." Consistent with Fleming's Cold War theme, however, this Scaramanga was Cuban rather than Greek. In the film adaptation of the book, Christopher Lee played Scaramanga. Ian Fleming, *The Man with the Golden Gun* (New York: Penguin Books, 1974 [1965]); *The Man with the Golden Gun*, Guy Hamilton, director (1974).

51 Gelina Harlaftis, *A History of Greek-Owned Shipping: The Making of an International Tramp Fleet, 1830 to the Present Day* (London: Routledge, 1996), 91.

52 Harlaftis, *History of Greek-Owned Shipping*, 52.

53 Stanley Chapman, *Merchant Enterprise in Britain: From the Industrial Revolution to World War I* (Cambridge: Cambridge University Press, 2004), 158–159.

54 I present pathways as both a social and spatial process, where movement helps forge social relationships, while also being shaped by the surrounding society, taking my understanding from geographer Allan Pred's work on space and structuration. See Pred, "Place as Historically Contingent Process: Structuration and the Time-Geography of Becoming Places," *Annals of the Association of American Geographers* 74:2 (1984), 279–297.

55 Christopher A. Long, "Family Group Sheet: Leonidas 'Leoni' (Pandély) Argenti," http://www.christopherlong.co.uk/gen/rallichaviaragen/fg01/fg01_120.html (accessed April 20, 2020).

56 He served in the House of Commons from 1875 to 1880. Christopher A. Long, "Family Group Sheet: Pandely (Toumazis) Ralli JP MP," http://www.christopherlong.co.uk/gen/rallichaviaragen/fg06/fg06_424.html (accessed April 20, 2020).

57 "List of Persons," BT 31/43736.

58 Leonore Davidoff and Catherine Hall, *Family Fortunes: Men and Women of the English Middle Class* (Chicago, IL: University of Chicago Press, 1987), 73.

59 "List of Persons," BT 31/43736.

60 Long, "Pandely."

61 The London Rallis were also likely connected to Leonidas Rodocanachi, an Alexandria-based merchant who purchased several thousand shares of Delta Land. "List of Persons," BT 31/43736.

62 "Egyptian Delta Land," IR 40/2968.

Chapter 3

1 This continued a long history of absentee landownership within the Ottoman empire. See, Chris Gratien, "The Ottoman Quagmire: Malaria, Swamps, and Settlement in the Late-Ottoman Mediterranean," *International Journal of Middle East Studies* 49 (2017): 583–604.

2 H.B.M. Consular Court–Cairo, "A. J. Wakeman Long and S. A. Brittain vs. The Egyptian Delta Land & Investment Co., Ltd.," Item 10, to Mr. Brittain from Mr. Louisidis, April 12, 1910, FO 841/135.

3 H.B.M. Consular Court–Cairo, "A.J. Wakeman Long and S.A. Brittain vs. The Egyptian Delta Land & Investment Co., Ltd.," FO 841/139.

4 H.B.M. Consular Court–Cairo, FO 841/139.

5 "EDLICO Annual Shareholders and Directors Reports," SRCARMPC.

6 "Title and Deeds Maadi 1914–1940, Source: Notary Public Office— Giza," SRCARMPC.

7 From the handwritten *Cahier des Charges* in 1909, to the printed copy from 1945 that had the company logo at the top, there were few changes to the specifications the document set out. *Cahier des Charges*, 1909, 1934, and 1945, SRCARMPC.

8 Letter from G. Dale to S. Raafat, June 8, 1992, Dale Family Correspondence, SRCARMPC.

9 "H.B.M. Consular Court–Cairo, Misc and Nos. 1–30, Item No. 2 of 1908, A. Adams (Egt. Delta Light Railways Ltd.) vs. Vincenzo Palmer," FO 841/96.

10 H.B.M. Consular Court–Cairo, "Suit No. 17 of 1915, A.J. Wakeman Long and S.A. Brittain, plaintiff, versus The Egyptian Delta Land & Investment Co., Ltd. and R.Q. Henriques, defendant," FO 841/135.

11 Thomas Dale's notes on Maadi are included in the letter to Andrew Holden. T. Dale, "Sidelights of Maadi, Beginnings," May 8, 1970, Tom Dale Papers, GB165-0073, MECA.

12 Adams purchased seventeen shares of Delta Land on May 19, 1904, and subsequently made two additional investments that year for a total of at least 718 shares. "List of Persons Holding Shares in the Egyptian Delta Land & Investment Co., Ltd. on the 9th of May 1904," BT 31/43736.

13 "H.B.M. Consular Court–Cairo, A. Adams (Egt. Delta Light Railways Ltd.) verse. Vincenzo Palmier," FO 841/96/105.

14 H.B.M. Consular Court–Cairo, FO 841/96/105.

15 "EDLICO Annual Shareholders and Directors Reports," SRCARMPC.

16 "EDLICO Annual Shareholders and Directors Reports."

17 Photographs Related to the Henriques Family, GB124.DPA/1068/1, Greater Manchester County Record Office, Manchester Archives; "Land Deeds and Titles, 1906–1940," SRCARMPC.

18 Other company leaders who came to Egypt via India included Ernest Lindsey Marryat and William Inglis Le Briton, member of the Public Works Department in Bombay, who resigned from Delta Land in 1907. "Copy of the Register of Directors and Managers of the Egyptian Delta Land & Investment Co., Ltd.," June 4, 1907, BT 31/43735.

19 Mordechai Arbell, *The Portuguese Jews of Jamaica* (Kingston: Canoe Press, 2000), 2.

20 For an extensive genealogy of the Henriques family, see, Martin Kurrein's Genealogy, "The Henriques Family Genealogy," http://www.kurrein. com/Henriques (accessed April 20, 2020).

21 Photographs, GB124.DPA/1068/1; Samir W. Raafat, *Maadi, 1904–1962: Society and History in a Cairo Suburb* (Cairo: Palm Press, 1994), 25–27.

22 *London Gazette*, January 4, 1898.

23 "List of Persons," BT 31/43736.

24 Reginald's estate, for instance, only had about half the value of that of his father Edward Micholls Henriques, whose investments were valued at £26,374 2s. 6p. upon his death in 1901. When Reginald died in 1916, his overall estate, including investments and property, was valued at £10,180 13s. 7p. British Consular Court, "Probate: Sir Reginald Q. Henriques," FO 841/161.

25 Photographs, GB124.DPA/1068/1.

26 "Land Deeds and Titles, 1906–1940," SRCARMPC.

27 "List of Persons," BT 31/43736; H.B.M. Consular Court–Cairo, FO 841/135.

28 "Land Deeds and Titles, 1906–1940," SRCARMPC.

29 The records for Delta Land deeds of sale show that the de Cramers purchased lots in Maadi in 1914, but newspaper records show that as of 1909 they were already in the same social circle as many other Maadi residents. It is likely that they moved to the town earlier and lived in an existing villa before building their own home. See, "Land Deeds and Titles, 1906–1940"; "Obituary: The Late Mrs. St. John Diamant," *Egyptian Gazette*, March 30, 1909.

30 Ministry of Finance, "Birthplace," table VII, in *The Census of Egypt* (Cairo: National Printing Department, 1909), 36–68.

31 Ministry of Finance, "Birthplace," table VII, in *The Census of Egypt.*

32 She was the daughter of United States Army General Samuel Comfort. Box 5, Folder 2, SCP.

33 Box 5, Folder 2, SCP.

34 Harry F.C. Crookshank went on to a successful career as a politician. He represented Gainsborough, Lincolnshire, in the House of Commons from 1924 to 1956. He also served as Austen Chamberlain's representative to the League of Nations in the 1930s, and Winston Churchill appointed him minister of health and leader of the House of Commons in 1951. He became deputy leader of the House of Lords in 1955 and accepted a peerage, being made viscount, in 1956. "Diaries, 1934–1961," Shelfmarks: MSS. Eng. hist. d. 359–61, Papers of Captain Harry Frederick Comfort Crookshank, Bodleian Library, Oxford University, United Kingdom. See also, Simon Ball, *The Guardsmen: Harold Macmillan, Three Friends, and the World They Made* (London: Harper Perennial, 2004).

35 Letter from S. Comfort to E. Crookshank, September 7, 1891, Box 4, Folder 8, SCP.

36 "Social and Personal," *Egyptian Gazette*, June 17, 1908.

37 Photographs, GB124.DPA/1068/1.

38 The company listed lot numbers for these people, but no property deed. In the case of Soliman Saad, it appears that he sold his property in Maadi to George Caruso in 1907. The increase in Egyptian residents in 1914 might partly be explained by the impact of the First World War, when the British declared Egypt a protectorate and sequestered German, Hungarian, and Turkish property. During these years, many Maadi residents became "enemy aliens" and lost their homes—a topic discussed at length in Chapter Three. "Land Deeds and Titles, 1906–1940," SRCARMPC.

39 Nadia Salem, personal interview, April 30, 2011.

40 Baedeker's 1902 guide to Egypt, for instance, purports to explain that "the Nubians are inferior to the Egyptians in industry and energy." *Egypt: Handbook for Travelers* (London: K. Beadeker, 1902), xiv.

41 Lanver Mak, "More than Officers and Officials: Britons in Occupied Egypt, 1882–1922," *Journal of Imperial and Commonwealth History* 39, no. 1 (2011): 21–46.

42 Maadi's dependence on domestic labor is a basic tenet of what James Ackerman describes in the "ideology of the villa." James S. Ackerman,

The Villa: Form and Ideology of Country Houses (Princeton, NJ: Princeton University Press, 1985), 10.

43　H.B.M. Consular Court–Cairo, FO 841/135.

44　H.B.M. Consular Court–Cairo, FO 841/135.

45　"EDLICO Annual Shareholders and Directors Reports," SRCARMPC.

46　H.B.M. Consular Court–Cairo, FO 841/139.

47　H.B.M. Consular Court–Cairo, FO 841/135.

48　Acte de Vente et d'Ouverture de Credit, Entre l'Egyptian Delta Land et Investment Company Limited Et Monsieur C. Major Spong, *Cahier des Charges* for Lots No. 200, 201, 221, 222, from May 7, 1909, SRCARMPC.

Chapter 4

1　Denis Winter, *25 April 1915: The Inevitable Tragedy* (St. Lucia: University of Queensland Press, 1994), 3–7.

2　"Australians at Meadi: A Visit to the Camps," *Egyptian Gazette*, December 15, 1914.

3　B2455 Personnel Dossiers for First Australian Imperial Force Ex-Service Members, Lexicographical series, CA 2001, Australian Imperial Force, Base Record Office, NAA.

4　James L. Gelvin, *The Modern Middle East: A History*, 4th ed. (Oxford: Oxford University Press, 2016), 189–190.

5　Amy Witherbee, *Fuad I* (2007), MasterFILE Premier (25181427). On widespread European interest in the position of the khedive, see, Donald M. McKale, "Influence without Power: The Last Khedive of Egypt and the Great Powers, 1914–1918," *Middle Eastern Studies* 33, no. 1 (1997): 20–39. On British interventions to preserve Fu'ad's royal line with the ascension of Faruq, see, Michael T. Thornhill, "Informal Empire, Independent Egypt and the Accession of King Farouk," *Journal of Imperial and Commonwealth History* 38, no. 2 (2010): 279–302.

6　B2455 Personnel Dossiers, NAA.

7　"Rena John Alfred," in B2455 Personnel Dossiers, NAA.

8　"Australians at Meadi: A Visit to the Camps," *Egyptian Gazette*, December 15, 1914.

9　"Gallipoli Casualties by Country," New Zealand History, https://nzhistory.govt.nz/media/interactive/gallipoli-casualties-country (accessed April 20, 2020).

10   A general description of Maadi and the house is included in "Recollections of Maadi," Australian War Memorial, Commonwealth Troops, SRCARMPC. A picture of the house was published in "Meadi Today," *Kia Ora Coo-Ee: The Official Magazine of the Australian and New-Zealand Forces in Egypt, Palestine, Salonica & Mesopotamia*, March 1918, http://nzetc.victoria.ac.nz/etexts/ReiKaOr/ReiKaOr029.gif (accessed April 20, 2020).

11   "Report on the Bungalow Hospital Maadi," February 22, 1916, Australian War Memorial, Canberra, Australia. Copies accessed from the SRCARMPC.

12   Michael Tyquin, "Doctors and Nurses: Gender Relations, Jealousy, and Maladministration in Wartime," *Health and History* 13, no. 1 (2011): 26–43.

13   Mario M. Ruiz, "Manly Spectacles and Imperial Soldiers in Wartime Egypt, 1914–19," *Middle Eastern Studies* 45, no. 3 (2009): 351–371.

14   "Routine Orders," by Lieutenant HCG Weston, OC, 7th Light Horse Details, June 10, 1915, AWM 25 707/S File 194, Australian War Memorial, Canberra, Australia. Copies accessed from the SRCARMPC.

15   "Routine Orders," June 11, 1915, AWM 25 707/S File 194, Australian War Memorial, Canberra, Australia. Copies accessed from the SRCARMPC.

16   "Routine Orders," June 11, 1915, AWM 25 707/S File 194.

17   Ruiz, "Manly Spectacles," 353; Beth Baron, *Egypt as a Woman* (Berkeley, CA: University of California Press, 2007), 53; Beth Baron, "Women, Honour, and the State: Evidence from Egypt," *Middle Eastern Studies* 42, no. 1 (2006): 1–20.

18   The house continued its association with the military though, later becoming the residence of Lt. Col. RBD Blakeney, RE, DSO, who had a long career in Egypt, previously serving as a lieutenant in the Royal Engineers, and participating in the Egyptian army's campaign in Sudan from 1896 to 1898. "Meadi Today," *Kia Ora Coo-Ee*; WO 100, War Office Campaign Medal and Award Rolls 1793–1949 (General Series), National Archives microfilm publication, WO 100, 241 rolls, BNA.

19   "Report on the Bungalow Hospital," SRCARMPC.

20   *Verbalnote*, Correspondence between the Foreign Office and Swedish Legation, May 7, 1919, FO 383/507.

21   International Committee of the Red Cross, *Turkish Prisoners in Egypt: A Report by the Delegates of the International Committee of the Red Cross* (2004

[1917]); "Turkish Prisoners of War: A Visit to the Meadi Camp," *Egyptian Gazette*, September 12, 1916.

22 All of the eight Egyptian POW camps housed male prisoners, except for an establishment in the Citadel, which housed more than four hundred women and children captured in the Hijaz, the region of present-day Saudi Arabia bordering the Red Sea. International Committee of the Red Cross, *Turkish Prisoners in Egypt*.

23 These Ottoman subjects included Arabs, Greeks, and Armenians, while the Austro-Hungarians also included Bulgarians, Czecho-Slovacs, and Poles. Red Cross, *Turkish Prisoners*; "Suspects Arrested in Salonica and interned in Egypt," FO 383/129.

24 "Turkish Prisoners of War," *Egyptian Gazette*. The Red Cross inspection report describes the camp as a former music school-turned-factory. Its description as a flour mill by the *Egyptian Gazette*, considering the rural landscape in Maadi and Tura, is likely more accurate.

25 International Committee of the Red Cross, *Turkish Prisoners in Egypt*.

26 *Verbalnote*, FO 383/507. Translation author's own.

27 The *Egyptian Gazette* depicted the POWs as unfortunate subjects of the Ottoman empire, reporting that the three groups were labeled "Turkish" because they "all have been compelled to take up arms under the Turkish flag." "Turkish Prisoners' Handiwork: Visit to the Cairo Depot," *Egyptian Gazette*, September 2, 1916.

28 A hundred Egyptian piasters, or *qirsh*, makes one Egyptian pound, *el-geneh el-masri*. At the time, the Egyptian pound was tied to the British pound sterling, and its value was based on the gold standard. Egypt remained part of the sterling area until 1962.

29 "Turkish Prisoners' Handiwork," *Egyptian Gazette*, September 2, 1916.

30 Private Papers of W.T. Smith, IWM.

31 "Prisoners Arrive in Egypt: Histrionics of German Officers," *Egyptian Gazette*, May 12, 1915.

32 Private Papers of W.T. Smith, Documents 15082, IWM.

33 Private Papers of W.T. Smith, IWM.

34 Private Papers of W.T. Smith, IWM. Grammar and punctuation are original to the diary.

35 Private Papers of W.T. Smith, IWM.

36 "Cholera in Egypt," *British Journal of Medicine* 1, no. 1828 (1896): 106–107, https://www-jstor-org.ezproxy.samford.edu/stable/20234488.

37   "Sanitary Matters in Cairo," *British Journal of Medicine 1, no. 2574 (1910)*:
     1057–1060, https://www-jstor-org.ezproxy.samford.edu/stable/25290485.
38   "Estate of Dr. Heinrich Hermann Bruno Bitter (German Subject), who
     died 23rd January 1918 in Germany," FO 847/66; "Maadi—Land Titles
     and Deeds—1906–1940," Dale Family Correspondence, SRCARMPC.
39   According to the 1907 census, there was a particularly large and growing
     population of Germans in Egypt in the early twentieth century, which
     increased by 44 percent after 1897. The census reports that the increase
     was largely due to increased immigration, rather than reproduction. The
     Bitters, however, indicate growth due to reproduction, where Europeans
     found other European spouses in Egypt and produced European chil-
     dren. In the case of the Bitters, three of these four "Germans" were born
     in Egypt. Ministry of Finance, "Nationality," in *Census of Egypt, Taken in
     1907: Under the Direction of C.C. Lowis, of the India Civil Service* (Cairo:
     National Printing Department, 1909), 130.
40   H.B.M. Supreme Court–Cairo, "Proclamations. – Letters & Orders
     issued respecting special courts for Germans, Austrians, Czeco-Slavs &
     Poles at Cairo," FO 841/215.
41   "Enemy Subjects in Egypt: The Case of the National Bank—Sir John
     Maxwell the Sole Arbiter," *Egyptian Gazette*, May 26, 1915.
42   "Baron Jacques de Menasce and Baron Charles de Mensace," FO 141/655/6.
43   "Baron Jacques de Menasce," FO 141/655/6.
44   The British Residency's careful differentiation between the individual
     members of the Menasce family became especially apparent when
     Jacques died in 1920. During the war, the British Public Custodian
     generally seized enemy property and liquidated it, making it nearly
     impossible for enemy subjects to receive an inheritance. When Menasce
     passed away and his seven children began making claims on his estate,
     however, the Public Custodian determined that all of the Menasce
     children could receive their share of the estate except the two living in
     Austria. "Baron Jacques de Menasce," FO 141/655/6.
45   The British Public Custodian's opinion on the Menasce family stands out
     in contrast to Krämer's description of the family, which she character-
     izes as deeply committed to their sense of European identity and their
     connection to the Austro-Hungarian empire. Gudrun Krämer, *The Jews
     of Modern Egypt, 1914–1952 (Seattle, WA: University of Washington Press,
     1989)*, 76–77.

46 "Baron Jacques de Menasce," FO 141/655/6.

47 Joel Beinin, *The Dispersion of Egyptian Jewry: Culture, Politics, and the Formation of a Modern Diaspora* (Berkeley, CA: University of California Press, 1998), 38.

48 The end of the pension payments coincided with a severe worsening of the war, with the devastating and totalizing effects of the Battle of the Somme and the Battle of Verdun, both unfolding in 1916. As John Morrow explains, 1916 was the watershed year, when it became a war of attrition, with no easy victory for either side. John H. Morrow, Jr., *The Great War: An Imperial History* (New York: Routledge, 2004), 175.

49 "Estate of Dr. Heinrich Hermann Bruno Bitter," FO 847/66.

50 In a letter to the Public Custodian, Kirby explained that she earned LE 25, as money "saved for rent out of the catering of the P of W billeted in the house." "Estate of Dr. Heinrich Hermann Bruno Bitter," FO 847/66.

51 Situations like Wanda Bitter's are part of the reason that nationality was a key concern for the international women's movement, initially taking precedent over suffrage. Leila J. Rupp, *Worlds of Women: The Making of an International Women's Movement* (Princeton, NJ: Princeton University Press, 1997), 41.

52 Rupp, *Worlds of Women*, 41.

53 Rupp, *Worlds of Women*.

54 Fouad Kamal paid LE 2,500 up front and agreed to repay the remainder to Delta Land at an annual interest rate of 7 percent, allowing Delta Land to resume charging interest on the house, this time to someone with the means to pay. "Estate of Dr. Heinrich Hermann Bruno Bitter," FO 847/66.

55 Ronald Robinson, John Gallagher, and Alice Denny use the term "official mind" to refer to the shared ideas and intentions of British government officials when shaping imperial objectives. Here I use it in a specific case, where British imperial aims in Egypt participated in the larger wartime strategies and objectives of the British government. See, Ronald Robinson, John Gallagher, and Alice Denny, *Africa and the Victorians: The Official Mind of Imperialism* (London: Macmillan, 1961).

56 Z. Khaled, "A Comparative Bacteriological Study of Bovine Abortion and Undulant Fever," *Journal of Hygiene* 22, no. 3 (1924): 335–342.

57 Cosmopolitanism can come to stand in for a number of complex meanings. In Maadi, it never represented the multinational and egalitarian

ideal of 'universal hospitality' articulated by Immanuel Kant. Instead, Maadi's cosmopolitanism incorporated elite social status and bourgeois tastes. Deborah Starr describes cosmopolitanism in Egypt as intertwined with imperialism. I would argue it is more connected to Ottoman systems, from which the British benefitted. Immanuel Kant, *Perpetual Peace: A Philosophic Essay*, translated by Benjamin Franklin Trueblood (Washington, DC: American Peace Society, 1897 [1795]); Deborah A. Starr, *Remembering Cosmopolitan Egypt: Literature, Culture, and Empire* (London: Routledge, 2009); Deborah A. Starr, "Recuperating Cosmopolitan Alexandria: Circulation of Narratives and Narratives of Circulation," *Cities* 22, no. 3 (2005): 217–228; David Harvey, "Cosmopolitanism and the Banality of Geographical Evils," *Public Culture* 12, no. 2 (2000): 529–564.

58 "Turkish Prisoners of War," *Egyptian Gazette*, September 12, 1916.

Chapter 5

1 "Directors Report for Financial Year Ending December 31, 1918," April 16, 1919, report from general meeting on April 10, 1919, "EDLICO Annual Shareholders and Directors Reports," SRCARMPC.

2 "Directors Report for Financial Year Ending December 31, 1918," April 16, 1919, report from general meeting on April 10, 1919, "EDLICO Annual Shareholders and Directors Reports," SRCARMPC; "Directors Report for Financial Year Ending December 31, 1920," May 5, 1921, report for meeting on April 4, 1921, "EDLICO Annual Shareholders and Directors Reports," SRCARMPC; Samir W. Raafat, *Maadi, 1904–1962: Society and History in a Cairo Suburb (Cairo: Palm Press, 1994)*, 33 and 47.

3 According to Geoffrey Dale, the Delta Land Company's manager from 1948 to 1956, the company's acquisition of the Luthy property constituted one of the biggest single land deals in its history. Letter from G. Dale to S. Raafat, SRCARMPC.

4 'Abd al-Rahman al-Raf'a, *Thawra sana 1919: Tarikh Misr al-qawmi min 1914 ila 1921*, 2nd ed. (Cairo: Maktabat al-Nahda al-Misriya, 1955), 6–7.

5 Joel Beinin and Zachary Lockman, *Workers on the Nile: Nationalism, Communism, Islam, and the Egyptian Working Class, 1882–1954 (Princeton, NJ: Princeton University Press, 1989)*, 122.

6 Lisa Pollard, *Nurturing the Nation: The Family Politics of Modernizing, Colonizing, and Liberating Egypt, 1805–1923* (Berkeley, CA: University of California Press, 2005); Wilson Chacko Jacob, *Working Out Egypt:*

Masculinity and Subject Formation in Colonial Modernity, 1870–1940 (Durham, NC: University of North Carolina Press, 2011).

7   See, Beth Baron, *Egypt as a Woman (Berkeley, CA: University of California Press, 2007)*; Margot Badran, *Feminists, Islam, and Nation: Gender and the Making of Modern Egypt* (Princeton, NJ: Princeton University Press, 1995).

8   On the *effendiya*, see, Michael Eppel, "Note about the Term *Effendiyya* in the History of the Middle East," *International Journal of Middle East Studies* 41, no. 3 (2009): 535–539; Arthur Goldschmidt, Jr., ed., *Egyptianizing Modernity through the 'New Effendiyya': Social and Cultural Constructions of the Middle Class in Egypt under the Monarchy* (Cairo: American University in Cairo Press, 2005); Noga Efrati, "The *Effendiyya*: Where Have All the Women Gone?" *International Journal of Middle East Studies* 43, no. 2 (2011): 375–377.

9   The continuity of Ottoman systems was not unique to Egypt and also took place in Syria. Nathan J. Brown, "The Precarious Life and Slow Death of the Mixed Courts of Egypt," *International Journal of Middle East Studies 25, no. 1 (1993): 47*; Philip S. Khoury, "Continuity and Change in Syrian Political Life: The Nineteenth and Twentieth Centuries," *The American Historical Review*, 96:5 (Dec., 1991), 1374–1395.

10   British Consular Court, "Probate: Sir Reginald Q. Henriques," FO 841/161; "Reginald Quixano Henriques, Deceased," *London Gazette*, December 26, 1916.

11   Photographs, GB124.DPA/1068/1.

12   "EDLICO Annual Shareholders and Directors Reports," SRCARMPC.

13   "Memorandum on EDLICO from G.D. Dale, No. 1," letter from G. Dale to S. Raafat, May 18, 1992, Dale Family Correspondence, SRCARMPC.

14   Letter from T. Dale to A. Holden, 12 March 1970, Andrew Holden Papers, GB165-0148, MECA.

15   Jo Guldi examines the development of highways in Britain during the eighteenth and nineteenth centuries to show how social segmentation resulted from the technical expertise behind infrastructure construction and often led to disproportionate allocation of resources. Jo Guldi, *Roads to Power: Britain Invents the Infrastructure State* (Cambridge, MA: Harvard University Press, 2011).

16   Saffeyah Moyine al-'Arab, *Saffeyah & Bin Bin: Growing Old Together* (Cairo: Trade Routes Enterprises International Publications, 1991), 55.

17 Letter from T. Dale to A. Holden, 8 May 1970, Andrew Holden Papers, GB165-0148, MECA.

18 T. Dale, "Sidelights at Maadi," Tom Dale Papers, GB165-0073, MECA.

19 *"Acte de Vente et Cahier des Charges,"* 7 May 1909, 11 June 1935, and 1944, SRCARMPC.

20 Ibrahim al-Bakistuni, "Reviewed Work: *Egyptian Service: 1902– 1946* by Thomas Russell Pasha," *African Affairs 48, no. 193 (1949): 335.*

21 "Egypt: Appeal Without Standing," *Time Magazine* 26, no. 23, December 2, 1935.

22 Beinin and Lockman, *Workers on the Nile,* 213.

23 T. Dale, "The Maadi–Cairo Road Lighting," Tom Dale Papers, GB165-0073, MECA.

24 "EDLICO Annual Shareholders and Directors Reports," SRCARMPC.

25 "EDLICO Annual Shareholders and Directors Reports," SRCARMPC.

26 Dale, "The Maadi–Cairo Road Lighting."

27 André Raymond, *Cairo: City of History (Cairo: American University in Cairo Press, 2007),* 326.

28 Dale, "The Maadi–Cairo Road Lighting."

29 Athar al-Nabi (Arabic for "traces of the Prophet") is just northwest of the heart of Old Cairo. Dale, "The Maadi–Cairo Road Lighting."

30 Dale, "The Maadi–Cairo Road Lighting."

31 *al-Ahram,* February 11, 1933, http://www.egy.com/maadi (accessed December 5, 2012).

32 The *Gazette* additionally reported that Elie Mosseri, Percy Stout, Edgard de Cattaoui, and Tom Dale were all present at the festivities. "Electric Lighting on Maadi Road: Inaugurated by Lady Loraine," *Egyptian Gazette,* February 10, 1933.

33 Brown, "The Precarious Life," 47.

34 While Egyptian women participated in their own public demonstrations during the 1919 revolution, when the Wafd created a new constitution in 1923, women's rights were excluded from the new government. Pollard, *Nurturing the Nation,* 177; Baron, *Egypt as a Woman,* 10–11. On women's similar exclusion from democratic politics in North America, see, Linda Kerber, *Women of the Republic: Intellect and Ideology in Revolutionary America* (New York: Norton, 1986), and on the maternalist politics of the French Revolution, see, Lynn Hunt,

The Family Romance of the French Revolution (Berkeley, CA: University of California Press, 1992). For a comparative discussion of maternalism, see, Seth Koven and Sonya Michel, eds., *Mothers of a New World: Maternalist Politics and the Origins of Welfare States* (New York: Routledge, 1993).

35 Beinin and Lockman, *Workers on the Nile*, 168.

36 Beinin and Lockman, *Workers on the Nile*, 170.

37 Pollard, *Nurturing the Nation*, 202–204.

38 Beinin and Lockman, *Workers on the Nile*, 163.

39 "EDLICO Annual Shareholders and Directors Reports," SRCARMPC.

40 Gabriel Josipovici, personal interview, March 29, 2011.

41 "Passing Notes: Maadi's New Club," *The Sphinx: The English Illustrated Weekly*, December 11, 1920 (Cairo: Sphinx Press), 138.

42 Mona Russell, "Marketing the Modern Egyptian Girl," *Journal of Middle East Women's Studies* 6, no. 3 (2010): 19–57.

43 Jacob, *Working Out Egypt*, 63.

44 "The Epistles of Peggy," *The Sphinx*, December 11, 1920.

45 Raafat, *Maadi*, 67.

46 Mrinalini Sinha, "Britishness, Clubbability, and the Colonial Public Sphere: The Genealogy of an Imperial Institution in Colonial India," *Journal of British Studies* 40, no. 4 (2001): 489–521.

47 Raafat, *Maadi*, 67.

48 Letter from T. Dale to A. Holden, March 12, 1970, Andrew Holden Papers, GB165-0148, MECA.

49 "EDLICO Annual Shareholders and Directors Reports," SRCARMPC.

50 Egyptian Delta Land & Investment Co Ltd. v Todd (Insp.): Question of Residence of an English Company Abroad and Liability under Schedule D on Mortgage Interest and Rents," Stamps and Taxes Division: Registered Files, IR 40/2968, BNA.

Chapter 6

1 Samir W. Raafat, *Maadi, 1904–1962: Society and History in a Cairo Suburb* (Cairo: Palm Press, 1994), 94.

2 "The Capitulations: Maitre Waheeb Doss Bey's Lecture," *Egyptian Gazette*, January 26, 1937.

3 "Obituary: Mr. John Williamson," *Egyptian Gazette*, March 29, 1932.

4 "Ahmad 'Abd al-Wahhab," *al-Ahram*, April 17, 1938.

5 "Ahmad 'Abd al-Wahhab"; Nathan J. Brown, "The Precarious Life and Slow Death of the Mixed Courts of Egypt," *International Journal of Middle East Studies* 25, no. 1 (1993): 45.

6 Malak Badrawi, *Isma'il Sidqi, 1875–1950: Pragmatism and Vision in Twentieth Century Egypt* (London: Curzon Press, 1996), 13.

7 Badrawi, *Isma'il Sidqi*, 35.

8 Naus Bey had been familiar with members of Egypt's Sephardic elite since at least 1909 and first met Sidqi during the First World War. Uri M. Kupferschmidt, *Henri Naus Bey: Retrieving the Biography of a Belgian Industrialist in Egypt* (Brussels: Academie Royale des Sciences d'Outre-Mer, 1998), 52.

9 "Henri Naus Bey," *al-Ahram*, September 24, 1938; Joel Beinin and Zachary Lockman, *Workers on the Nile: Nationalism, Communism, Islam, and the Egyptian Working Class, 1882–1954 (Princeton, NJ: Princeton University Press, 1989), 184*; Gudrun Krämer, *The Jews of Modern Egypt, 1914–1952 (Seattle, WA: University of Washington Press, 1989)*, 123.

10 Beinin and Lockman, *Workers on the Nile*, 193–194.

11 Brown, "The Precarious Life," 46–47.

12 P.J. Cain and A.G. Hopkins, *British Imperialism, 1688–2000, 2nd ed. (Harlow: Longman, Pearson Education, 2002)*, 68.

13 Brown, "The Precarious Life," 46–47.

14 "EDLICO Annual Shareholders and Directors Reports," SRCARMPC.

15 "EDLICO Annual Shareholders and Directors Reports," SRCARMPC.

16 Krämer, *The Jews of Modern Egypt*, 43.

17 Krämer, *The Jews of Modern Egypt*, 157–158.

18 Gianluca Paolo Parolin, *Citizenship in the Arab World: Kin, Religion, and Nation-State* (Amsterdam: Amsterdam University Press, 2009), 81.

19 Parolin, *Citizenship in the Arab World*.

20 Joel Beinin, *The Dispersion of Egyptian Jewry: Culture, Politics, and the Formation of a Modern Diaspora* (Berkeley, CA: University of California Press, 1998), 38.

21 Krämer, *The Jews of Modern Egypt*, 43.

22 "List of Persons Holding Shares in the Egyptian Delta Land & Investment Co., Ltd. on the 9th of May 1904," BT 31/43736.

23 Beinin and Lockman, *Workers on the Nile*, 212–213.

24 Laila Morsy, "The Military Clauses of the Anglo-Egyptian Treaty of Friendship and Alliance, 1936," *International Journal of Middle East Studies* 16 (1984): 67.

25 Women were initially excluded from the group to accommodate Islamic conservatism, but its leaders anticipated that with the growth of the women's movement among younger Egyptians, they would be able to join soon after its founding. Letter from Robert to Elgood, April 15, 1937, FO 141/645.

26 Letter from Robert to Elgood, 15 April 1937, FO 141/645; "Ahmad ʿAbd al-Wahhab Pasha," *al-Ahram*, April 17, 1938.

27 "An Anglo-Egyptian Union," *Egyptian Gazette*, January 21, 1937.

28 "An Anglo-Egyptian Union."

29 "Ahmad ʿAbd-al-Wahhab Pasha," *al-Ahram*.

30 "Ahmed Abdel Wahab Pasha: Financier and Organiser," *Egyptian Gazette*, April 17, 1938.

31 "Excerpt from Minute Book of Proceedings at Annual General Meetings of the Egyptian Delta Land and Investment Co., Ltd.," Binder 3, SRCARMPC.

32 Mary's stepmother Martha Evelyn Stone (née Stevens) was among the survivors of the sinking of the Titanic in 1912. Lyn Longridge (granddaughter of Percy and Mary Stout), email message to the author, June 15, 2011; Malc King, "Percy Stout," Gloucester Rugby Heritage, http://www.gloucesterrugbyheritage.org.uk/page_id__201_path__0p3p17p.aspx (accessed September 14, 2012).

33 "The Cairo Exchange, Ltd.," May 21–22, 1907, Issues: A Reprint of the Prospectuses of Public Companies, Etc., Advertised in the *Times* 33, p. 174.

34 Percy Wyfold Stout, "British Army WWI Medal Rolls Index Cards, 1914–1920," Army Medal Office, WWI Medal Index Cards, database online, Ancestry.com (accessed September 18, 2012); "Obituary: Mr. Frank M. Stout," *Egyptian Gazette*, June 1, 1926.

35 Sir Robert Greg, KCMG, preface to *Gardening for Egypt and Allied Climates*, by Mary Stout (Cairo: Egyptian Horticultural Society, 1935), 7.

36 Agar was already well-known for her gardening expertise at the time, having published two guidebooks in England: *A Primer for School Gardening* in 1909 and *Garden Design in Theory and Practice* in 1911. Her most famous project came shortly after her collaboration with Stout, when she helped design the War Memorial Garden at Wimbledon. Agar designed the memorial with Brenda Colvin, one of her students in garden design at Swanley Horticultural College. Brenda was born in Simla, India, and was the niece of Sir Auckland Colvin. "Brenda Colvin," in *The Northeastern*

Dictionary of Women's Biography, 3rd ed., edited by Jennifer S. Uglow and Maggy Hendry (London: MacMillan, 1998), 135.

37 "Egyptian Horticultural Society," SRCARMPC.

38 "Flower Show at Cairo: Some Fine Exhibits," *Egyptian Gazette*, December 15, 1919.

39 "List of Persons Holding Shares in the Egyptian Delta Land & Investment Co., Ltd. on the 9th of May 1904," BT 31/43736; Dale Family Correspondence, SRCARMPC.

40 Mary Stout, *Gardening for Egypt and Allied Climates (Cairo: Egyptian Horticultural Society, 1935)*, 17.

41 Stout, *Gardening*, 18.

42 Stout, *Gardening*, 19.

43 Stout, *Gardening*, 21.

44 Stout, *Gardening*, 19.

45 Stout, *Gardening*, 34.

46 Work on the history of science has devoted extensive study to differentiating between explicit and implicit knowledge, arguing that modern scientific experimentation and knowledge production often efface the "gestural" knowledge that cannot be easily articulated and relies upon years of practice. Heinz Otto Sibum, "Reworking the Mechanical Value of Heat: Instruments of Precision and Gestures of Accuracy in Early Victorian England," *Studies in the History and Philosophy of Science* 26, no. 1 (1995): 73–106. In a related argument, Steven Shapin and Simon Schaffer suggest that early modern science was successful because of "invisible technicians" whose work is effaced in the scientific documentation. See, Steven Shapin and Simon Schaffer, *Leviathan and the Air-Pump: Hobbes, Boyle, and the Experimental Life* (Princeton, NJ: Princeton University Press, 1985). For women's contributions to science as "invisible technicians," see, Chapter Three of Londa Schiebinger, *The Mind Has No Sex? Women in the Origins of Modern Science* (Cambridge, MA: Harvard University Press, 1989).

47 Stout, *Gardening*, 34.

48 Stout, *Gardening*, 40–41.

49 Stout, *Gardening*, 41–42.

50 Beinin and Lockman, *Workers on the Nile*, 153.

51 The Devonshires were married at the British embassy in Paris on 26 May 1887. "Silver Wedding," *Egyptian Gazette*, May 24, 1912.

52 "Land Deeds and Titles, 1906–1940," SRCARMPC.

53 Commonwealth War Graves Commission, "Devonshire, Feray Vulliamy," http://www.cwgc.org/find-war-dead/casualty/1437026/DEVON-SHIRE,%20FERAY%20VULLIAMY (accessed August 31, 2012).

54 "Death of Mr. Devonshire," *Egyptian Gazette*, July 16, 1921.

55 Henriette Devonshire, *Rambles in Cairo* (Cairo: E. and R. Schindler, 1931), I.

56 In presenting her history on these terms, Devonshire participated in some of the hallmark activities of early women historians. Bonnie Smith argues that women's amateur work anticipated cultural and social history by focusing on travel, the details of daily life, and emotionally cathartic elements of their subjects. Bonnie Smith, *The Gender of History: Men, Women and Historical Practice* (Cambridge, MA: Harvard University Press, 1998).

57 Devonshire, *Rambles*, 1.

58 Devonshire, *Rambles*, 2.

59 Devonshire, *Rambles*, 3.

60 Devonshire, *Rambles*, 3.

61 Yi-Fu Tuan, *Space and Place: The Perspective of Experience* (Minneapolis, MN: University of Minneapolis Press, 1977), 159.

62 Devonshire, *Rambles*, 7.

63 Mehmet Ozan Aşik and Aykan Erdemir, "Westernization as Cultural Trauma: Egyptian Radical Islamist Discourse on Religious Education," *Journal for the Studies of Religions and Ideologies* 9, no. 25 (2010): 111–132.

64 Abd Al-Fattah M. El-Awaisi, "Jihadia Education and the Society of the Egyptian Muslim Brothers: 1928–49," *Journal of Beliefs & Values: Studies in Religion & Education* 21, no. 2 (2000): 213–225; Beth Baron, *The Orphan Scandal: Christian Missionaries and the Rise of the Muslim Brotherhood* (Stanford, CA: Stanford University Press, 2014), 144–147.

65 Baron, *Orphan Scandal*, 144.

66 "Works by the Same Author," in Devonshire, *Rambles*. Devonshire continued writing into the 1930s and 1940s. In 1940, she published *Abu Bekr ibn Muzhir et sa mosquée au Caire* through the Institut Francais d'Archéologie Orientale.

67 "Lecture by Mrs. Devonshire," *Egyptian Gazette*, January 12, 1925.

68 "Social and Personal," *Egyptian Gazette*, April 19, 1924.

69 "Social and Personal," *Egyptian Gazette*, May 16, 1927; "Mrs. Devonshire Honoured by King Farouk," *Egyptian Gazette*, April 6, 1944.

70 Stout, *Gardening*, 8; Devonshire, *Rambles*, v–vi.

Chapter 7

1 "Meadi," in *Egypt Today: Published in the Interests of Egyptian Finance, Industry and Commerce, 1937–38*, 2nd ed. (London: Bemrose & Sons, Ltd. 1938), 171.

2 "Meadi," *Egypt Today*.

3 Robert Vitalis, *When Capitalists Collide: Business Conflicts and the End of Empire in Egypt (Berkeley, CA: University of California Press, 1995)*, 41.

4 Marius Deeb, "Bank Misr and the Emergence of the Local Bourgeoisie in Egypt," *Middle Eastern Studies* 12, no. 3 (1976): 71; Eric Davis, *Challenging Colonialism: Bank Misr and Egyptian Industrialization, 1920–1941* (Princeton, NJ: Princeton University Press, 1983).

5 "Egyptian Finance and Enterprise," in *Egypt Today: Published in the Interests of Egyptian Finance, Industry and Commerce, 1937–38*, 2nd ed. (London: Bemrose & Sons, Ltd., 1938).

6 Michael T. Thornhill, "Informal Empire, Independent Egypt and the Accession of King Farouk," *Journal of Imperial and Commonwealth History* 38, no. 2 (2010): 279–302.

7 "Table IX. Total Population during the Last Seven Censuses (1882–1947) and Changes in Figures by Governate (included within the Present Boundaries)," in "Movement of the Population," *Population Census of Egypt, 1947: General Tables*, AARR.

8 André Raymond, *Cairo: City of History (Cairo: American University in Cairo Press, 2007)*, 339.

9 "Table I-E. Population by Nationality," in "Area, Density, Occupied Dwellings," *Population Census of Egypt, 1947: General Tables*, AARR.

10 Raymond, *Cairo*, 341.

11 Raymond, *Cairo*, 341–342.

12 Robert Ilbert, "Heliopolis: Colonial Enterprise and Town Planning Success?" in *Coping with the Urban Growth of Cairo, edited by Ahmet Evin (Singapore: Concept Media and Aga Khan Award for Architecture, 1985)*, 36–42.

13 Letter from G. Dale to S. Raafat, June 8, 1992, SRCARMPC.

14 Nona Orbach, email message to the author, May 18, 2012.

15 Letter from G. Dale to S. Raafat, June 8, 1992, SRCARMPC.

16 Letter from G. Dale to S. Raafat, June 8, 1992, SRCARMPC; Samir W. Raafat, *Maadi, 1904–1962: Society and History in a Cairo Suburb (Cairo: Palm Press, 1994)*, 59.

17 Letter from G. Dale to S. Raafat, June 8, 1992, SRCARMPC.

18 "Villa: Propriété Kipnis à Maadi," image courtesy of Nona Orbach.

19 Samir Raafat, "A Snapshot of Egypt's Postal History," Egy.com, December 3, 1994, http://www.egy.com/historica/94-12-03.php (accessed April 20, 2020).

20 Raafat, *Maadi*, 258.

21 "Memorandum of Association of the Egyptian Delta Land & Investment Company, Limited," Board of Trade (BT) 31/43735, BNA; "List of Persons Holding Shares in the Egyptian Delta Land & Investment Co., Ltd. on the 9th of May 1904," BT 31/43736.

22 "EDLICO Directors, 1904–1956," SRCARMPC.

23 Art deco architecture from this period often used circular and rounded patterns, which were inspired by similar stylings used in ocean liner, automobile, and airplane design at the time. "Art Deco's Dynamic Style," *Herald Sun* (Melbourne, Australia), November 4, 2000.

24 "Villa à Maadi—Mazloum Pacha," image courtesy of Nona Orbach.

25 "Letters Received in 2005," Bassatine News, http://bassatine.net/letters2005.php (accessed April 20, 2020).

26 "Contrat de location avec option de vente," from Church of St. John the Baptist.

27 "St. John's Church," from Church of St. John the Baptist.

28 "St. John's Church," from Church of St. John the Baptist.

29 "Contrat de location avec option de vente," from Church of St. John the Baptist.

30 "St. John's Church," from Church of St. John the Baptist.

31 "St. John's Church," from Church of St. John the Baptist.; letter from G. Dale to S. Raafat, June 8, 1992, SRCARMPC.

32 Williams Whyte, "How Do Buildings Mean? Some Issues of Interpretation in the History of Architecture," *History and Theory* 45 (2006): 173.

33 Letter from G. Dale to S. Raafat, June 8, 1992, SRCARMPC.

34 Meyr Y. Biton Synagogue, Maadi, correspondence between Nona Orbach and the author, June 7, 2012.

35 Raafat, *Maadi*, 258.

36 Dale explained that he was well acquainted with all three men, particularly Fouad Kamal Bey, whom he considered a friend. "El Farouk Mosque—Maadi," included in letter from T. Dale to A. Holden, Andrew Holden Papers, GB165-0148, MECA.

37 "El Farouk Mosque—Maadi," included in letter from T. Dale to A. Holden, Andrew Holden Papers, GB165-0148, MECA.

38 "Jalalat al-Malak yaftatah Masjid Faruq al-Awwal bil-Maadi," *al-Ahram*, February 18, 1939. Little information remains about Ittihad al-Maadi, but it had formed by at least 1937, when the *Egyptian Gazette* reported that the group's administrative council met to discuss ways to improve Maadi. "Maadi Union," *Egyptian Gazette*, April 7, 1937.

39 "Jalalat al-Malak yaftatah Masjid Faruq al-Awwal bal-Maadi," *al-Ahram*, February 18, 1939; "List of Persons," BT 31/43736.

Chapter 8

1 "Misr laysat fi harb wa-lakinnaha tasta'id li-l-harb," *al-Ahram*, April 2, 1940.

2 "Misr laysat fi harb wa-lakinnaha tasta'id li-l-harb," *al-Ahram*.

3 "Cairo Jew Starts Libel Suit against 'German League,'" Jewish Telegraphic Agency, August 6, 1933, https://www.jta.org/1933/08/06/archive/cairo-jew-starts-libel-suit-against-german-league (accessed April 20, 2020); "Alleged Libel of Jews," *Egyptian Gazette*, January 23, 1934, 5.

4 "Garden Party at Maadi," *Egyptian Gazette*, April 12, 1938.

5 "Alleged Libel of Jews," *Egyptian Gazette*.

6 "To Appeal Decision of Egypt Tribunal on Jew's Libel Suit," Jewish Telegraphic Agency, January 26, 1934, https://www.jta.org/1934/01/26/archive/to-appeal-decision-of-egypt-tribunal-on-jews-libel-suit (accessed April 20, 2020); "Germans Win Cairo Lawsuit," *Egyptian Gazette*, January 25, 1934, 5.

7 "Germans Win Cairo Lawsuit," *Egyptian Gazette*.

8 "Germans Win Cairo Lawsuit," *Egyptian Gazette*.

9 During the initial hearing, Kamal Sidqi Bey, one of Van Meeteren's lawyers, criticized Castro's use of a 1732 English case in his argument. The invocation of a foreign precedent, Kamal Sidqi argued, was evidence of the weakness of the Egyptian judicial system. The entire nature of the case, he argued, pointed to the ill effects of foreign interference on Egyptian governance. For some Egyptian nationalists, identifying Jews as foreign interlopers would serve as a new platform for asserting independence. Castro's description of Egypt as a "country containing many minorities" would figure less and less prominently as part of Egyptian national identity. "Alleged Libel of German Jews," *Egyptian Gazette*, January 24, 1934, 6.

10 "Anti-Semitism in Egypt," *Egyptian Gazette*, June 15, 1938.

11 Samir Raafat, "When Doctor Goebbels Came to Town," *Egyptian Mail*, September 30, 1995, republished on http://www.egy.com/historica/95-09-30.php (accessed June 18, 2019).

12 Alex Hendley, with Megan Hutching, *Fernleaf Cairo: New Zealanders at Maadi Camp, the Fascinating Story of New Zealanders in Wartime Egypt* (Auckland: HarperCollins, 2009), 16.

13 Hendley with Hutching, *Fernleaf Cairo*.

14 Hendley with Hutching, *Fernleaf Cairo*, 17, 24.

15 Hendley with Hutching, *Fernleaf Cairo*, 108–109.

16 Hendley with Hutching, *Fernleaf Cairo*, 25.

17 Hendley with Hutching, *Fernleaf Cairo*; "Sun Print 2," Nona Orbach: Blog as Artwork, http://nonaorbach.com/blog/?p=1024 (accessed April 20, 2020).

18 Orbach, "Sun Print 2."

19 Private papers of H.W. Hainsworth, Documents 12578, IWM.

20 Nona Orbach, correspondence with the author, May 19, 2012.

21 Gabriel Warburg, "Lampson's Ultimatum to Faruq, 4 February, 1942," *Middle Eastern Studies* 11, no. 1 (1975): 30.

22 Warburg, "Lampson's Ultimatum to Faruq," 24–32; Charles D. Smith, "4 February 1942: Its Causes and Its Influence on Egyptian Politics and on the Future of Anglo-Egyptian Relations, 1937–1945," *International Journal of Middle East Studies* 10, no. 4 (1979): 453–479.

23 Warburg, "Lampson's Ultimatum to Faruq," 25.

24 Hendley, with Hutching, *Fernleaf Cairo*, 13.

25 Salem, personal interview, November 12, 2009.

26 "The English School, Cairo: Maadi Branch," *Egyptian Gazette*, June 4, 1932.

27 Salem, personal interview, November 12, 2009; Maggie Safwat, personal interview, January 13, 2011, and May 5, 2011.

28 Salem, personal interview, April 30, 2011.

29 Salem and Safwat, personal interview, November 12, 2009.

30 Safwat, personal interview, May 5, 2011.

31 Salem, personal interview, April 30, 2011.

32 "Worst Storm in 23 Years," *Egyptian Gazette*, January 2, 1945.

33 "When the Wadi Digla flooded Maadi," Tom Dale Papers, GB165-0073, MECA.

34 "When the Wadi Digla flooded Maadi," Tom Dale Papers, GB165-0073, MECA.

35 "Worst Storm in 23 Years," *Egyptian Gazette.*

36 "When the Wadi Digla flooded Maadi," Tom Dale Papers, GB165-0073, MECA.

37 "King's Gift for Storm Victims," *Egyptian Gazette,* January 3, 1945.

38 Arthur Goldschmidt, Jr., "'Abbud, [Muhammad] Ahmad (2 May 1889–28 December 1963)," *Biographical Dictionary of Modern Egypt* (Boulder, CO: Lynne Rienner Publishers, 2004), https://login.ezproxy.samford.edu/login?url=https://search.credoreference.com/content/entry/bdmodegypt/abbud_muhammad_ahmad_2_may_1889_28_december_1963/0?instituti onId=3477 (accessed June 21, 2019).

39 "When the Wadi Digla flooded Maadi," Tom Dale Papers, GB165-0073, MECA.

40 James Steele, *An Architect for People: The Complete Works of Hassan Fathy* (Cairo: American University in Cairo Press, 1997), 6.

41 Hassan Fathy Architectural Archives, Rare Books and Special Collections Library, American University in Cairo, Egypt.

42 Hassan Fathy, *Architecture for the Poor: An Experiment in Rural Egypt* (Chicago, IL: University of Chicago Press, 1971), 6. The book was originally published in 1969 by Egypt's Ministry of Culture as *Gourna: A Tale of Two Villages.*

43 Fathy, *Architecture for the Poor,* 5.

44 Steele, *An Architect for People,* 6.

45 Fathy, *Architecture for the Poor,* 12.

46 Arthur Goldschmidt, Jr., "Sirri, Husayn (12 December 1892–15 December 1960)," *Biographical Dictionary of Modern Egypt* (Boulder, Co: Lynne Rienner Publishers, 2004), https://login.ezproxy.samford.edu/login?url=https://search.credoreference.com/content/entry/bdmode-gypt/sirri_husayn_12_december_1892_15_december_1960/0?institutio nId=3477 (accessed June 20, 2019).

47 Fathy, *Architecture for the Poor,* 5 and 12.

48 Fathy, *Architecture for the Poor,* 13.

49 Fathy, *Architecture for the Poor, 13.*

50 Fathy, *Architecture for the Poor,* 134.

51 Steele, *An Architect for People.*

52 Tom Dale Papers, GB165-0073, MECA.

53 "Villa Aziza Hassanein," Hassan Fathy Architectural Archives.

54 "Fila hadara sahibat al-asma 'Aziza Hanem Hassanein 'ala al-Nil bi-nahi-yat al-Maadi," Hassan Fathy Architectural Archives.

55 Fathy, *Architecture for the Poor*, 14.

Chapter 9

1 Gabriel Josipovici, *A Life* (London: London Magazine Editions, European Jewish Publication Society, 2001), 17.

2 Joel Beinin, *The Dispersion of Egyptian Jewry: Culture, Politics, and the Formation of a Modern Diaspora* (Berkeley, CA: University of California Press, 1998), 258.

3 Nathan J. Brown, "The Precarious Life and Slow Death of the Mixed Courts of Egypt," *International Journal of Middle East Studies* 25, no. 1 (1993): 48.

4 André Raymond, *Cairo: City of History* (Cairo: American University in Cairo Press, 2007), 327.

5 For a discussion of more recent iterations of cosmopolitanism in Cairo in the early-twentieth century, see Diane Singerman and Paul Amar, eds. *Cairo Cosmopolitan: Politics, Culture, and Urban Space in the New Globalized Middle East* (Cairo: American University in Cairo Press, 2006).

6 Gabriel Josipovici, "Gabriel Josipovici, 1940–," *Contemporary Authors Autobiography Series*, vol. 8, edited by Mark Zadrozny (Detroit, MI: Gale, 1988), 145–154.

7 Josipovici, "Gabriel Josipovici," 150.

8 "Descendants of Eliahu Rossi," http://www.geocities.com/rainforest/vines/5855/rossi.htm (accessed January 29, 2013); Josipovici, *A Life*, 25; "Obituary: Sacha Rabinovitch," *Independent*, April 9, 1996.

9 The girls were baptized by Sister Margaret Clare, a prominent English missionary and devotee to the British community in Cairo in the early twentieth century. Josipovici, "Gabriel Josipovici," 145; Josipovici, *A Life*, 24. Sister Margaret Clare was particularly influential in establishing English schools in the city, and a fund was created in her name to provide scholarships in 1917. "Sister Margaret Clare Fund: A Worthy Object," *Egyptian Gazette*, February 16, 1917. On Sister Margaret Clare, also see, Letter from Sister Margaret Clare, Honorable Secretary of the Anglo-Egyptian Aid Society, to Sir Ronald Campbell, British Ambassador to Egypt, July 5, 1946, with attached Anglo-Egyptian Aid

Society Brochure, "British Community: Post-war Reconstruction," FO 141/1112; "Women's Organizations: White Slave Trade," FO 141/790.

10 Josipovici, "Gabriel Josipovici," 145.

11 Josipovici, *A Life*, 93.

12 Josipovici, *A Life*, 93.

13 Josipovici, *A Life*, 93.

14 Anna Joannides also recalled that the family's permanent reunion was further suspended when her paternal grandmother had an illness, and her father lived with her for a stint. Anna Joannides, personal interview, April 11, 2011.

15 Anna Joannides, personal interview, April 11, 2011.

16 Samir W. Raafat, *Maadi, 1904–1962: Society and History in a Cairo Suburb* (Cairo: Palm Press, 1994), 40.

17 Josipovici, personal interview, March 29, 2011.

18 Josipovici, personal interview, March 29, 2011.

19 Josipovici, personal interview, March 29, 2011.

20 Joannides, personal interview, April 11, 2011.

21 Josipovici, personal interview, March 29, 2011.

22 "*Amm*" is Arabic for uncle and is used as a term of respect and endearment for older men. Nadia Salem, Maggie Safwat, and Ingy Safwat, personal interview, January 13, 2011.

23 Raafat, *Maadi*, 267; "Ism al-Nadi," *Nadi al-Maadi al-Riyad wa al-Yakht*, SRCARMPC.

24 'Adl Nimatallah and Maggie Zaki, personal interview, January 13, 2011.

25 Downtown was less obscure to Salem, who traveled through downtown for school every day after she finished at the Maadi English School. She would take the train from the Maadi station to the town center, then board a bus to Ramses College for Girls. Salem, Safwat, and Safwat, personal interview, January 13, 2011.

26 "*Ya'ni*" is an Egyptian colloquial expression, which literally translated means "I mean" or "to mean," but is used similarly to English speakers' "um" or "like" in everyday speech. Safwat and Safwat, personal interview, May 5, 2011.

27 Bernard Reich, ed., *Arab–Israeli Conflict and Conciliation: A Documentary History* (Westport, CT: Greenwood Press, 1995), 82.

28 Benny Morris, *The Birth of the Palestinian Refugee Problem Revisited* (Cambridge: Cambridge University Press, 2004), 522.

29 James Jankowski, "The Government of Egypt and the Palestine Question, 1936–1939," *Middle Eastern Studies* 17, no. 4 (1981): 427–453.

30 Cattaoui's insistence on his allegiance to Egypt might also have been a product of the difficulty Jews had in acquiring Egyptian nationality after 1929. The new citizenship law passed that year required that Jews trace their lineage in Egypt to before 1848. While most elite Jewish families had European citizenship at this time, the Cattaouis lost their Austro-Hungarian nationality after the First World War and gained Egyptian citizenship after 1922. Had their loyalties fallen into question, they were at risk of becoming stateless. Beinin, *The Dispersion of Egyptian Jewry*, 250.

31 "Baron Jacques de Menasce and Baron Charles de Mensace," FO 141/655/6; "Cattaoui, Yusuf (Pasha)," FO 141/759/20.

32 "The Zionist Movement in Egypt," FO 141/790.

33 Nona Orbach, correspondence with the author, May 18, 2012.

34 By 2010, it is estimated that only a hundred Jews remained in the city, all of whom were women, making it impossible to perform their religious ceremonies without the assistance of men at the Israeli embassy. Carmen Weinstein, president of the Cairo Jewish Community, speech to the Cairo Women's Association, October 27, 2010; Gudrun Krämer, *The Jews of Modern Egypt, 1914–1952 (Seattle, WA: University of Washington Press, 1989)*, 221.

35 Josipovici, *A Life*, 4.

36 Josipovici, *A Life*, 30.

37 Krämer, *The Jews of Modern Egypt*, 42.

38 In response to the domestic bombings, Israeli planes bombed a predominantly Muslim neighborhood in Cairo, which resulted in a Muslim march on the city's Jewish *hara*. Beinin, *The Dispersion of Egyptian Jewry*, 68.

39 Raafat, *Maadi*, 195.

40 Letter from G. Dale to S. Raafat, June 8, 1992, SRCARMPC.

41 Samia Zaytun, personal interview, November 12, 2009.

42 Safwat and Safwat, personal interview, May 5, 2011.

43 Zaytun, personal interview, November 12, 2009.

44 Edward Said, *Out of Place: A Memoir* (New York: Alfred A. Knopf, 2000), 23.

45 The school later changed its name to Cairo American College and remains one of the most prestigious international schools in Maadi. "History of CAC," 1958, SRCARMPC.

46 Said, *Out of Place*, 22.

47 Said, *Out of Place*, 11; Raafat, *Maadi*, 63.
48 Said, *Out of Place*, 6–7.
49 Said, *Out of Place*, 87.
50 Said went on to be instrumental in articulating a critique of imperialism's cultural and psychological impact. The intellectual critique of colonialism's far-reaching significance began with the publication of Frantz Fanon's *Black Skin, White Masks* in 1952. Said most famously applied these concepts to the particular experiences of Middle Eastern and Asian cultures in his critique of western literature, first in *Orientalism* in 1978 and later with *Culture and Imperialism* in 1993.
51 Said, *Out of Place*, 22.
52 Said, *Out of Place*, 115.
53 Said, *Out of Place*.

Chapter 10

1 Letter from G. Dale to S. Raafat, May 18, 1992, SRCARMPC.
2 "EDLICO Directors, 1904–1956," SRCARMPC. See also the list of Maadi Sporting Club presidents, secretaries, and committee members, SRCARMPC.
3 "Maadi—Land Titles and Deeds—1906–1940," Dale Family Correspondence, SRCARMPC; letter from G. Dale to S. Raafat, May 18, 1992, SRCARMPC.
4 Samir W. Raafat, *Maadi, 1904–1962: Society and History in a Cairo Suburb* (*Cairo: Palm Press, 1994*), 198.
5 John Freeman, "A Brief Account of the Church of St. John the Baptist, Maadi," 1955, SRCARMPC.
6 Sir Richard Vaux, "Egyptian and Other Episodes: Personal, Political, and Legal," unpublished memoir (1941), GB165-0293, MECA.
7 Henriette Caroline Devonshire, "England, Andrews Newspaper Index Cards, 1790–1976," database online, Ancestry.com (accessed July 11, 2020).
8 Ami Ayalon, "Christian 'Intruders,' Muslim 'Bigots': The Egyptian-Syrian Press Controversy in Late-Nineteenth Century Cairo," in *Jews, Muslims, and Mass Media: Mediating the 'Other'*, eds. Tudor Parfitt and Yulia Egorova (London: Routledge Curzon, 2004), 15–27; Tiysir Abu 'Araja, *al-Muqattam: Jaridat al-Ihtilal al-Britani fi Misr, 1889–1952* (Cairo: al-Hiy'ia al-Misriyya al-'Ama lil-Kitab, 1997), 29; Raafat, *Maadi*, 267.

9 André Raymond, *Cairo: City of History* (Cairo: American University in Cairo Press, 2007), 346.

10 Janet L. Abu-Lughod, *Cairo: 1001 Years of the City Victorious* (Princeton, NJ: Princeton University Press, 1971), 201.

11 Raymond, *Cairo*, 346.

12 Letter from G. Dale to S. Raafat, June 8, 1992, SRCARMPC.

13 Raafat, *Maadi*, 203.

14 Safwat and Safwat, personal interview, May 5, 2011.

15 "New Maadi Village to be Built in Four Zones," *Egyptian Gazette*, February 14, 1947.

16 Rabatat al-Maadi/Maadi Association, "Jiaghrafiat al-Maadi"/"The Geography of Maadi," in *The Maadi Guide* (Cairo: Minerbo Press, 1956), 24 (Arabic).

17 Rabatat al-Maadi, *Maadi Guide*, 24 *(Arabic) and 23 (English)*.

18 Rabatat al-Maadi, *Maadi Guide*, 24 *(Arabic) and 23 (English)*.

19 Lawrence Wright, *The Looming Tower: Al-Qaeda and the Road to 9/11* (New York: Vintage Books, 2006), 38–42.

20 It is worth noting that the intellectual father of al-Qaeda, Sayyid Qutb, also experienced a sense of dislocation within the rapidly transforming social and physical landscape of greater Cairo, albeit further south in Helwan. Wright, *The Looming Tower*, 11–12.

21 Rabatat al-Maadi, *Maadi Guide*, 24 (Arabic) and 23 (English).

22 "Princess Fawzia Fuad of Egypt," *Telegraph*, July 5, 2013.

23 "Prospects and Needs of Victoria College, Cairo," FO 141/1172.

24 "Prospects and Needs of Victoria College, Cairo," FO 141/1172.

25 Said, *Out of Place*, 182.

26 "Prospects and Needs of Victoria College," FO 141/1172.

27 Sahar Hamouda and Colin Clement, eds., *Victoria College: A History Revealed* (Cairo: American University in Cairo Press, 2004), 169.

28 "Prospects and Needs of Victoria College," FO 141/1172.

29 Robert Fishman, *Urban Utopias in the Twentieth Century: Ebenezer Howard, Frank Lloyd Wright, Le Corbusier* (Cambridge, MA: Massachusetts Institute of Technology Press, 1982), 163–164.

30 On Wright and Le Corbusier, see James S. Ackerman, *The Villa: Form and Ideology of Country Houses* (Princeton, NJ: Princeton University Press, 1985), 253–285.

31 Said, *Out of Place*, 185–186.

32 Josipovici, personal interview, March 28, 2011.

33 Josipovici, personal interview, March 28, 2011.

34 Freeman, "A Brief Account."

35 Tim Sullivan, "The Education of Americans in Egypt," 1986, unpublished manuscript, SRCARMPC.

36 "Memorandum of Association of the Egyptian Delta Land & Investment Company, Limited," BT 31/43735, "List of Persons Holding Shares in the Egyptian Delta Land & Investment Co., Ltd. on the 9th of May 1904," BT 31/43736.

37 "List of Persons," BT 31/43736

38 Letter from G. Dale to S. Raafat, June 8, 1992, SRCARMPC.

39 "Letters: Maadi's Trees Are Being Cut Down," *Egyptian Gazette*, February 6, 1948.

40 Letter from G. Dale to S. Raafat, June 8, 1992, SRCARMPC.

41 Nancy Y. Reynolds, *A City Consumed: Urban Commerce, the Cairo Fire, and the Politics of Decolonization in Egypt* (Stanford, CA: Stanford University Press, 2012), 2; "1952: Britons Killed in Cairo Riots," *BBC*, January 26, 1952, http://news.bbc.co.uk/onthisday/hi/dates/stories/january/26/newsid_2506000/2506301.stm (accessed July 12, 2019).

42 James Jankowski, *Nasser's Egypt, Arab Nationalism, and the United Arab Republic* (Boulder, CO: Lynne Rienner Publishers, 2002), 17.

43 Laila A. Morsy, "American Support for the 1952 Egyptian Coup: Why? (Free Officers Coup of 1952)," *Middle East Studies* 31, no. 2 (1995): 307–317.

44 Joel Gordon, *Nasser's Blessed Movement: Egypt's Free Officers and the July Revolution* (Oxford: Oxford University Press, 1992), 194.

45 Gamal Abdel Nasser, foreword to Anwar Sadat, *Revolt on the Nile* (New York: John Day, 1957), 6.

46 Zdenek Müller, "Nasserism: The Shaping of the Ideology of the Egyptian Leadership after 1952," *Archiv Orientiani* 50, no. 1 (1982): 22–42.

47 Salem, personal interview, November 12, 2009.

48 Josipovici, personal interview, March 29, 2011.

49 Safwat and Safwat, personal interview, May 5, 2011.

50 Rabitat Sukkan wa Mullak al-Maadi, "Khatawat ta'sis al-rabita," SRCARMPC.

51 Rabitat Sukkan wa Mullak al-Maadi, "Khatawat ta'sis al-rabita," SRCARMPC.

52 "EDLICO Directors, 1904–1956," SRCARMPC.

53 Raafat, *Maadi*, 226.

54 Letter from G. Dale to S. Raafat, June 26, 1993, SRCARMPC.

55 The Free Officers recruited Naguib, an older, more accomplished general, to lend their movement legitimacy. While he became Egypt's first president and held initial power, Nasser and the other members of the RCC soon isolated him politically, making him a symbolic figurehead. By February 1954, he resigned, and in his place Nasser was elected as president in a national plebiscite. Peter Mansfield, "Nasser and Nasserism," *International Journal* 28, no. 4 (1973): 670–688.

56 Ray Bush, "Politics, War and Poverty: Twenty Years of Agricultural Land Reform and Market Liberalisation in Egypt," *Third World Quarterly* 28, no. 8 (2007): 1599–1615.

57 Salem, personal interview, April 30, 2011.

58 Charles B. Selak, Jr., "The Suez Canal Base Agreement of 1954: Its Background and Implications," *American Journal of International Law* 49, no. 4 (1955): 487–505; G.C. Peden, "Suez and Britain's Decline as a World Power," *Historical Journal* 55, no. 4 (2012): 1073–1096.

59 Jankowski, *Nasser's Egypt*, 29.

60 Josipovici, personal interview, March 29, 2011.

Chapter 11

1 Juliet Tabet and Mona Tabet, personal interview, May 14, 2011.

2 Robert Tignor, *Capitalism and Nationalism at the End of Empire: State and Business in Decolonizing Egypt, Nigeria, and Kenya, 1945–1963* (Princeton, NJ: Princeton University Press, 1998), 108–109.

3 Robert Tignor explains that the full dismantling of the Egyptian private sector unfolded in the five years that followed the canal crisis. Tignor, *Capitalism and Nationalism*, 113.

4 Peden, "Suez and Britain's Decline," 1073–1096.

5 Diane B. Kunz, *The Economic Diplomacy of the Suez Crisis* (Chapel Hill, NC: University of North Carolina Press, 1991), 188; Robert Tignor, "Decolonization and Business: The Case of Egypt," *Journal of Modern History* 59, no. 3 (1987): 479–505.

6 Joannides, personal interview, April 11, 2011.

7 Lucette Lagnado, an Egyptian Jew who grew up in Garden City, wrote a memoir of her family's experiences in Egypt and then the United States

during the mid-twentieth century and later. She recalled that after 1956, many of her relatives fled Egypt with a sense of panic. Her own immediate family left after Nasser unleashed the full scale of his nationalization plan in the early 1960s. The Suez Canal Crisis had been the turning point, after which "it was no longer a question of whether to leave Egypt, but when." Lucette Lagnado, *The Man in the White Sharkskin Suit: My Family's Exodus from Old Cairo to the New World* (New York: HarperCollins, 2007), 94.

8   Howard M. Sachar, *A History of Israel from the Rise of Zionism to Our Time*, 2nd ed. (New York: Alfred A. Knopf, 1996), 515.

9   Tabet did not mention the nationality of these people, only that they had to leave the country quickly. Juliet Tabet and Mona Tabet, personal interview, May 14, 2011.

10   Juliet Tabet and Mona Tabet, personal interview, May 14, 2011.

11   Juliet Tabet and Mona Tabet, personal interview, May 14, 2011.

12   Juliet Tabet and Mona Tabet, personal interview, May 14, 2011.

13   Jehan Sadat, *A Woman of Egypt* (New York: Pocket Books, 1987), 166.

14   Josipovici, personal interview, March 29, 2011.

15   Nancy Reynolds makes a similar argument regarding the local impact of the Cairo Fire, as foreign-owned businesses and institutions were targeted. Nancy Y. Reynolds, *A City Consumed: Urban Commerce, the Cairo Fire, and the Politics of Decolonization in Egypt* (Stanford, CA: Stanford University Press, 2012), 2.

16   John Sakkas, "Greece and the Mass Exodus of Egyptian Greeks, 1956–66," *Journal of the Hellenic Diaspora* 35, no. 2 (2009): 101–115.

17   They participated in a large exodus of Greeks from Egypt, which unfolded after the 1952 coup. Alexander Kitroeff notes that there were more than forty-seven thousand Greeks in Egypt in 1960 and that the number dwindled to roughly seventeen thousand following the 1967 war. Alexander Kitroeff, *The Greeks and the Making of Modern Egypt* (Cairo: American University in Cairo Press, 2019), 16–17.

18   Joannides, personal interview, April 11, 2011.

19   Joannides, personal interview, April 11, 2011.

20   John Freeman, "A Brief Account of the Church of St. John the Baptist, Maadi," 1955, SRCARMPC.

21   Rabatat al-Maadi, *The Maadi Guide*.

22   Rabitat Sukkan wa Mullak al-Maadi, "Khatawat ta'sis al-rabita," SRCARMPC.

23　It appears that the original text was in Arabic, and the English version was secondary, but written by someone who was fluent in the language. Rabatat al-Maadi, *The Maadi Guide*, 22 (Arabic) and 20 (English).

24　Rabatat al-Maadi, *The Maadi Guide, 22 (Arabic) and 20 (English)*.

25　Salem, personal interview, November 12, 2009.

26　"*Acte de Vente et Cahier des Charges*," June 11, 1935, SRCARMPC.

27　Rabatat al-Maadi, *The Maadi Guide*, 29.

28　Rabatat al-Maadi, *The Maadi Guide*, 29.

29　Rabitat Sukkan wa Mullak al-Maadi, "Khatawat ta'sis al-rabita," SRCARMPC.

30　Samir W. Raafat, *Maadi, 1904–1962: Society and History in a Cairo Suburb (Cairo: Palm Press, 1994)*, 268.

31　"Ijra'at jadida fi tariq al-ishtirakiya," *al-Ahram*, July 21, 1961.

32　Arthur Goldschmidt, Jr., "'Abbud, [Muhammad] Ahmad (2 May 1889–28 December 1963)," *Biographical Dictionary of Modern Egypt (Boulder, CO: Lynne Rienner Publishers, 2004)*, https://login.ezproxy.samford.edu/login?url=https://search.credoreference.com/content/entry/bdmodegypt/abbud_muhammad_ahmad_2_may_1889_28_december_1963/0?institutionId=3477 (accessed June 21, 2019).

33　Raafat, *Maadi*, 229 and 251.

34　Samia Zeitoun, "Tree Lovers Needed," *Al-Ahram Weekly Online* 794 (May 11–17, 2006), http://weekly.ahram.org.eg/2006/794/sc131.htm (accessed April 27, 2012).

35　Saffeyah Moyine al-'Arab, *Saffeyah & Bin Bin: Growing Old Together (Cairo: Trade Routes Enterprises International Publications, 1991)*, 21.

36　Moyine al-'Arab, *Saffeyah & Bin Bin*, 53.

37　Moyine al-'Arab, *Saffeyah & Bin Bin*, 96.

38　Moyine al-'Arab, *Saffeyah & Bin Bin*, 55.

39　Moyine al-'Arab, *Saffeyah & Bin Bin*, 53.

40　Salem, personal interview, April 30, 2011.

41　Josipovici, personal interview, March 29, 2011.

42　Safwat and Safwat, personal interview, May 5, 2011.

43　Yi-Fu Tuan, *Space and Place: The Perspective of Experience (Minneapolis, MN: University of Minneapolis Press, 1977)*, 10.

Postscript

1　"View of the Schuler House from the Wolff House," Photo Collection, SRCARMPC.

2 Samir W. Raafat, *Maadi, 1904–1962: Society and History in a Cairo Suburb* *(Cairo: Palm Press, 1994),* 216; Huda Shaarawi, *Harem Years: The Memoirs of an Egyptian Feminist, 1879–1924, translated by Margot Badran (New York: Feminist Press of City University of New York, 1987).*

3 "My Beloved Home in Maadi, Where I Grew Up," Photo Collection, SRCARMPC.

4 J. Hugo Cota-Sánchez, "Taxonomy, Distribution, Rarity Status and Uses of Canadian Cacti," *Haseltonia* 9 (2002): 17–25.

BIBLIOGRAPHY

Archival Material and Abbreviations

AARR: Asia and Africa Reading Room, British Library, London, United Kingdom.

BNA: British National Archives, Kew, Surrey, United Kingdom.

BT: Board of Trade, BNA, Series BT 31.

BW: British Council, BNA, Series BW 29, BW 43.

FO: Foreign Office, BNA, Series FO 141, FO 307, FO 370, FO 371, FO 383, FO 407, FO 841, FO 847.

HF: Hassan Fathy Architectural Archives, Rare Books and Special Collections Library, American University in Cairo, Egypt.

HFCC: Papers of Captain Harry Frederick Comfort Crookshank, Viscount Crookshank, 1925–1961, MSS. Eng. hist. b. 223; c. 596–606; d. 359–61, Bodleian Library, Oxford University, United Kingdom.

IWM: Imperial War Museum, London, United Kingdom. Private papers.

IR: Board of Inland Revenue, BNA, Series IR 40.

MECA: Middle East Centre Archives, St. Antony's College, Oxford, United Kingdom. Private papers.

NAA: National Archives of Australia, Canberra, Australia.

RBSCL: Rare Books and Special Collections Library, American University in Cairo, Egypt.

SCP: Samuel Comfort Papers, No. C0407, Rare Books and Special Collections, Firestone Library, Princeton University, United States.

SRCARMPC: Samir Raafat Cairo Architecture Research Materials and Photograph Collection (formerly Maadi Collection), Rare Books and Special Collections Library, American University in Cairo, Egypt.

Contemporary Periodicals

"Ahmad 'Abd al-Wahhab." *al-Ahram*, April 17, 1938.

al-Ahram, February 11, 1933, http://www.egy.com/maadi (accessed December 5, 2012)

"Alleged Libel of German Jews." *Egyptian Gazette*, January 24, 1934, 6.

"Alleged Libel of Jews." *Egyptian Gazette*, January 23, 1934, 5.

"An Anglo-Egyptian Union." *Egyptian Gazette*, January 21, 1937.

"Anti-Semitism in Egypt." *Egyptian Gazette*, June 15, 1938.

"Australians at Meadi: A Visit to the Camps." *Egyptian Gazette*, December 15, 1914.

"Death of Mr. Devonshire." *Egyptian Gazette*, July 16, 1921.

"Death of Sir E. Palmer, Prominent Local Financier, Sketch of Successful Career." *Egyptian Gazette*, January 29, 1906.

"Death of Sir E. Palmer." *Egyptian Gazette*, Jan. 30, 1906.

"Enemy Subjects in Egypt: The Case of the National Bank—Sir John Maxwell the Sole Arbiter." *Egyptian Gazette*, May 26, 1915.

"The English School, Cairo: Maadi Branch." *Egyptian Gazette*, June 4, 1932.

"The Epistles of Peggy." *The Sphinx*, December 11, 1920.

"Flower Show at Cairo: Some Fine Exhibits." *Egyptian Gazette*, December 15, 1919.

"Garden Party at Maadi." *Egyptian Gazette*, April 12, 1938.

"Germans Win Cairo Lawsuit." *Egyptian Gazette*, January 25, 1934, 5.

"Henri Naus Bey." *al-Ahram*, September 24, 1938.

"Ijra'at jadida fi tariq al-ishtirakiya." *al-Ahram*, July 21, 1961.

"'Ilan," *al-Muqattam*, December 22, 1904.

"Jalalat al-Malak yaftatah Masjid Faruq al-Awwal bil-Maadi." *al-Ahram*, February 18, 1939.

"King's Gift for Storm Victims." *Egyptian Gazette*, January 3, 1945.

"Lecture by Mrs. Devonshire." *Egyptian Gazette*, January 12, 1925.

"Letters: Maadi's Trees Are Being Cut Down." *Egyptian Gazette*, February 6, 1948.

"Maadi Union." *Egyptian Gazette*, April 7, 1937.

"Misr laysat fi harb wa-lakinnaha tasta'id li-l-harb." *al-Ahram*, April 2, 1940.

"Mr. John Williamson: A Pioneer in Cyprus and Maadi." *Egyptian Gazette*, March 29, 1932.

"Mrs. Devonshire Honoured by King Farouk." *Egyptian Gazette*, April 6, 1944.

"New Maadi Village to be Built in Four Zones." *Egyptian Gazette*, February 14, 1947.

"Obituary: Mr. Frank M. Stout." *Egyptian Gazette*, June 1, 1926.

"Obituary: The Late Mrs. St. John Diamant." *Egyptian Gazette*, March 30, 1909.

"Passing Notes: Maadi's New Club." *The Sphinx: The English Illustrated Weekly*, December 11, 1920 (Cairo: Sphinx Press), 138.

"Prisoners Arrive in Egypt: Histrionics of German Officers." *Egyptian Gazette*, May 12, 1915.

"Sharikat al-Delta." *al-Ahram*, January 9, 1904.

"Silver Wedding." *Egyptian Gazette*, May 24, 1912.

"Sister Margaret Clare Fund: A Worthy Object." *Egyptian Gazette*, February 16, 1917.

"Social and Personal." *Egyptian Gazette*, April 19, 1924.

"Social and Personal." *Egyptian Gazette*, June 17, 1908.

"Social and Personal." *Egyptian Gazette*, May 16, 1927.

"Turkish Prisoners of War: A Visit to the Meadi Camp." *Egyptian Gazette*, September 12, 1916.

"Turkish Prisoners' Handiwork: Visit to the Cairo Depot." *Egyptian Gazette*, September 2, 1916.

"The Wardan Company." *Egyptian Gazette*, January 18, 1916.

"Worst Storm in 23 Years." *Egyptian Gazette*, January 2, 1945.

Zeitoun, Samia. "Tree Lovers Needed." *Al-Ahram Weekly Online* 794 (May 11–17, 2006).

Published Primary Sources

Baring, Evelyn. *Modern Egypt*. London: MacMillan & Co., 1908.

Colvin, Auckland. *The Making of Modern Egypt*, 4th ed. London: Seeley & Co., 1906.

_____. *John Russell Colvin: The Last Lieutenant Governor of the Northwest Company*. Oxford: Clarendon Press, 1895.

"Cholera in Egypt." *British Journal of Medicine* 1, no. 1828 (1896): 106–107. https://www-jstor-org.ezproxy.samford.edu/stable/20234488.

De Guerville, A.B. *New Egypt*. London: William Heinemann, 1906.

Devonshire, Henriette. *Rambles in Cairo*. Cairo: E. and R. Schindler, 1931.

Egypt: Handbook for Travelers. London: K. Beadeker, 1902.

Fathy, Hassan. *Architecture for the Poor: An Experiment in Rural Egypt*. Chicago, IL: University of Chicago Press, 1971.

Howard, Ebenezer. *Garden Cities of To-morrow*, edited by F.J. Osborn. Cambridge, MA: Massachusetts Institute of Technology Press, 1965.

Josipovici, Gabriel. *A Life*. London: London Magazine Editions, European Jewish Publication Society, 2001.

Moyine al-'Arab, Saffeyah. *Saffeyah & Bin Bin: Growing Old Together*. Cairo: Trade Routes Enterprises International Publications, 1991.

Rabatat al-Maadi. *The Maadi Guide*. Cairo: Minerbo Press, 1956 (bilingual: English and Arabic).

Sadat, Anwar. *Revolt on the Nile*. New York: John Day, 1957.

Sadat, Jehan. *A Woman of Egypt*. New York: Pocket Books, 1987.

Said, Edward. *Out of Place: A Memoir*. New York: Alfred A. Knopf, 2000.

"Sanitary Matters in Cairo." *British Journal of Medicine* 1, no. 2574 (1910): 1057–1060. https://www-jstor-org.ezproxy.samford.edu/stable/25290485

Seligman, Edwin Robert Anderson. *The Crisis of 1907 in the Light of History*. New York: Columbia University Press, 1908.

Stout, Mary. *Gardening in Egypt and Allied Climates*. Cairo: Egyptian Horticultural Society, 1935.

Books and Articles

Abu 'Araja, Tiysir. *Al-Muqattam: Jaridat al-Ihtilal al-Britani fi Misr, 1889–1952*. Cairo: al-Hiy'ia al-Misriyya al-'Ama lil-Kitab, 1997.

Abu-Lughod, Janet L. *Cairo: 1001 Years of the City Victorious*. Princeton, NJ: Princeton University Press, 1971.

Ackerman, James S. *The Villa: Form and Ideology of Country Houses*. Princeton, NJ: Princeton University Press, 1985.

AlSayyad, Nezar. *Cairo: Histories of a City*. Cambridge, MA: Harvard University Press, 2011.

Arbell, Mordechai. *The Portuguese Jews of Jamaica*. Kingston: Canoe Press, 2000.

Aşik, Mehmet Ozan, and Aykan Erdemir. "Westernization as Cultural Trauma: Egyptian Radical Islamist Discourse on Religious Education." *Journal for the Studies of Religions and Ideologies* 9, no. 25 (2010): 111–132.

el-Awaisi, Abd Al-Fattah M. "Jihadia Education and the Society of the Egyptian Muslim Brothers: 1928–49." *Journal of Beliefs & Values: Studies in Religion & Education* 21, no. 2 (2000): 213–225.

Ayalon, Ami. "Christian 'Intruders,' Muslim 'Bigots': The Egyptian-Syrian Press Controversy in Late-Nineteenth Century Cairo." In *Jews, Muslims, and Mass Media: Mediating the 'Other'*, edited by Tudor Parfitt and Yulia Egorova, 15–27. London: Routledge Curzon, 2004.

Aymes, Marc. "The Port-City in the Fields: Investigating an Improper Urbanity in Mid-Nineteenth-Century Cyprus." *Mediterranean Historical Review* 24, no. 2 (2009): 133–149.

Badran, Margot. *Feminists, Islam, and Nation: Gender and the Making of Modern Egypt*. Princeton, NJ: Princeton University Press, 1995.

Badrawi, Malak. *Isma'il Sidqi, 1875–1950: Pragmatism and Vision in Twentieth Century Egypt*. London: Curzon Press, 1996.

al-Bakistuni, Ibrahim. "Reviewed Work: Egyptian Service: 1902–1946 by Thomas Russell Pasha." *African Affairs 48, no. 193 (1949): 335.*

Ball, Simon. *The Guardsmen: Harold Macmillan, Three Friends, and the World They Made*. London: Harper Perennial, 2004.

Baron, Beth. *The Orphan Scandal: Christian Missionaries and the Rise of the Muslim Brotherhood*. Berkeley, CA: Stanford University Press, 2014.

_____. *Egypt as a Woman: Nationalism, Gender, and Politics*. Berkeley, CA: University of California Press, 2007.

_____. "Women, Honour, and the State: Evidence from Egypt." *Middle Eastern Studies* 42, no. 1 (2006): 1–20.

Batchelor, Peter. "The Origins of the Garden City Concept for Urban Reform." *Journal of the Society of Architectural Historians* 28, no. 3 (1969): 184–200.

Beinin, Joel. *The Dispersion of Egyptian Jewry: Culture, Politics, and the Formation of a Modern Diaspora*. Berkeley, CA: University of California Press, 1998.

Beinin, Joel, and Zachary Lockman. *Workers on the Nile: Nationalism, Communism, Islam, and the Egyptian Working Class, 1882–1954*. Princeton, NJ: Princeton University Press, 1989.

Brown, Nathan J. "The Precarious Life and Slow Death of the Mixed Courts of Egypt." *International Journal of Middle East Studies* 25, no. 1 (1993): 33–52.

Bush, Ray. "Politics, War and Poverty: Twenty Years of Agricultural Land Reform and Market Liberalisation in Egypt." *Third World Quarterly* 28, no. 8 (2007): 1599–1615.

Cain, P.J., and A.G. Hopkins. *British Imperialism, 1688–2000*, 2nd ed. Harlow: Longman, Pearson Education, 2002.

Chapman, Stanley. *Merchant Enterprise in Britain: From the Industrial Revolution to World War I.* Cambridge: Cambridge University Press, 2004.

Cole, Juan R.I. *Colonialism and Revolution in the Middle East: Social and Cultural Origins of Egypt's 'Urabi Movement.* Cairo: American University in Cairo Press, 1999.

Cota-Sánchez, J. Hugo. "Taxonomy, Distribution, Rarity Status and Uses of Canadian Cacti." *Haseltonia* 9 (2002): 17–25.

Darwin, John. *The Empire Project: The Rise and Fall of the British World-System, 1830–1970.* Cambridge: Cambridge University Press, 2009.

Davidoff, Leonore, and Catherine Hall. *Family Fortunes: Men and Women of the English Middle Class, 1780–1850.* Chicago, IL: University of Chicago Press, 1987.

Davis, Eric. *Challenging Colonialism: Bank Misr and Egyptian Industrialization, 1920–1941.* Princeton, NJ: Princeton University Press, 1983.

Deeb, Marius. "The Socioeconomic Role of Local Foreign Minorities in Modern Egypt, 1805–1961." *International Journal of Middle East Studies* 9, no. 1 (1978): 11–22.

———. "Bank Misr and the Emergence of the Local Bourgeoisie in Egypt." *Middle Eastern Studies* 12, no. 3 (1976): 69–86.

Dobrowolska, Agnieszka, and Jaroslaw Dobrowoski. *Heliopolis: Rebirth of the City of the Sun.* Cairo: American University in Cairo Press, 2006.

Efrati, Noga. "The *Effendiyya*: Where Have All the Women Gone?" *International Journal of Middle East Studies* 43, no. 2 (2011): 375–377.

Eppel, Michael. "Note about the Term *Effendiyya* in the History of the Middle East." *International Journal of Middle East Studies* 41, no. 3 (2009): 535–539.

EzzelArab, AbdelAziz. "The Experiment of Sharif Pasha's Cabinet (1879): An Inquiry into the Historiography of Egypt's Elite Movement." *International Journal of Middle East Studies* 36, no. 4 (2004): 583–584.

Fishman, Robert. *Urban Utopias in the Twentieth Century: Ebenezer Howard, Frank Lloyd Wright, Le Corbusier.* Cambridge, MA: Massachusetts Institute of Technology Press, 1982.

Frangakis-Syrett, Elena. "Banking in Izmir in the Early Twentieth Century." *Mediterranean History Review* 24, no. 2 (2009): 132–155.

———. "The Making of an Ottoman Port: The Quay of Izmir in the Nineteenth Century." *Journal of Transport History* 22, no. 1 (2001): 23–46.

Gelvin, James L. *The Modern Middle East: A History,* 4th ed. Oxford: Oxford University Press, 2016.

Gillies, Warna D. "Children on the Move: Third Culture Kids." *Childhood Education* 75, no. 1 (1998): 36–38.

Gratien, Chris. "The Ottoman Quagmire: Malaria, Swamps, and Settlement in the Late-Ottoman Mediterranean." *International Journal of Middle East Studies* 49 (2017): 583–604.

Goldschmidt Jr., Arthur, ed. *Egyptianizing Modernity through the 'New Effendiyya': Social and Cultural Constructions of the Middle Class in Egypt under the Monarchy*. Cairo: American University in Cairo Press, 2005.

_____. *Biographical Dictionary of Modern Egypt*. Boulder, CO: Lynne Rienner Publishers, 2004.

Gordon, Joel. *Nasser's Blessed Movement: Egypt's Free Officers and the July Revolution*. Oxford: Oxford University Press, 1992.

Grossi, Patricia, and Robert Muir-Wood. *The 1906 San Francisco Earthquake and Fire: Perspectives on a Modern Super Cat*. Newark, NJ: Risk Management Solutions, 2006.

Guldi, Jo. *Roads to Power: Britain Invents the Infrastructure State*. Cambridge, MA: Harvard University Press, 2011.

Hamouda, Sahar, and Colin Clement, eds. *Victoria College: A History Revealed*. Cairo: American University in Cairo Press, 2004.

Hansen, Bent. "Interest Rates and Foreign Capital in Egypt under British Occupation." *Journal of Economic History* 43, no. 4 (1983): 867–884.

Harlaftis, Gelina. "Mapping the Greek Maritime Diaspora from the Early Eighteenth to the Late Twentieth Centuries." In *Diaspora Entrepreneurial Networks: Four Centuries of History*, edited by Ina Baghdiantz McCabe, Gelina Harlaftis, and Ioanna Pepelasis Minoglou, 147–172. London: Berg Publishers, 2005.

_____. *A History of Greek-Owned Shipping: The Making of an International Tramp Fleet, 1830 to the Present Day*. London: Routledge, 1996.

Harvey, David. "Cosmopolitanism and the Banality of Geographical Evils." *Public Culture* 12, no. 2 (2000): 529–564.

Hausman, William J. *Global Electrification: Multinational Enterprise and International Finance in the History of Light and Power, 1878–2007*. Cambridge: Cambridge University Press, 2008.

Hendley, Alex, with Megan Hutching. *Fernleaf Cairo: New Zealanders at Maadi Camp, the Fascinating Story of New Zealanders in Wartime Egypt*. Auckland: HarperCollins, 2009.

Fleming, Ian. *The Man with the Golden Gun*. New York: Penguin Books, 1974 [1965].

Hunt, Lynn. *The Family Romance of the French Revolution*. Berkeley, CA: University of California Press, 1992.

Hunter, Archie. *Power and Passion in Egypt: A Life of Sir Eldon Gorst, 1861–1911*. New York: I.B. Tauris, 2007.

Ilbert, Robert. "Heliopolis: Colonial Enterprise and Town Planning Success?" In *Coping with the Urban Growth of Cairo*, edited by Ahmet Evin. Singapore: Concept Media and Aga Khan Award for Architecture, 1985.

———. *Héliopolis, le Caire 1905–1922: Genèse d'une ville*. Marseille: Centre National de la Recherche Scientifique, 1981.

Jackson, Maureen. "'Cosmopolitan' Smyrna: Illuminating or Obscuring Cultural Histories?" *Geographical Review* 102, no. 3 (2012): 337–349.

Jacob, Wilson Chacko. *Working Out Egypt: Masculinity and Subject Formation in Colonial Modernity, 1870–1940*. Durham, NC: University of North Carolina Press, 2011.

Jankowski, James. *Nasser's Egypt, Arab Nationalism, and the United Arab Republic*. Boulder, CO: Lynne Rienner Publishers, 2002.

———. "The Government of Egypt and the Palestine Question, 1936–1939." *Middle Eastern Studies* 17, no. 4 (1981): 427–453.

Kant, Immanuel. *Perpetual Peace: A Philosophic Essay*, translated by Benjamin Franklin Trueblood. Washington, DC: American Peace Society, 1897 [1795].

Kerber, Linda. *Women of the Republic: Intellect and Ideology in Revolutionary America*. New York: Norton, 1986.

Khaled, Z. "A Comparative Bacteriological Study of Bovine Abortion and Undulant Fever." *Journal of Hygiene* 22, no. 3 (1924): 335–342.

Khoury, Philip S. "Continuity and Change in Syrian Political Life: The Nineteenth and Twentieth Centuries." *American Historical Review* 96, no. 5 (1991): 1374–1395.

Kitroeff, Alexander. *The Greeks and the Making of Modern Egypt*. Cairo: American University in Cairo Press, 2019.

Koven, Seth, and Sonya Michel, eds. *Mothers of a New World: Maternalist Politics and the Origins of Welfare States*. New York: Routledge, 1993.

Krämer, Gudrun. *The Jews of Modern Egypt, 1914–1952*. Seattle, WA: University of Washington Press, 1989.

Kunz, Diane B. *The Economic Diplomacy of the Suez Crisis*. Chapel Hill, NC: University of North Carolina Press, 1991.

Kupferschmidt, Uri M. *Henry Naus Bey: Retrieving the Biography of a Belgian Industrialist in Egypt.* Brussels: Academie Royale des Sciences d'Outre-Mer, 1998.

Lagnado, Lucette. *The Man in the White Sharkskin Suit: My Family's Exodus from Old Cairo to the New World.* New York: HarperCollins, 2007.

MacFadyen, Dugald. *Sir Ebenezer Howard and the Town Planning Movement.* Manchester: Manchester University Press, 1970.

Mahfouz, Naguib. *Palace Walk.* New York: Random House, 1990.

Mak, Lanver. "More than Officers and Officials: Britons in Occupied Egypt, 1882–1922." *Journal of Imperial and Commonwealth History* 39, no. 1 (2011): 21–46.

Mansfield, Peter. "Nasser and Nasserism." *International Journal* 28, no. 4 (1973): 670–688.

McKale, Donald M. "Influence without Power: The Last Khedive of Egypt and the Great Powers, 1914–1918." *Middle Eastern Studies 33, no. 1 (1997): 20–39.*

Meacham, Standish. *Regaining Paradise: Englishness and the Early Garden City Movement.* New Haven, CT: Yale University Press, 1999.

Meinardus, Otto F.A. *The Historic Coptic Churches of Cairo.* Cairo: Philopatron, 1994.

Morris, Benny. *The Birth of the Palestinian Refugee Problem Revisited.* Cambridge: Cambridge University Press, 2004.

Morrow, John H., Jr. *The Great War: An Imperial History.* New York: Routledge, 2004.

Morsy, Laila A. "American Support for the 1952 Egyptian Coup: Why? (Free Officers Coup of 1952)," *Middle East Studies* 31, no. 2 (1995): 307–317.

_____. "The Military Clauses of the Anglo-Egyptian Treaty of Friendship and Alliance, 1936." *International Journal of Middle East Studies* 16 (1984): 67–97.

Müller, Zdenek. "Nasserism: The Shaping of the Ideology of the Egyptian Leadership after 1952." *Archiv Orientiani* 50, no. 1 (1982): 22–42.

Oshima, Ken Tadashi. "Denenchōfu: Building the Garden City in Japan." *Journal of the Society of Architectural Historians* 55, no. 2 (1996): 140–151.

Owen, E.R.J. "The Attitudes of British Officials to the Development of the Egyptian Economy, 1882–1922." In *Studies in the Economic History of the Middle East: From the Rise of Islam to the Present Day*, edited by M.A. Cook, 485–500. Oxford: Oxford University Press, 1970.

Owen, Roger. *Lord Cromer: Victorian Imperialist, Edwardian Proconsul.* Oxford: Oxford University Press, 2005.

Parolin, Gianluca Paolo. *Citizenship in the Arab World: Kin, Religion, and Nation-State.* Amsterdam: Amsterdam University Press, 2009.

Peden, G.C. "Suez and Britain's Decline as a World Power." *Historical Journal* 55, no. 4 (2012): 1073–1096.

Pollard, Lisa. *Nurturing the Nation: The Family Politics of Modernizing, Colonizing, and Liberating Egypt, 1805–1923.* Berkeley, CA: University of California Press, 2005.

Pred, Allan. "Place as Historically Contingent Process: Structuration and the Time-Geography of Becoming Places." *Annals of the Association of American Geographers* 74, no. 2 (1984): 279–297.

Raafat, Samir W. *Maadi, 1904–1962: Society and History in a Cairo Suburb.* Cairo: Palm Press, 1994.

al-Raf'a, 'Abd al-Rahman. *Thawra sanat 1919: Tarikh Misr al-qawmi min 1914 ila 1921,* 2nd ed. Cairo: Maktabat al-Nahda al-Misriya, 1955.

Raymond, André. *Cairo: City of History.* Cairo: American University in Cairo Press, 2007.

Reich, Bernard, ed. *Arab–Israeli Conflict and Conciliation: A Documentary History.* Westport, CT: Greenwood Press, 1995.

Reimer, Michael J. "Urban Government and Administration in Egypt, 1805–1914." *Die Welt des Islams* 39, no. 3 (1999): 289–318.

Reynolds, Nancy Y. *A City Consumed: Urban Commerce, the Cairo Fire, and the Politics of Decolonization in Egypt.* Stanford, CA: Stanford University Press, 2012.

Robinson, Ronald, John Gallagher, and Alice Denny. *Africa and the Victorians: The Official Mind of Imperialism.* London: Macmillan, 1961.

Rodogno, Davide. *Against Massacre: Humanitarian Interventions in the Ottoman Empire, 1815–1914.* Princeton, NJ: Princeton University Press, 2011.

Ruiz, Mario M. "Manly Spectacles and Imperial Soldiers in Wartime Egypt, 1914–19." *Middle Eastern Studies* 45, no. 3 (2009): 351–371.

Rupp, Leila J. *Worlds of Women: The Making of an International Women's Movement.* Princeton, NJ: Princeton University Press, 1997.

Russell, Mona. "Marketing the Modern Egyptian Girl." *Journal of Middle East Women's Studies* 6, no. 3 (2010): 19–57.

Sachar, Howard M. *A History of Israel from the Rise of Zionism to Our Time,* 2nd ed. New York: Alfred A. Knopf, 1996.

Said, Edward W. *Culture and Imperialism*. New York: Vintage Books, 1993.

Said, Edward W. *Orientalism*. New York: Vintage Books, 1994 [1978].

Sakkas, John. "Greece and the Mass Exodus of Egyptian Greeks, 1956–66." *Journal of the Hellenic Diaspora* 35, no. 2 (2009): 101–115.

Schiebinger, Londa. *The Mind Has No Sex? Women in the Origins of Modern Science*. Cambridge, MA: Harvard University Press, 1989.

Selak, Charles B., Jr. "The Suez Canal Base Agreement of 1954: Its Background and Implications." *American Journal of International Law* 49, no. 4 (1955): 487–505.

Shaarawi, Huda. *Harem Years: The Memoirs of an Egyptian Feminist, 1879–1924*, translated by Margot Badran. New York: Feminist Press of City University of New York, 1987.

Shapin, Steven, and Simon Schaffer. *Leviathan and the Air-Pump: Hobbes, Boyle, and the Experimental Life*. Princeton, NJ: Princeton University Press, 1985.

Sibum, Heinz Otto. "Reworking the Mechanical Value of Heat: Instruments of Precision and Gestures of Accuracy in Early Victorian England." *Studies in the History and Philosophy of Science* 26, no. 1 (1995): 73–106.

Singerman, Diane, and Paul Amar, eds. *Cairo Cosmopolitan: Politics, Culture, and Urban Space in the New Globalized Middle East*. Cairo: American University in Cairo Press, 2006.

Sinha, Mrinalini. "Britishness, Clubbability, and the Colonial Public Sphere: The Genealogy of an Imperial Institution in Colonial India." *Journal of British Studies* 40, no. 4 (2001): 491–493.

Smith, Bonnie. *The Gender of History: Men, Women and Historical Practice*. Cambridge, MA: Harvard University Press, 1998.

Smith, Charles D. "4 February 1942: Its Causes and Its Influence on Egyptian Politics and on the Future of Anglo-Egyptian Relations, 1937–1945." *International Journal of Middle East Studies* 10, no. 4 (1979): 453–479.

Starr, Deborah A. *Remembering Cosmopolitan Egypt: Literature, Culture, and Empire*. London: Routledge, 2009.

_____. "Recuperating Cosmopolitan Alexandria: Circulation of Narratives and Narratives of Circulation." *Cities* 22, no. 3 (2005): 217–228.

Steele, James. *An Architect for People: The Complete Works of Hassan Fathy*. Cairo: American University in Cairo Press, 1997.

Tabak, Faruk. "Imperial Rivalry and Port-Cities: A View from the Top." *Mediterranean Historical Review* 24, no. 2 (2009): 79–81.

Thornhill, Michael T. "Informal Empire, Independent Egypt and the Accession of King Farouk." *Journal of Imperial and Commonwealth History* 38, no. 2 (2010): 279–302.

Tignor, Robert. *Capitalism and Nationalism at the End of Empire: State and Business in Decolonizing Egypt, Nigeria, and Kenya, 1945–1963*. Princeton, NJ: Princeton University Press, 1998.

———. "Decolonization and Business: The Case of Egypt." *Journal of Modern History* 59, no. 3 (1987): 479–505.

———. *State, Private Enterprise, and Economic Change in Egypt, 1918–1952*. Princeton, NJ: Princeton University Press, 1984.

Tuan, Yi-Fu. *Space and Place: The Perspective of Experience*. Minneapolis, MN: University of Minneapolis Press, 1977.

Tyquin, Michael. "Doctors and Nurses: Gender Relations, Jealousy, and Maladministration in Wartime." *Health and History* 13, no. 1 (2011): 26–43.

Van den Boogert, Maurits H. *Capitulations and the Ottoman Legal System: Qadis, Consuls and Beraths in the 18th Century*. Leiden: Brill, 2005.

Vitalis, Robert. *When Capitalists Collide: Business Conflict and the End of Empire in Egypt*. Berkeley, CA: University of California Press, 1995.

Warburg, Gabriel. "Lampson's Ultimatum to Faruq, 4 February, 1942." *Middle Eastern Studies* 11, no. 1 (1975): 24–32.

Whyte, William. "How Do Buildings Mean? Some Issues of Interpretation in the History of Architecture." *History and Theory* 45 (2006): 153–177.

Winter, Denis. *25 April 1915: The Inevitable Tragedy*. St. Lucia: University of Queensland Press, 1994.

Wright, Lawrence. *The Looming Tower: Al-Qaeda and the Road to 9/11*. New York: Vintage Books, 2007.

Uglow, Jennifer S., and Maggy Hendry, eds. *The Northeastern Dictionary of Women's Biography*, 3rd ed. London: MacMillan, 1998.

Useem, Ruth H., and Richard D. Downie. "Third Culture Kids." *Today's Education* 65, no. 3 (1976): 103–105.

Zadrozny, Mark, ed. *Contemporary Authors Autobiography Series*, vol. 8. Detroit, MI: Gale, 1988.

Websites

Al-Ahram Weekly Online, http://english.ahram.org.eg/Index.aspx

Ancestry.com, https://www.ancestry.com/

BBC, "On This Day, 1950–2005," http://news.bbc.co.uk/onthisday/default.stm

Bassatine News, http://bassatine.net

Biographical Dictionary of Egypt, Credo Reference, https://search-credoref-erence-com.ezproxy.samford.edu

Brill Online, https://referenceworks.brillonline.com/subjects

Christopher Aidan Long, British Journalist, http://www.christopherlong.co.uk

Commonwealth War Graves Commission, https://www.cwgc.org

Descendants of Eliahu Rossi, http://www.geocities.com/rainforest/vines/5855/rossi.htm

Egy.com, http://www.egy.com

Gloucester Rugby Heritage, https://www.gloucesterrugbyheritage.org.uk

Jewish Telegraphic Agency, https://www.jta.org

JSTOR, https://www.jstor.org

Keeping Cairo, (I'atni Balqahira), http://www.keepingcairo.org

Levantine Heritage Foundation, http://www.levantineheritage.com

Martin Kurrein's Geneaology, http://www.kurrein.com/index.html

New Zealand Electronic Text Collection, http://nzetc.victoria.ac.nz

New Zealand History, https://nzhistory.govt.nz

Nona Orbach: Blog as Artwork, http://nonaorbach.com/blog/

Trove, National Library of Australia, https://trove.nla.gov.au

Wikimedia Commons, https://commons.wikimedia.org/wiki/Main_Page

INDEX